THE PRECINCT OF RELIGION

THE
PRECINCT OF RELIGION
IN
THE CULTURE OF HUMANITY

BY
Prof. CHARLES GRAY SHAW, B.D., Ph.D.
PROFESSOR OF PHILOSOPHY IN NEW YORK UNIVERSITY
AUTHOR OF "CHRISTIANITY AND MODERN CULTURE"

WIPF & STOCK · Eugene, Oregon

Wipf and Stock Publishers
199 W 8th Ave, Suite 3
Eugene, OR 97401

The Precinct of Religion in the Culture of Humanity
By Shaw, Charles Gray
Softcover ISBN-13: 978-1-7252-9629-9
Hardcover ISBN-13: 978-1-7252-9631-2
eBook ISBN-13: 978-1-7252-9630-5
Publication date 1/4/2021
Previously published by Swan Sonnenschein, 1908

This edition is a scanned facsimile of
the original edition published in 1908.

TO
MY DAUGHTER
WINIFRED CLARKE SHAW

PREFACE

THE following work contains the substance of the lectures delivered in the Graduate School of New York University in the course entitled, Philosophy of Religion. As the title will suggest, the purpose of this essay is to indicate the limits of religion in human culture, although, as a reading of the succeeding pages will show, the principle of limitation is to be understood in a manner acceptable to a genuine conception of faith. The spirit in which the precinct of religion has been examined is not that of the older noumenalism, still less that of the newer phenomenalism; both metaphysics and psychology are here set aside for the sake of a humanism which seems best adapted to defining the essence of human worship. Thus it is not with antipathy towards certain popular tendencies that we make this departure, but rather with sympathy for living religion whose rich intellectual content seems to be most faithfully conserved when expressed through the culture of humanity.

C. G. S.

TABLE OF CONTENTS

HISTORICAL INTRODUCTION

PAGES

Philosophy of religion a modern idea. 1. The Age of Enlightenment. Metaphysical dualism with Descartes. Moral diremption with Hobbes. The regressus to fundamentals in thought, in life. Emancipation of religion. Its inness and universality. The error of deism corrected. 2. The Age of Culture. Moralism and pessimism in Kant. Hegel's intellectualism and positivism. Schleiermacher as epoch-maker. Schleiermacher and Spinoza . 1–16

PART I

THE ESSENCE OF RELIGION

Religion, Philosophy, and Science

Threefold view of the world and the soul. 1. The world of nature. The cosmos of philosophy. Religion and the world of spirit. Threefold attitude toward the world. 2. The problem of life. Science and utility. Philosophy and value. Religion and blessedness. 3. Methods. Science and mathematics. Philosophy and logic. The method of religion. 4. Limits. The temporal and spatial in science. The eternal in philosophy. Religion and history 17–33

2. The Limitation of Religion

Effect of secularism and sacerdotalism. 1. The ramification of modern philosophic disciplines. The independence of religion. 2. Limitation of religion. Its internal and qualitative aspects. Religion limited by itself. The precinct of religion. 3. Interaction between religion and other forms of culture. Speculative and practical forms of interaction . . . 33–53

3. *Religious Consciousness*

1. The precinct of religion and religious consciousness. Historic consciousness of the race. Hindu and Hebrew. Religious consciousness of the soul. Idea of a world-whole peculiar to religion. God a religious notion. 2. Religion no simple element of the mind. The faculty of judgment. Religion both passive and active. The totality of the soul . . . 53–69

4. *Religion, the Self-Affirmation of the Soul*

What is desirable in definition ? 1. The inness of religion. Its foundation in the ego. Self-doctrine in Descartes, Fichte, and Schleiermacher. 2. Attitude of soul toward world. The spontaneity of religion. Affirmation of the World-Soul. 3. Motive for self-affirmation. The humanistic principle. The place of pessimism in religion 69–82

PART II

THE CHARACTER OF RELIGION

A. THE RELIGIOUS VIEW OF THE WORLD

1. *Religion as Knowledge*

1. Modern logic and religion. Value of Herbert's "De Veritate." Scepticism of Hume. The case of Kant. Conflict between intellectualism and moralism. 2. Religion not irrational. Place of knowledge in religion. Living ideas of religion. 3. Cognitive, conception, and communication of religion. Israel and India. Religion as faith 83–102

2. *Religion as Æsthetic Intuition*

The essential nature of art. 1. Origin of æsthetics in Plotinus. Value of Gothicism. Theology of Romanticism. 2. Religious significance of art. Æsthetic unity of spiritual life. Religious nature of the artistic deed. Their common idealism. 3. Positive form of art and religion. Artistic furtherance of faith. The religious element in the fine arts. The intelligible nature of intuition 103–116

B. THE RELIGIOUS INTERPRETATION OF LIFE

1. *Religion and Ethics*

The half-work of Kant. 1. The formal distinction between religion and ethics. Range of ethics. Theoretical nature of the ethical.

Table of Contents

The positive form of religion. Its historical essence. Spiritual religion pessimistic. World-despair. Religion *infra* and *supra* moral. 2. Actual connection between religion and morality. Position of Jesus and Socrates. Nature of religious conduct. Specific and sacred character of righteousness. 3. Value of morality for religion. The ethical the highest means of self-affirmation. Moral destiny of man . . . 116–139

2. Religion and Rights

The practical side of religion juristic. 1. Common origin of *jus naturale* and *religio naturalis*. Effect of natural rights upon deism. 2. Parallel history of rights and religion. The forensic in Christianity. 3. Substantial bond between religion and rights. The metapolitical in religion. The humanistic in jurisprudence. 4. Metaphysical realism of rights. Religion and law the sanction of ethics. *Lex talionis* and non-resentment . . 139–154

PART II

THE REALITY OF RELIGION

1. The Origin of Religion

1. The *argumentum a tergo*. The beginning of religion genuine. Fallacy of supernaturalism. Insufficiency of rationalism. 2. Naturism and spiritism. Humanistic quality in primitive worship. The poetical element in naturism. Value of the disorderly in nature. Sundering of man from nature . 155–168

2. The Development of Religion

Modern genetic thinking. 1. Opposition to development in logic and ethics. The progressive in religion, art, and law. Hegel's treatment of history. History the mere vehicle of religion? Spiritual meaning of history. Value of historical events to Israel and India. 2. How history realizes the essence of religion. Self-affirmation of the soul cumulative. Stages in the development of idea of God 168–181

3. World-Religions

Three types of universal religion. 1. Chinese religion of nature. The hexagrams of the Yi-King. Eternal recurrence. Taoism as world-religion. Naturistic nihilism. Quiescence and non-resentment. 2. Intellectualism of the Veda. " *Tat tvam asi* "— " *aham brama asmi*." The Self without and within. Aim of

Vedanta. Empirical ego and the Self. Spirit of non-resistance.
3. Christianity a religion of spirit. The living World-Soul.
Transcendental needs. The Christian deed positive. "That
art Thou" in the eternal Gospel 181–200

4. *The Revelation of Religion*

Revelation and the Christian religion. 1. Revelation a communion
of human and divine. Relation to universal religion. God,
redemption, and revelation. Revelation communion not communication. 2. Goal rather than source of religion in revelation.
History an eternal present. Participation of man in history of
humanity. Christianity as revelation. Revelation not abrupt.
Pedagogical analogy. The order of revelation . . 200–214

PART IV

THE RELIGIOUS WORLD-ORDER

1. *The Religious Value of Theism*

Idea of God humanistic. 1. Interpretation of being. Theism and
religion. Theology and metaphysics. Striving toward the Godhead. 2. World Ground and law of identity. Empirical scruples against "immanence." Possibility of atheism. Theism
and monotheism. World of things versus world of spirits.
3. Theistic "demonstrations." Career of the ontological argument. Religious world-order the unity of religion and theism 215–231

2. *The Affirmation of Absolute Life*

Religion more than theism. 1. Real significance of thought. Logic
and life. 2. Æsthetical yearning for reality. Genuine culture
metaphysical. Significance of human ecstasy. Communion of
beauty and truth. 3. Metaphysical moment in ethics. Meaning
of conscience. Psychology of remorse. 4. Rights and eternal
justice. Logic of non-resentment. Problem of evil. Vicarious
suffering and Absolute Life 231–247

3. *The World of Humanity*

Idea of humanity not primitive. 1. The "Gunas" of Sankhya philosophy. Humanism in the Occident. Contrast between ancient
and modern ideals. 2. The ontological in man. Phenomena,
noumena, and pneumata. Place of persons in the world of humanity. Illusion of individuality. Consciousness of humanity.
Problem of death. 3. The historical in humanity. History and
the individual. Temporal and eternal considerations. Destiny
of man 248–263

4. Unity of Finite and Infinite

Various phases of the problem. 1. Sense and reason in philosophy. Spinoza's solution. The religious method. Dualism of conscious and unconscious in religion. The individual and the Absolute. Immortality of man. Unity of temporal and eternal. Relation of man to God. 2. Ethical unity of life. Synthesis of fate and freedom. Moral units of man and God. Man's participation in the infinite. Final unity of life . . . 263–279

THE PRECINCT OF RELIGION
IN THE CULTURE OF HUMANITY

HISTORICAL INTRODUCTION

RELIGION is as old as man; philosophy of religion is confined to modern thought. The religious consciousness may be traced as far back as human culture and civilization, but the problem of religion was not raised until the opening of the seventeenth century. The vast orient which gave the religious fact, and which, once for all, performed the religious deed, did not possess the intensity necessary for deducing the religious idea. From the East comes the content of religion, from the West its form. Among ancient Mediterranean speculations, we find that Plato, with his worthy views of the human mind, and Aristotle, with his extensive comprehension of human nature, did not isolate and discuss the religious problem as such, but remained content in the plastic and contemplative spirit peculiar to the antique. Stoicism, the earnestness of whose thinking gave us ideas of nature, humanity, conscience, rights, and progress, as well as suitable terms for the expression of their meaning, likewise contributed the idea of religion. This service, however, was largely confined to terminology, and the result of the invention of the word was expended wholly upon the side of etymology. Philology is not philosophy, and the idea and consciousness of religion remained implicit until the natural religious discussion of modern times.

In modern philosophy, two periods have contrived to produce a philosophy of religion : first, there came the age of enlightenment which covered the seventeenth and eighteenth centuries ; then, there followed the period of culture from the French Revolution to the present. Here there was analysis which culminated in the Kantian philosophy ; there was found synthetic movement which had its beginning with German idealism. For religion the propelling force was, first, a juristic tendency which had its source in the philosophy of natural rights ; secondly, an æsthetical influence incident upon the current problem of culture. That modernity should evince the religious idea should not be deemed paradoxical, nor must it be assumed that the problem of religion arose serenely as one question among several. The very bent of modernity was destined to call forth the thought of religion, and the programme which the modern laid down for himself made this a necessary part.

In seeking to account for those modern conditions which have made religious thought possible, history must investigate something more than clearly marked periods and leading personalities. The very tendency and direction of modern philosophy incline toward religion in a manner no less forceful and direct. Here may be noted the strong dualistic movement which acted as the cause of our modern philosophic science, and that equally invincible impulse on the part of thought to return to first principles. In each case the religious principle was involved in both a general and specific manner, and the undercurrent of modern speculation seems to have been directed toward the religious precinct. The reason for this consists in the fact that religion lies in the depths of man's spiritual nature, and when thought creates vast divisions in the human understanding and returns to fundamental principles in the life of mankind, the connection between living religion and speculative philosophy is more easily made out. Breach with the world of appearance and tradition and the return to a fundamental ground are the very elements which religious speculation needs, and hereby does religion itself become a problem.

1. So invariable is the dualism which pervades our modern thought that it may be regarded as essential to our problem. Upon the psychological side, a beginning could not be made until Descartes created a fundamental distinction between mind and body. It is true that the way in which this distinction is expressed, as the contrast between two substances known as *res cogitans* and *res extensa*, can hardly satisfy our psychical and physical theories to-day, but the Cartesian dualism was necessary for presenting the psychological problem. In the same way, modern dualism appears in Kant where it assumes the form of sense and understanding, or phenomenon and noumenon. Here again, we may dissent from the peremptory fashion in which Kant seeks to solve the problems of empiricism and rationalism, yet we cannot fail to observe how germane to the modern was the distinction between appearance and reality. So far as historical facts in philosophy may indicate necessary thought, it may be said that problems of mind and of thought could arise and be discussed only as the thinker separated mind from matter and thought from sensation. The vigour with which this was done caused a shock, the reverberation of which we feel even to-day.

Nor were the practical problems of life exempt from this diremptive tendency, for here as well was made distinction which set the speculator against himself and divided the moderns into party-thinkers. The ethical problem, introduced by Hobbes and thoroughly presented by the thinkers who opposed or corrected his doctrines, was subject to the same influence. Here was a hedonism which based all moral sanction upon some heteronomous principle, while there was an intuitionism appealing to the autonomy of reason. Thus the modern took sides in the conflict between natural desire and rational duty. In the field of æsthetics, there was aroused somewhat the same conflict and there appeared the same dualistic agency. Accordingly, taste was defined in terms of pleasure which appealed to the senses, or after the manner of perfection which partook of reason and spirit. Likewise the philosophy of rights which set up abiding contrasts between *jus* and *lex*. When Puffendorf, from his chair of international law, endeavoured to adjust the claims of ego and society, as these had been set forth by Hobbes and Grotius, he evinced the keen nature of the problem at hand. Thus the issues of man's life which would be expected to leave him happy in the sense of his humanity, move against him and make his life a problem.

Religion itself, which naturally profited by a view which separated man from the world about him and emancipated him from his immediate consciousness, was to participate in exactly the same spirit of dualism. Here it became something more than an academic dispute, and assumed the form of a great religious conflict. On the one side was the newly discovered principle of reason, which was set at variance with the medieval idea of tradition, and this contrast between *ratio* and *traditio* was destined to emancipate human nature. In perfect keeping with this strident separation of reason and culture was the conflict between freedom and authority. In this distinction between *libertas* and *auctoritas*, there was involved the principle of free-thought, as also the whole programme of toleration. Hereby the religious consciousness of man was liberated and philosophy of religion became a possibility. Tradition which had been the guide of the fathers, and authority which played the same part with the Schoolmen, were now set at naught; no longer was it argued *de religionis non est disputandam*, but the essence of religion became a leading problem. Thus with mind and body, noumenon and phenomenon, *jus* and *lex*, religion and revelation, the modern inaugurated the religious problem.

In immediate connection with this dualistic tendency was that philosophical impulse which led the early modern thinker to retrace his principle to its source. It cannot be said that the characteristic thinker of the seventeenth century was possessed of any genetic motive or historical spirit, for no greater conflict with history than that which developed in the Enlightenment can be noted. What the pioneer speculator was doing consisted in reducing accepted philosophical dicta to their appropriate grounds, so far as his rationalistic methods could discover these. It was at this point that religion was destined to gain, for religion manifests itself as a principle of thought only when the superficial view of things gives way before the fundamental. Problems of physics and politics, questions concerning thought and action were taken up as soon as the Enlightenment came to consciousness. Then the way for religion was prepared, and the religious problem itself was adjusted to this vast retroactive tendency. The path of this *regressus* was not far removed from that of the dualistic movement, and in each case the modern assumed his characteristic attitude.

As Descartes had proposed the dualism of mind and matter, so he was practically the first modern to point out the way toward fundamentals. The scepticism and subsequent rationalism of Descartes are well known and sufficiently estimated, yet their bearing upon religion is not properly appreciated. With a sceptical spirit and a logical method, Descartes found the fundamental principle to consist in self-consciousness, *cogito, ergo sum.* To him this was convincing, and he was satisfied with the discovery of the soul as *res cogitans;* yet his thought could not rest until it had evinced the validity of the idea of God, and Descartes, who imitates Augustine's scepticism, rehabilitates the realism of Anselm with his famous ontological argument. Upon the same speculative side, Locke deduced the fundamental of the understanding after the manner of an empiricist. The soul viewed in its primitive form is not a *res cogitans*, but a *tabula rasa*, upon which experience traces its objective elements. Locke, who invests the mind with more content and gives it more life, still agrees with Descartes in seeking the fundamental. The extremes to which these advocates of rationalism and empiricism went only evince the vigour of their thought and fundamental character of their common problem.

The first and fundamental thing in human life was none the less an object of investigation, and the speculative impulse which urged the thinker to discover the primary principle of thought, also acted to lead him to investigate the original impulse in human life. Grotius thus set about to evince the indigenous in human life. This he found to consist in an original form of rights, *jus naturale*, which in its independence of tradition as a source of authority as its sanction was conceived by him to hold valid of itself and *non esse deum*. The extreme to which Grotius went in his endeavour to lay bare the primary character of rights was imitated by Hobbes in his theory of the *status naturalis*. In this condition of mere nature, man has a natural right to everything and a legal right to nothing, while he acts in response to motives which are egoistic in their courses and pessimistic in their consequences. Indeed, Hobbes was so unflinching in his determination to reveal the essential impulses of man that he put them upon a materialistic basis and brought about a union of physics and politics. In this spirit, problems of mind and problems of man were reduced to prime numbers of the natural.

Meanwhile religion had not failed to participate in the great return to nature, and when the Enlightenment set up the sharp contrast between liberty and authority, it completed this by conceiving of human worship in the form of *religio naturalis*. This was the original form of modern philosophy of religion. It is no difficult task to indicate the obvious imperfections of such a crass system of religious thinking. Ignoring intuition in its zeal for inference, flouting history in its enthusiasm for reason, natural religion failed to penetrate to the psychological essence and

Historical Introduction

spiritual character of human worship. Thus Deism failed in its search for the actual as well as in its alignment of the ideal ; its concept of religion was lacking in content, while its standard was wanting in worth. Natural religion could no more explain positive cults than it could satisfy speculative demands. In such a manner, *res cogitans, tabula rasa, status naturalis* and *religio naturalis* became by-words in the seventeenth century, and they indicate a thorough faith in the ideals of reason and nature to which they gladly returned.

German philosophy, which was not so premature, but was more profound, did not follow the regressive course which modern philosophy elsewhere had been outlining. Nevertheless, the systematic speculation which developed from Leibnitz to Schopenhauer had its method of sounding the depths of human understanding. To pass in review over the limits of German idealism is to see how the gifted intellect of mankind pauses in the presence of the insoluble. Leibnitz' rationalism covers the domain of speculation and includes things both human and divine, yet it finds obstruction in the idea of certain *vérités de faits* which could not be intellectualized. Kant's abhorrence of the thing-in-itself betrays the limits of his transcendental system. The intrepid systems which followed Kant in his categorical reasoning, but refused to accept the limits which he found in phenomena, found other obstacles no less insurmountable. Fichte's self-propelled ego cannot explain the blind " Deed-act " of the world. Schelling's " Absolute " is a dark and unfathomable world-ground, while Hegel's magnificent phenomenology of nature, man and philosophy is not broad enough to include the contingent facts of human experience (" Das Zufällige "). Schopenhauer's idealism, which reduces the phenomenal world to illusion, no less really postulates a blind, irrational will as the basis of all reality.

In the midst of these ineradicable modern tendencies, religion was making a history for itself. The career of natural religion during the Enlightenment exemplifies the actual course which philosophy of religion was to follow. It was at the outset nothing but a blind affirmation of religion as something free and natural. Having discovered the general principle of rights, Deism deduced the particular idea of the right to think as a special application of the same. Then toleration was demanded as the natural consequence when the emancipated and enlightened thinker desired to express his new opinions. The limitation which legal toleration prescribed for the natural freedom of thought was further reduced to definite proportions in the form of a natural religion and a rational Christianity. These were rapidly formulated by an age which felt its own internal freedom, but which further desired to live in harmony with the principles of some established religion. That which was decided upon as the most suitable religion was not the orthodoxy of the Church, but the abstract Deism of the natural religion school. Deism arose as a practical movement created by a philosophy which sought to unite right and law in the form of free-thought and toleration.

The immediate result of such a movement was to isolate religion and to arouse the religious consciousness; at the same time, the subject of religion as a matter for speculation was distinguished from the non-religious. This was made possible by the modern philosophy of natural rights. By virtue of its internal nature as something belonging to man while distinct from the state, the principle of rights served to express the inward nature of religion. It was under such forensic auspices that Spinoza, as jurist, distinguished between the legal fields of reason and religion: *ratio regnum sapientiæ et vertatis, theologia autem obedientiæ et pietatis.* The principle of this distinction was found in the idea of rights, upon the basis of which it was decided what in a practical way may be included in and excluded from the precinct of religion. For religion, the importance of Spinoza consists not merely in making a distinction, but in elaborating a definition, according to which the vital

Historical Introduction

nature of religion was interpreted in terms of piety and according to another conclusion of Spinoza, mercy.

What Deism, with Spinoza, accomplished was twofold; it pointed out the inness of religion, and marked out its universal character. The first principle which concerned the intrinsic quality of religion was masked under the idea of *jus naturale*, which enabled the pioneer thinker to develop his *religio naturalis;* the second principle was the work of reason, which, along with the principle of rights, made religion co-ordinate with the human soul. While the crass arguments for liberty of thought did not succeed in identifying the peculiar essence of religion, they did not fail to put the latter upon the basis of independent speculation, just as the method of rationalism was able only in part to relate religion to the world-order established by human speculation. Where Deism failed was in its lack of psychological analysis, as well as in its antipathy to historical thinking.

Assuming, as we may safely do, that history teaches philosophy in an exemplary fashion, a glance at the counter-Enlightenment will aid in clarifying the modern concept of religion. This period, while not marking out the religious precinct, sufficed to negate the false ideal of the rationalists and served to prepare the way for Kant and the modern constructive thinkers. Here may be noted the attack upon the Enlightenment inaugurated by Vico and Voltaire, Hume and Lessing. One hundred years after the appearance of Herbert's "De Veritate," Vico produced "Scienza Nuova" as a foundation work in the philosophy of history. Vico criticizes Grotius, Hobbes, and Puffendorf among the jurists as those who indicated a false beginning for civilization, while he himself returns to the actual beginning of human culture in the naive idea of the primitive man. From such a genuine beginning, which saw the poetical rather than the political in original man, he proceeds to outline the development of mankind according to the threefold plan of naturistic, heroic, human. To the plan of Vico's new science Voltaire adds no substantial principle, yet his " Essai sur les mœurs des nations " reflects a historical spirit counter to Deism and directed towards the scientific ideals of the present.

Hume and Lessing nullify the programme of natural religion, when one points out that, not reason, but " custom is the great guide of human life," and the other regards revelation as " the education of the human race." Hume's scepticism which ends in his reposing his faith in habit and custom, fits him for the work of religious thinking which is ever marked by the positive. In a restricted sense, Hume may be regarded as the finisher of Deism and the founder of the modern science of religion. Lessing's service was not so vast, but more intimate. To an age given up to static views of the world, he announces that it is only after a long process that man is able to produce from within and receive from without such vast ideas as those of the unity of God and the immortality of the soul. Lessing adds to the Spinozistic ideas of unity and rationality, Leibnitzian principles of individuality and development. Thus he concludes that the knowledge of God as one and of the soul as immortal was gradual in its development and marked by successive steps toward the *dénouement* in the Eternal Gospel of the future. As Hume's work is marred by naturalism, so Lessing's is of oblique influence, because it never advances beyond the intellectualistic ideal that religion is *knowledge* of God and immortality. Yet the ideas of custom and education serve to prepare the way for the second period, which consists of culture. Under the auspices of this age, the fate of religion was destined to be more happy.

2. The succeeding age profited by the errors of Deism. Just as the French Revolution changed the course of civilization, so it created the problem of culture as the writings of Rousseau and Fichte clearly show. In this age of culture, religion receives a more satisfactory treatment than that which the age of Enlightenment had been able to afford, and it is also the idea of culture, rather than that

Historical Introduction

of rights, which is calculated to express the nature and function of religion. The thinkers who formulated the theory of religion were Kant, Schleiermacher, and Hegel. Kant bases his idea of religion upon the ethical, and defines it by saying, " it is recognition of duty as a divine command." Hegel resorts to a method equally logical, and regards religion as the " finite spirit's consciousness of itself as infinite." Schleiermacher mediates between the two, when he makes use of the æsthetical analogy. For him, religion consists of intuition and feeling, a feeling of absolute dependence. It was the artistic spirit of Schleiermacher which enabled him to advance beyond Kant and Hegel, and to put religion upon a satisfactory basis.

Not only in the romantic " Discourses " of Schleiermacher, but in the ethical views of Kant and the logical constructions of Hegel does the æsthetical appear. Kant's point of view in the " Critique of Pure Reason " finds its most significant feature in the part fitly styled " transcendental æsthetic," and while this foundation of the critical philosophy does not include a doctrine of the beautiful, it is not wanting in that metaphysical view of time and space, as intuitions, which in the " Critique of Judgment," reappears in the form of that which is universal without the concept. Thus, in order to comprehend the logical intuitions of Kant's greater work, one can do no better than to absolve the argument for æsthetical intuition which the " Critique of Judgment " puts forth. With Kant, the æsthetical plays also a teleological part in the interpretation of the actual world, and the critic who turns away from abstract ontology finds some value in the argument from design. In the case of the Hegelian dialectic, the æsthetical terms a stage in the self-development of the absolute in the form of image, representation, and concept or art, religion, and philosophy.

With particular reference to Kant's moralistic system, it may be said that its religious and æsthetical ideas contained in the final portion of his philosophy give answer to the third of his critical questions, " What may I hope ? " One cannot fail to note the serious, if not abject, tone in Kant's " Religionsphilosophie." The "Critique of Pure Reason " relegates the mind of man to such a central position in the universe that it is concluded that the understanding gives unto nature her laws. In similar confidence, " the Critique of Practical Reason " urges man to act so that by his act of writing his maxims may become universal laws. Thus do the category of causality and the categorical imperative glorify the human understanding and will. Kant's " Religionsphilosophie " abandons this imperious view and humbly presents man as a creature of radical evil who stands in need of redemption !

The message from this *vox clamantis in deserto* is that of repentance and the Kingdom of God. First it is declared that man is possessed of a nature radically evil. Such evil is not due to a perversion of sense, which would make man simply bestial ; nor is it due to a depravity of reason, which would make him devilish, but may be explained as an ineradicable tendency to subordinate reason to sense. To the correction of this radical tendency, man must become the subject of redemption, which involves, not good works, but a complete reversal of human impulses. In order that this may be accomplished, man must have a redeemer in the form of the Son of God, who, Himself having conquered evil, is able to save man by means of the influence coming from example. Finally, when we observe that the fact of human salvation is contained in history and recorded in religious literature, we may conclude that thereby is made necessary an established church as repository of such traditions as also priesthood to facilitate their interpretation.

In dealing with positive religion, it may be said that Kant is hardly just, since he regards religion as a means to an end purely ethical. As Schiller proclaimed the æsthetical education of man, who is above sense yet below pure ethics, so Kant seems to observe that the human being, whom he has relegated to the theoretical world of phenomena, cannot live in the noumenal world of duty. To effect the transition from one realm to another man must have religious education. It is the pessimistic tone of Kant's system which adapts him to the subject of religion and which puts him *en rapport* with biblical ideals. This note, melancholy as it may appear, forms the residuum in a system of religious thinking which is warped upon the ethical side.

The Hegelian philosophy, which everywhere manifested the tendency towards phenomenology, was prejudiced in favour of religion. Hegel's career begins with the writing of a " Leben Jesu," his system falls into discredit upon the publication of Strauss's " Leben Jesu," in 1835. It was the dialectical method of reconciliation which put Hegel in the attitude where he could view, as one mind and matter, God and man. In itself, the dialectical plan contains a tripartite movement which involves the religious consciousness, first in its naive immediacy, secondly in the form of spiritual individuality, and, finally, as a happy synthesis of the two apposites, in the form of the absolute religion. Where subsequent philosophy departed from Hegel, it was partly on account of the artificial character of his method, and also because of the complete intellectualism which envelops his system.

Religion, which is itself a step in the development of absolute spirit, possesses similar stages in its own peculiar evolution. First in order comes the immediate nature-religion, which betrays its features in various primitive peoples. Upon the same plane, but in a more advanced form, Chinese, Sanskrit, and Pali cults set forth the same general trait of naturism. Such is the way in which Confucianism, Brahmanism, and Buddhism are styled respectively religions of measure, of phantasy, and of self-absorption. Transition from this lowest stage to the next higher one is made by means of the Persian dualism, the Phœnician religion of pain, and the Egyptian religion of mystery.

Sundered from nature, spiritual life sets up the contrast of light and darkness, this dualism invades man's soul only to cause world-pain, which, as he broods upon it, resolves itself into a mystery whose Sphinx-like silence is never broken. The second stage, that of individualistic religion, appears in Judaism, where God is everything and man nothing, in Grecian religion, where man is all and the gods are naught apart from him, and in the Roman religion of utility, which, in the spirit of apotheosis, unites divinity with humanity. The culmination of religion is found in Christianity, the absolute religion. Here may be found a dialectical motive in the respective domains of Father, Son, and Spirit.

The valuable element in the doctrine of Hegel is that of the positive, which, however, does not fare so well when the philosopher assumes the rôle of historian. So far as the literature of oriental religion is concerned, nothing would seem to justify Hegel in putting Brahmanism or Buddhism upon so low a plane. The inherent power of Vedic religion and the adaptability of Buddhism to China and of Vedanta to European thought would seem to indicate that the Hegelian treatment is of value only in a general and suggestive manner. It tends to inculcate belief in the value of history, but does not enable the student to gain insight into particular periods of religious history.

The position of Schleiermacher's system is unusually noteworthy. Written after Kant's work and before Hegel's, it recalls the moralism of the one, while it anticipates the intellectualism of the other. At the same time, the psychological tendency which everywhere pervades the system, relates the author to Herbart's intellectualistic view and Schopenhauer's voluntarism. The first position is assumed in Schleiermacher's "Discourses on Religion," wherein he adjusts both Kantianism and Hegelianism to their proper positions to the right and left of the religious precinct. The second position appears later in the psychology, where Schleiermacher exalts feeling as the essence of the soul, in distinction from cognition and volition. In the plan which Schleiermacher lays down, the adjustment of religion to morality and metaphysics is no less marked than the description of the essence of religion itself. This adjustment is made in the " Reden uber Religion," while the definition, in its complete form, is developed in " Der Christliche Glaube."

At the outset, Schleiermacher's system is marked by wholly negative elements, which culminate in the bold statement that, " Piety cannot be an instinct craving after a mess of metaphysical and moral crumbs." Insight rather than argument marks the method of Schleiermacher ; true it is that he urges against logic by saying that quantity of knowledge is not quantity of piety, and distinguishes between morality and religion by regarding one as active, the other as passive, but the thought is genial rather than convincing. If logic emphasizes thought, religion depends upon intuition; if ethics leads to action, religion consists of feeling. To these general characterizations, Schleiermacher adds certain important qualifications, which end in a definition : " Religion is sense and taste for the Infinite." Such is the burden of the all-important second discourse of the brilliant theologian of the " Romantik." The " Glaubenslehre " tends to unify the conception of religion, and is able to do this because the issue is no longer with moralism and intellectualism. Religion, accordingly, is regarded as a sense of absolute dependence, in the elaboration of which idea Schleiermacher distinguishes religion from the Fichtean conception, a feeling of absolute independence. The value of Schleiermacher's work is more general than that of either Kant or Hegel. Like Spinoza, he indicates the independence of religion from philosophy, as his predecessor had separated it from science ; together they proclaim that genuine religion consists in piety.

Slow as was the emancipation of the religious precinct, it appears finally that the means which effected this were those of rights and æsthetics. The Enlightenment had tried to show that religion consists in the knowledge of God and the performance of such ethical duties as follow from the same. But Spinoza points out that the legal conception of human faith involves no element of speculative *veritas* or practical *sapientia*. As if in imitation of this, Schleiermacher addresses himself to an age, not so much of rights, as of culture, for which he separates religion from an alien morality and metaphysics. His method was that of art, and, on the ground of intuition and taste, he defines the religious precinct. The typical personality of the age of Enlightenment was wont to unite religion and rights as he exclaims, in revolutionary tones : " *Dieu et mon droit !* " The more contemplative romanticist approached the Deity in a nobler way and, like Schelling, said, " Kunst ist Gott." The thinker of the Enlightenment had the good fortune to state the religious problem and to evince the nature of religion ; the age of culture invested this with a rich content, the fruits of which are still enjoyed.

When at last the emancipated idea of religion appears, it proposes a problem which, by virtue of its historical career as well as its internal character, is peculiar to religion. In no other department of culture is there presented such an issue, for nowhere else is human interest so directly involved. In order to survey and evaluate the religious principle, we must devote the whole philosophy of religion to the subject alone, and must everywhere resist the temptation to turn aside into the paths of either ethics or metaphysics. A complete discussion of religion will involve : (1) An analysis of the essence of religion in human nature ; (2) An evaluation of the character of religion in human life ; (3) A view of religion as positive reality ; (4) A contemplation of the world-order of religion.

PART I

THE ESSENCE OF RELIGION

IN determining the essence of religion, philosophy may be helped by the career which the subject has had in modern times. Both the period of Enlightenment and the age of culture have revealed the independence of religion in the life of human reason; the first epoch evinced abstractly the inness and universality of worship, while the second invested this with moral and metaphysical elements. The age of naturism emancipated religion and commenced the work of modern philosophy; the period of humanism elaborated faith and brought the subject to a temporary conclusion. Such is the status of the problem as it now confronts us, and it is in keeping with modern conditions that it must be discussed; for this reason, it is manifestly erroneous to relegate religion to some form of metaphysical or moralistic study, just as it is fatal to reduce it to the phenomenalistic principles of psychology and sociology. Philosophy must keep upon the plane of spiritual life, and it is in the spirit of culture that the values of humanism are to be conserved. The particular method which is to be applied to the problem of religion's essence involves four considerations, which extend from the external limits to the internal definition of human worship. Religion must first be distinguished from both science and philosophy. Then the precincts of worship may fitly be determined. On the constructive side of the question, it will appear that living consciousness fills out the precinct of religion and prepares the way for a definite determination of its nature.

1. *Religion, Philosophy, and Science*

The reason for comparing religion with science and philosophy is vital, not academic. Together, these three disciplines have characteristic views of the world and equally marked estimates of human life, and this field of inner and outer thought is one which must be divided in a sufficient fashion. If each form of human speculation were complete, it might appear that their common perfection would result in a single view of man and nature, but since we are dealing with imperfect and progressive factors, we must make some practical distinctions among them. What is here attempted is to relate religion to both philosophy and science in general; not with the aim of reconciling any supposed conflict, but rather with the hope of indicating how these naturally adjust themselves to one another in the consciousness and life of mankind. The distinctions are felt there; and by following out the lines of thought indicated by human instinct, we may perhaps be able to apprehend the nature of religion, as we seek to mark out its limits.

Religion may be said to claim, as its peculiar field, the soul; science, the world; philosophy properly consists in a view of both soul and world. Both religion and science, from their own points of view, apprehend their problems directly; religion seeks to help the soul, while science desires to make of the world practical use. Philosophy, however, yields chiefly a view of these realms of spirit and nature, and seeks, by an indirect method, to indicate the ultimate meaning of life and the final essence of the world. For the decision upon these ultimate questions—and are they yet settled?—religion and science do not wait. Instinct and feeling cause the soul to develop its religion; perception and experience lead to scientific culture. In

The Essence of Religion

all this philosophy is needed to rehabilitate the immediate facts of inner and outer perception, and to make possible a more or less consistent view of the human soul and the world of nature. When we set out to compare these three most general forms of human, spiritual life, we do not consider philosophy as the overarching principle between the extremes of the soul and the world, but we rather regard all three disciplines as upon about the same level; at the same time, our interest in instituting the comparison is the religious one.

The position of religion may now be indicated in connection with these two other methods of thought. It is very natural to speak of "philosophy of religion," and it is not unusual to use the expression, "science of religion." There is a sense, then, in which the religious experience of mankind may assume the general form of a philosophy; just as it is possible, by noting the various details of human faith, to construe these in the form of a science. Such a philosophy may not have a complete metaphysical cast; such a science may not measure up to the demands of mathematics; but the examination of the religious life which is to-day being made, is carried on according to the methods of reflection and research, and the study of religion is to be regarded as a distinct philosophical discipline. Accordingly, the independence of religion is to be considered as the point of departure in the discussion of that theme, and in connection with the subjects of philosophy and science should this all the more strikingly appear. Religion has its own source in human nature, and, in developing this, an independent method is followed. The inner reference which, by religion, is made to the human spirit is peculiar to this subject; so is also the outer reference, where the religious consciousness projects itself upon the screen of the world; according to these two views do the method and limits of human faith vary.

Whatever may result from a comparison of religion with cognate forms of culture, it must be noted quite clearly that religion has its source in itself. Ultimately, its existence does not depend upon the evidence of science; nor does its validity hinge upon the dictum of philosophy. But, since the larger human life puts forth these several impulses to perceive, to understand, and to believe, it becomes necessary, or at least desirable, for religious thought to find its own place in connection with the scientific and philosophical tendencies. Yet religion is not a conclusion to be reached after one has made empirical investigations; nor does it wait for philosophy to make its deductions; meanwhile, the fact of religion abides. Science, in the form of psychology, may, perhaps, offer some criticism as to religion's source in human nature; while philosophy may similarly adjust its metaphysical principles to religion's foundation in human reason. But religion has its own life, and that life develops according to its own principles; and this very independence of religion is all the more assured when the latter is compared with these parallel phases of culture.

When we speak of the independence of the religious idea, as this is defended in philosophy of religion—then, the order of development is made quite different, and religion accordingly is to be viewed as the last, rather than the first, in the triple series. With philosophy established in the days of Plato and Aristotle, and science made possible by Copernicus and Newton, philosophy of religion began to consider the independence of its subject about the year 1800, when Schleiermacher wrote his " Discourses on Religion." Religion as a philosophical discipline has thus had a career, although not a long one. And it is this form of religion chiefly which offers comparison to science and philosophy. Religion as such is a life, founded upon impulse and instinct, and manifested immediately in the individual and the race. But philosophy of religion, like philosophy of æsthetics, consists of something more than the mere sentiments of worship and of the beautiful, respectively.

The Essence of Religion

Reflection upon the religious consciousness, therefore, makes manifest distinct points of view, and, in connection with them, we are able to note the lines of divergence from both science and philosophy. The general nature of religion is very different from these, being more akin to ethics and rights; but philosophy of religion, by virtue of its form, at once suggests various comparisons with general empirical and speculative methods. These appear in connection with the view of the world and the conception of human life, as well as in the particular methods which are entertained and the limitations which are felt. In each of these four points of comparison a threefold view may be maintained, wherein the peculiar character of religion becomes quite clear.

1. The "world," as a term, signifies something the exact nature of which the human mind cannot indicate. In the case of science, of philosophy, and of religion, characteristic views are projected upon reality, and, hereby, we are able more perfectly to discern the exclusive differences among them. Not only the view of the world, but the attitude toward it, is peculiar to each of these three forms of human culture. In general, it may be noted that science expresses its opinion of the world in general postulates, a "nature" which is characterized by uniformity in the realm of matter and conservation in the world of energy; such is the scientific world of perceptions. Philosophy sums up its world of conceptions by assuming the existence of substance and the activity of causality. In the scientific "nature," consisting of matter and motion, in the philosophic cosmos of being and change, empirical and speculative thought everywhere participates.

The religious world-order is *sui generis*. True it may be that as knowledge becomes more and more perfect it will eliminate these poetical views of science, philosophy and religion will see one and the same world, but the present state of human knowledge does not permit of any such magnificent system of unity. Hence, the religious "world" must stand alone. Among advanced cults, there are not wanting sufficient ideas of a religious world-order. Among the Chinese, Tao stands for the reality of the world when its nature is finally perceived, and while Taoism is more or less nihilistic, its view of the universe is self-contained and in many ways consistent. In a similar way and toward the same end does the Hindoo conception of Brahm direct itself. Brahm is the world among a group of thinkers who are as acosmic as the Taoists are nihilistic. The Vedantist development is more striking and more valuable for our purpose, for here the universe is the personal world of the soul. Accordingly, it is affirmed that celestial and terrestrial object is nothing but illusion, whose deceptive character is discovered by the soul within. Christianity may not despair of nature, yet it does not trust the external appearance of things. Christianity postulates a Kingdom of God which is not of this world. Such oriental views make manifest the reality of a religious world, which is as much a matter of human culture as the ancient philosophic cosmos or modern scientific nature.

Of the three, science was the last to formulate a conception of the world-whole; this it accomplished in modern times chiefly by the aid of the new physics. Here, we cannot pause to inquire into the ultimate validity of the scientific theory of the world, where we might go on to ask whether as a view it is supported by that which gives absolute certainty or merely a working hypothesis. We take these views as they are, and regard them as expressing one great tendency in human reason; the tendency to universalize certain impressions. In various ways has science expressed its faith in just this impulse, and our current conception of the world is modified by appropriate scientific formulations. Mathematico-physical science in the seventeenth and eighteenth centuries construed the world in the form of energy, the exact sum of which is ever maintained in the universe. In the nineteenth and twentieth centuries chemistry and biology have added somewhat to

The Essence of Religion

this rather quantitative and static view; and they have, as science, given currency to the ideas of process and development. Perhaps, then, the scientific " world " may be identified by styling it a system of energy or of evolution. At any rate, one complete view of the universe is entertained under auspices similar to these. In this world, science assuredly believes.

For philosophy, the " cosmos " is somewhat different and less easy to identify; this may at once be seen when we bring up the question, " What is reality ? " In the largest sense, this latter term may afford an example of how our modern view of things is formulated. Other and earlier ideals were found in connection with " substance " and " being." All of them are attempts, on the part of the understanding, to universalize its conceptions; and upon the basis of some such view, philosophy, in its speculative form, is built up. More definite formulations of the philosophical cosmos may be found contained in particular theories, like the " world of ideas " in Plato's system, and the ethical " world-order " in Fichte's " Science of Knowledge." Such conceptions have behind them vast logical constructions, of which they are the incarnations; where they are lacking is in connection with human experience, and man can only confess some doubt as to whether these things are so. But, for centuries, the best intellectual life of the race has entertained such thoughts, and their presence has been felt in more than one phase of human culture and civilization. Science persists without a far-reaching logic; philosophy goes on with but a slender connection with experience; and each has its definite construction of the universe to offer.

Religion's feeling toward the world is decisive. In general, this attitude is one of opposition. When handling the cosmos, human faith does not proceed as science has ever done; the world of sense is for religion a matter of decided distrust. The world of philosophical forms is regarded by religion as only a finer conception of the general idea of nature. That which condemns both of them is intellectualism : here it is expressed in terms of sense ; there, in the forms of understanding ; and from all such adjustments must the religious consciousness turn away. In this way, it comes to pass that the distinctly religious conception of the world offers defiance to the more general conception of the universe. Thus it has been with the Hindoo belief in Brahman, and the Christian principle of the Kingdom of God. These, however unreal they may seem in comparison with a scientific " nature " and a philosophical " cosmos," must be regarded as genuine competitors in the great tendency to explain the world. But religion has a more arduous task than that of mere explanation. In postulating such spiritual realm as the " Kingdom," Christianity fulfils the demand of universality ; at the same time, in denying the value of the natural order of things, it shows that it conceives the meaning of the idea couched in the term " world-whole."

The attitude toward the world varies in each of the subjects engaging our attention. Certainly, science, as well as philosophy and religion, makes some kind of departure from the world-idea of naive realism. Nature is no landscape, but a system of laws, and any genuine form of intellectual or spiritual effort, on the part of man, makes it necessary to break with that which is immediately perceived in the manifold forms of sense. What is the true attitude of science ? Science may be said to adjust itself to the world, when it has expressed its conviction in the form of a mathematical formula. Thus, science measures the world. It is essential to philosophy that it should present what is distinctly to be understood as a *view* of the world. Herein, it differs from science, and that chiefly because philosophy involves larger considerations. A scientist like Copernicus completely changes the geometrical conception of the universe, finding a new centre for it in the sun. A philosopher like Kant may style himself a " second Copernicus," but the change which the great

Königsberger effected in philosophy was a change in the relation of subject and object, of thought and thing. An epoch in science is one thing ; in philosophy another.

The spirit of religion, in dealing with the world, is very different. A modern scientist may cause a vast wrench in the world of sense ; an advanced philosopher may set up a dualism in all reality. But religious thought is still more vigorous in apprehending the world, which it does not hesitate to negate. Religion, when it realizes itself, involves the principle of victory over the world of time and space. This is effected in more than one way. By virtue of its fundamental judgment, religion concludes that, when compared with the soul, the world is of no value. At the same time, religious consciousness evinces a certain distrust of physical reality, and a corresponding inclination for the world of spiritual life. As the natural result of this feeling, and the corresponding thought of the supersensible, religion wakens within the soul an unwonted aspiration for something not of the world. It is for some such reasons as these that universal religions, like Buddhism and Christianity, ever suggest acosmism, in one or another form. Yet religious faith has not run the risk of mere subjectivism ; it has considered itself to be the substance of things hoped for. But the distinction which comes out in connection with the religious realm is this : science is at home in the natural world ; philosophy distinguishes its field from the world, as in the idea of the incorporeal ; religion's attitude is one of opposition, for it finds the world inimical. From such a point of view the conception of life is determined.

2. " Life," when taken up by these three forms of spiritual activity, receives a creative treatment, varying with the power and character of the particular discipline. This effect, surely wrought upon human existence, is such as to affect the work, as well as the thought, of mankind. We here leave unnoticed the vast interrogation, " What is life ? " and seek rather to answer three distinct questions : " What does science do for human living ? How does

philosophy consider it ? What is the fate of life in the hands of religion ? In each case a characteristic answer can be given ; and, hereby, we can in some way determine again the limit of religion, as well as the latter's relation to the two other forms of human thought. In the most direct manner, it may then be said that science, in serving man's existence, has done this in the form of *utility*. An exact study of natural phenomena results in the production of helpful devices ; discovery leads to invention. Philosophy has ever had its own method of getting life, and has generally tried to contribute the principle of *value ;* this it has treated as an ideal. So far as religion is concerned, it may be observed that the service rendered is different from both of these others. Religion has not stopped, until it has construed man's existence in the form of *blessedness ;* this it has aspired to bestow.

The scientific treatment of life affects, at once, theoretical considerations and practical goals. The nineteenth century especially witnessed an attempt to apprehend the ultimate essence of organic existence. It is alien to our purpose of comparison even to touch upon the field of biological research ; but let it be said that the evolutionary view of nature, systematized by Darwin, and the organic conception of society, as brought out by Spencer, seem both of them to stand in contradiction to the now popular view that, instead of a principle of " vitalism," life is made up and governed by mechanico-chemical elements. The extreme application of the term " organism " seems to offer glaring contradiction to the antipathetical treatment of the theory of vitalism. Science, however, concerns us here as creating in thought and fact the principle of utility. Modern industrialism — nay, modern life — depends upon the scientific conception of the world. Invention, device, and contrivance, made possible by the application of mathematical science, have had a helpful effect upon man's painful career in the realm of time and space. A moment's reflection will show how all this has

The Essence of Religion

come about; deeper consideration can only reveal the other fact—that the complete service of science is bounded by the principle of utility; science pays.

In the hands of philosophy, life has been idealized and its intrinsic value made manifest. This has come about in both a speculative and an ethical manner. The facts of experience, as these are considered in science, are not ignored by any means; but in the merely actual, the philosophy of life does not abide. Its thought aims to ascertain that which is prior to experience; while practical impulse, when it is thus idealized, aspires to reach the transcendental. Philosophy, when it attacks the problem of life, does not fail to idealize its subject. It shows what is thinkable and demonstrates what is desirable; the perceived fact and the felt desire are only points of departure for some higher ground. With especial reference to the question of life, philosophy makes a distinct advance beyond the standpoint of science. That which is involved is the *character* of life, not its mere existence. Philosophy thus dignifies human existence, which it invests with meaning; it does this by evincing the value of the soul.

When religion makes use of the term " life," it expands this idea, while investing it with an unwonted meaning. It is thus with awe the New Testament speaks of eternal life as a spiritual element which, present in the existence of man, is also the very essence of God. Life is in this way magnified, by virtue of a new point of view. So vast becomes the idea, that it is not easy to relate this life to history or to the conditions of earthly existence. The further thought of destiny may enter in as explaining life as eternal; the mere fact of science, as well as the speculative ideal of philosophy, is here transfigured by the thought of purpose. In some ways the religious view of life reconciles the realism of science with the idealism of philosophy. For religion, man's existence is no crude fact, yet it is not an abstraction; religion begins with the actual world, but does not end there or anywhere, until it rests in some absolute condition of things. But, all the while, it keeps *en rapport* with the facts of human life and history.

Blessedness, however, is the more definite principle which characterizes the religious view of man's existence. This is not the actual condition of human life in the world, yet is not a mere ideal. The religious subject feels that for him blessedness is obtainable ; at any rate, thus is religion guided. No other principle than this may be applied to the one thing which religion has ever judged as being needful ; and whether we consult the actual history of human faith, or the reflective views of religious thought, we can only find that religion seeks those things which are above. Such an idea is not an empty one. Christ spoke of the Kingdom of Heaven as consisting of blessedness ; but he did not fail to add that that kingdom is as seed sown in the ground. He described it as the highest object of man's destiny ; yet those who were among the first to enter in were publicans and harlots. Blessedness, at once idealistic and realistic, blessedness, as belonging to both the highest and the lowest phases of mankind, is the religious principle of life as brought out by such a religion as Christianity. It is true that, in religion, the sense of usefulness is not lost, nor yet the conception of value ; but with these foundations of life-activity the religious consciousness cannot remain content. For it, a new and heavenly realm is made necessary.

3. A comparison of the *methods* of science, philosophy, and religion will bring out the intrinsic difference of religious thought. Science, to realize its ideal, must be exact, and for this realization it demands mathematics. As a rule it may be said, then, that a perfect science does not exist, unless it can express its data in the form of an equation. Certain classes of scientific research, however, only approximate to this ideal. The method of philosophy, when we consider the latter's speculative form, is parallel to this. A philosophical truth cannot claim validity, unless it be expressed in the form of a judgment. Logic

The Essence of Religion

is, therefore, the perfected form of all philosophy. Not all philosophy measures up to this criterion, it is true; but such is the ideal of the understanding. Religion can, of course, make use of no such methods; yet it has its way of expressing its conviction.

Knowledge is for both science and philosophy the acknowledged goal. Religion has usually been supposed to content itself with faith. It is by no means a settled question whether faith, as a definite element in religion, relates itself to the speculative, or the practical, side of human reflection; and in the light of present thought, it may perhaps be ventured that religious belief tends to assume an ethical rather than a logical form. It is thus that Höffding has recently defined religion as "*Der Glaube an die Erhaltung der Werte in der Welt.*" Such a definition of religion, and such a general conception of faith as is now being brought forward, seem to show that the attitude of religious belief is a decidedly practical one. The faith philosophy of Jacobi and Herder represents a form of belief very different from that actually encountered in religion. If religion does not follow the method of knowledge, it employs something very like the latter. What is knowledge? This is a question which has puzzled modern thought, especially since the days of Kant; and it is an open question as to what is the source of knowledge in the cogenitive process, as well as to what is the criterion of logical truth. Thus the question, "What is knowledge?" is about on the parallel of the other question, "What is religion?" The old logic can no longer dogmatize; syllogistic argumentation can hardly commend itself to current methods. Religion has ideas of its own. Among these ideas are the world, the soul, and God; these have been deduced and elaborated by the religious consciousness. Knowledge, in the largest sense, would seem to have an extra-logical significance; and so long as the single aim is to find the truth, the difference in points of detail may wellnigh be ignored. In the two forms of historical tradition and theological doctrine the actual content of religious knowledge may be found. Knowledge is something more than the mere relation of ideas; in addition to these, it has a vital substance which relates it to human thought. Motives toward knowledge may be found in the feeling of curiosity as well as in the appreciation of truth; and because religion emphasizes the general anxiety of life and its concerns, it can only strengthen the feeling for knowledge.

Knowledge is for religion an important consideration, because the denial of the ability to attain to absolute truth threatens the supernatural realm, without which spiritual religion cannot exist. Religion apprehends the spiritual, and it does this in independence of both science and philosophy. But any positivistic limitation on the part of science, or agnostic prescription from the camp of philosophy, is inimical to that transcendental principle which is surely demanded by religious faith. The fate of religion is, accordingly, somewhat the same as that of speculation, and if absolute knowledge is impossible, absolute religion would seem to be in danger. It is for religious thought to realize that a part of the burden of truth rests upon it; and to note, further, that the deliverances of religion are such as to constitute true knowledge, and not sheer faith. In connection with the idea of spirit does this appear. The spiritual is the religious concept deduced in independence of experience or speculation; faith produces it in response to some vital demand of the religious life where there is postulated a distinct " there " in opposition to the " here." Particular developments of the principle of spirit may be found in the ideas of the soul and God, as these are advanced by religious belief and worship. The spiritual soul is free. Its freedom, however, does not consist in an arbitrary will, but in a complete emancipation from the field of matter. Inner experience, which characterizes the nature of the soul, is the thought of a religious mind intent upon realizing its destiny. God is spirit.

The Essence of Religion

But such an idea is the result of monotheistic belief, not of theistic speculation. God is an only God, and as such he commands the worship of free spirits. Religion has learned this lesson for itself, and has not had an education from the masters of science or philosophy. And thus, self-taught, it has produced the two ideas which have been mentioned, as it has also contributed to the knowledge of the world-whole. The method of religion is a self-respecting one, which is seen when the fruits of its labours are examined.

4. *Limitation* is a fate which besets any form of thought as soon as it becomes at all definite ; and hence it is that science and philosophy outline their own precincts. For scientific investigation the limits are to be found within the forms of time and space, which are the types of all arithmetical and geometrical reasoning. Within the temporal and spatial limits are to be found the phenomena of physical science. These boundaries are not transgressed, and scientific thought does not affect to answer the questions, " What is time ? " " What is space ? " Philosophy, however, finds in these two questions two very important problems, and, along with the question of causation, they make up the most characteristic phases of metaphysics. In itself, philosophical thought assumes to regard its problems in independence of these cosmological limits ; and speculation, when it perfects itself, assumes the attitude *sub specie aeterni*. Such was Spinoza's conception of true knowledge. In theory, the conception of eternity signified relief from the limits of time and space, rather than a mere regressus into infinity.

The field of religion may not be indicated so easily. It may perhaps be said that the career of religion has ever been within the field of the temporal ; for, of all things, religion is pre-eminently an historical matter. But this is not all ; religion has some relation to the eternal, certainly in the idea of God. And hereby it offers a parallel to the precinct of philosophy. To relate the contingent and temporal to the necessary and eternal has, for more than two centuries, been a problem for religious thought. The Enlightenment's testimony was to the effect that true religion is a matter of eternal significance ; and, convinced of the soundness of this idea, this period did not fail to set positive religion at naught. Current thought has concluded differently, and thus seems inclined to rest in the temporal phenomena of religion to the partial exclusion of speculative principles. The proper attitude of religion can only be found when the temporal and eternal are reconciled ; how this may be done is a special question for philosophy of religion. But the fact remains that religion, departing from the realm of time and space, does not pause until it has reached that which does not suffer change ; its limitation is peculiar to itself, and does not offer analogy to the cases of science and philosophy.

History, as the peculiar synthesis of time and eternity, is the province within which religion finds its limits. But hereby religion realizes itself. An abstract conception of a static endlessness cannot attain it ; nor can the opposite view of science, which abides in the contingent fact. When the religious life expands within the field of the historical, it reacts upon the latter and brings out the inner meaning of development. Science is essentially a matter of the present, and the old abides only as it is transformed into an acceptable form ; astronomy discards astrology ; chemistry, alchemy. Philosophy has its present, but ever returns to the past for guidance ; the historical element, however, is only one among many others. But, for religion, the historical is essential, and as a method it is employed in a characteristic manner. Past and present have a vital connection, and without the historical content religion is as nothing. The result of this comparison of religion with philosophy and science now appears, religion is possessed of a spirit and method of its own just as it is marked by certain limitations, which constitute the religious precinct. The sincere spirit and the essential limitations of religion must now be examined.

2. *The Limitation of Religion.*

The spirit of religious thought in the present has been that of construction rather than controversy. Until the dawning of the nineteenth century the method in religion had consisted either in attack or defence, and nowhere was to be witnessed a calm consideration of those things which are essential to religion and vital to its character. Yet the construction of philosophy of religion was not destined to shake off entirely the skirts of the long conflict, and in more than one way has religious inquiry been warped and otherwise rendered ineffective. Two tendencies have contrived to hinder the progress of sincere religious thinking ; one is secularism, the other sacerdotalism ; the first characterizes theology, the second, science. Sacerdotalism has given religion such an elevation that it has made it unsteady; it has done this by taking away its foundation in human nature and human culture, leaving it in mid-air. On the other hand, secular science of religion has allowed its zeal for facts and phenomenological generalization to lower religion to the level of mere anthropology. Both the ideal and the real must be surveyed sincerely in the history of ethnic religion. Not only the flower but the root must be surveyed and analysed. Sacerdotalism has turned away from positive, psychological religion, just as secularism has spurned everything but these humanistic products. Both of these points of departure must be abandoned by philosophy of religion.

Sacerdotalism pursues the subject of religion in the spirit of idealism, but it does not do justice to positive religion as a fact in the individual's consciousness, or as an element in the history of the race. Religion, as conceived of by sacerdotalism, seems to be a subject closed to investigation. Here a fatal mistake is made. Subordinate as the general subject of positive religion may be, the natural history of the religious consciousness must be regarded as essential to religious thought. Religious customs, as well as the phenomena of worship in general, must be made the subject of research. Only then may we hope to comprehend the mysteries of faith. True it is that we cannot remain among the ruins of ancient beliefs, any more than we can content ourselves with these torsos of a faith, once living, but now passed and gone ; yet, the positive, as such, plays its part in religious inquiry. Now, it is from the positive that sacerdotalism has turned away.

As scientific research is thus set at naught, so also is reflection, in the philosophic sense of the same. Religion appears to be a subject too holy for thought ; indeed, it seems to be above any parallel which speculation can produce, so that it becomes difficult to detach it from its usual theological environment and set it down in the philosophical curriculum. But this false sanctity is unjust to the superlative merits of the subject ; by study we do not make void the works of religion ; nay, we establish religion. In a word, just as the customs developed in the history of positive religion must become subjects of scientific research, so the concepts which are manifest in religion, as a form of spiritual life, must be subjected to philosophical reflection. To the test of validity and value must these concepts be put, and this need not be esteemed as endangering the character and content of such a spiritual subject. The ideas which reflection thus seeks to identify and develop are not obscure abstractions to be pursued after the manner of ratiocination, but are vital and vivid products of the religious life, and these are naturally destined to become the subjects of thought. Particularization has thus been the natural result of sacerdotalism's treatment ; not religion, as such, but a particular form of worship has been regarded as all-sufficient for consideration. From a purely practical point of view this may, perhaps, be just. We are Christians ; the elements of this faith are wrought into our occidental life and civilization, and these can in no wise be changed by any data derived from the phenomenology of ethnic religion. But our thought and our philosophy of religion may not proceed in this way; here, we must settle accounts with science and adjust ourselves to the data of comparative religion. To adjust Christianity to its strategic position in the history of humanity, it becomes necessary to orient that faith to the other religions of the East. Rightly to divide the history of religion and, at the same time, to bring out the characteristic nature of Christianity, is one of the most critical questions which, to-day, may be presented to our minds. At the same time, the products of historical religion, because they represent facts and present material which command our attention, must in some wise be explained. And it is just this explanation which religious thought has overlooked or neglected. When positive religion has been investigated, when its history has been so divided that various cults may be properly classified, then the singular destiny of Christianity may appear.

But religion in general and Christianity in particular have not received straightforward treatment. What has not the particularizing tendency of sacerdotalism done! Among other things it has failed to derive religion from its proper source in human consciousness, having had too much to say about reason as a logical faculty and revelation as an abruptness on the part of the divine. Religion must be viewed as organic to human nature, just as its history must not fail to be esteemed as constructive in the development of humanity. Now, sacerdotalism has never penetrated to the depth of this sentiment, whose flower it would nourish and cherish; where it has departed from a strictly theological point of view, it has been to embrace a rationalism which is equally far removed from the manifest nature of religion itself. It has done this as though intellectualism were in harmony with the affairs of faith. It is true that the products of pure thought tend to exalt the intrinsic quality of human life above that which is purely natural, and thus thought may rise to meet religion in the latter's own spiritual atmosphere. But religion suffers from such contact, and practically all of human worship is now subsumed under the thought-process; where faith enters in, it is only as an inferior form of knowledge. Secularism thus sharpens into intellectualism; the end is not thus reached.

Does secularism come any nearer the heart of this painful problem? Secularism follows a course in some ways antithetical to sacerdotalism, and has its advantages for science. Yet it is not without limitation. Appeal is made to experience, and there is witnessed an effort to penetrate to the human soul. Religion, as believed on in the world and not simply as an idea which man's mind may entertain, is now made the subject of study. To the individual, the method of psychology is applied; when dealing with the race, history and social science are brought in. At first sight it appears as though the heart of man were at variance with his intellect; for, where, in the actual history of humanity, are the concepts and logical relations which, in human thought, have been so majestically paraded? Such concrete concepts as may be identified in connection with positive religion are very different from ordinary theological ideas. But they have this advantage over the latter: they possess a certain rough reality, and thus become amenable to investigation. But, unfortunately, the science of religion has not always appreciated the integrity of its subject. Under such ill-favoured auspices did the modern scientific study of religion begin. As a work in this line, what has been more important than Hume's " Natural History of Religion "? Yet how hopeless was the conclusion with which Hume's study is crowned; it was couched in the following words: " Examine the religious principles which have in fact prevailed in the world. You will scarce be persuaded that they are anything but sick-men's dreams." Such words as these show how the realism

The Essence of Religion

of religious inquiry may deepen into pessimism, yet they should not be taken as signifying anything contrary to the conception that religion is a normal product of human nature. The "sick-man's dream"! Is it not a dream of health? The wretchedness which thus cries out in the soul of the man, is it not a cry for deliverance from this body of death? From the mere fact our thought must press on to the ultimate significance. The positivist treatment is ever pursued with a cardinal difficulty; when we assume a purely anthropological point of reference we are in danger of considering religion as all-too-human. We dwell upon that which it has been the singular fate of religion to disclose—the imperfection of human nature; as a result, our psychology becomes pathology.

Secularism aspires to explain religion; does it not likewise desire to explain it away? A psychology of religion is developed, but only with the result of showing the subjective and superficial nature of the question under treatment. Thus, the fact of religion is admitted, while its value is denied. Where sacerdotalism pointed toward religion as a supra-logical sentiment, secularism tends to regard it as infra-rational feeling on the part of humanity. Was it not so a generation ago, with Feuerbach, and is it not the case to-day, with Spencer and many another contributor to modern religious science? The scientific view is content with phenomenology, having no place for a philosophy of religion. Such a tendency manifests itself in the perpetual desire to retrace the course of religion to its immediate beginning in prehistoric times. Thus it is argued, here is the source of the sentiment—animism, dendrolatry, litholatry—and here is the secret to be found. But surely this is not the whole matter; there is another question which, entering into the consideration, tends to change the direction of logic. This is the question of destiny. Religion has its origin in man's nature, but its place is not a subordinate one. It arises and asserts itself, and thus determines what man's life shall be. If the origin be human, the goal which religion creates for humanity is more than human. Can the science of religion content this demand? Certainly there is something more to this study than these purely phenomenological traits.

Generalization has ever been the science of religion's foe. Following a line of thought about the opposite of that which guided sacerdotalism, this other spirit of religious inquiry has fallen into a difficulty which is none the less fatal. In both cases the integrity of the religious principle has been impugned. Secular and scientific thinking has endeavoured to complete its study of the religious sentiment by exalting a generalization from empirical data to the elevation of a supreme religious principle. The result has been emptiness; the universal in religion has been denied; the character of the sentiment neglected. No matter how faithful may have been the study of phenomena, or how conclusive the induction may have been, the worship which appeals to the heart can be no "perception of the infinite." To produce that which shall be religion for us, this method of study is wholly unsuited. What will be the most likely result? In the place of a barren intellectualism there will be only a cross naturalism—the alleged glory of the statue would seem to be found not in the form but only in the stone.

By the proffered aid of neither of these methods does the veritable nature of religion appear; a sacerdotalism which resorts to rationalism, a secularism which relinquishes all to a purely empirical treatment of human religion, alike fail to show what religion justly may be esteemed to be. The first duty in the philosophy of religion is to express the integrity of the subject with which it deals. To do this various forms of expression may be employed. As a form of spiritual life, religion may be regarded as occupying a distinct province in human thought; in comparison with other philosophical sciences, that of religion must be considered as self-centred and complete; in the individual as well as in the race, the natural history of the

The Essence of Religion

religious consciousness may be traced. When such essential features of the religious principle have received recognition, the way is prepared for a sincere consideration of the problem itself. Let it not be said that this only indicates the starting-point; if current thought can keep in mind, that religion proceeds from a source peculiar to itself, it may be fairly well satisfied with its performance.

If religion is not an independent phase of human life, and philosophy of religion is not a valid form of human reason, it is because there is no religious precinct. Perhaps religion is in vain, and consists of crude beliefs and vague impulses on the part of primitive man, or is a moribund type of modern life. But religion must be itself; must appreciate its peculiar character, and indicate its own goal. Thus its fate lies in its own hands. Among the many problems incident upon the development of an independent religious view, nothing is more necessary, while other things may be more entertaining, than the idea of religion's own precinct. This must be defined. In discussing the field of religion, it becomes necessary to observe, first, the tendency of modern philosophy to radiate into special sciences; second, the impulse of religion to differentiate itself and prescribe its limits; third, the method by which independent and self-contained religion adjusts itself to these other branches of human speculation. This threefold task is made easier when it is assumed in connection with the religious precinct.

1. *Ramification.* When we consider the suggestions of non-religion, we can easily be struck with a sense of wonder. Why should the present, whose psychological and sociological genius has enabled it to identify the peculiar nature of religion, begin to speak of the passing of this principle? It is only to-day that spiritual religion has begun to be appreciated by European and American; and the independent study of Christianity is something which has just occurred to us as being worth while. Monotheism, or the belief in an only and spiritual God, is a conception which,

even to-day, is expressed with great imperfection. Spiritual life and destiny in man are ideas to whose significance the present has hardly awakened. When we begin to explain religion, we fancy we are explaining it away; as a matter of fact, we are only becoming conscious of an ineradicable instinct. At the dawn of the twentieth century, thought had been sufficiently aroused to notice the presence and power of religion in individual and race. Religion, rather than non-religion, is the most likely tendency; and to study the former, it becomes necessary to outline the religious precinct, so that, among the ramifications of modern thinking, the independent character of worship and belief may be seen.

The emancipation of the various philosophical sciences is one of the most interesting phases of current thought. To recognize the fact, that practically every speculative discipline has declared its independence, is a duty thrust upon the student of contemporary thought; while to provide for some vital method of interrelation, which shall unify all of these in the human spirit, is a task which should not long be put off. The ramification of the philosophical realms is a modern performance, comparable to that political system of internationalism which has taken the place of medieval cosmopolitanism and ancient nationalism. Indeed, the analogy between the modern effort, on the part of the social spirit, to break up into various nations, between which the rights of war and peace should obtain, and the attempt made by the scientific consciousness to differentiate the precincts of culture, is a very significant one. What is lost thereby is the unity of spiritual life; but the loss is only an apparent and temporary one, and the tendency to constitute independent precincts is a healthy development. A glance at the career of certain philosophical sciences will show that we are confronted by no theory, but by actual conditions.

Since the social consciousness seems to have been the means of emancipating the scientific consciousness, it was natural that the conception of rights should have been one of the first to detach itself from the staid course of history, and affirm its independence as a human consideration. This was brought about by Grotius, creator of the science of rights and the philosophy of international law. For Hobbes, the performance of Grotius was inspiring and useful, and he was thereby enabled to emancipate the ethical consciousness of the English people. Morality received an explanation, but not a sufficient justification. Yet Hobbes deserves credit for having appealed to human nature and human motives. Grotius's theory of rights finds its counterpart in that sense of corporate spirit represented in Rembrandt's " Night Watch," while Hobbes's ethics was objectified in the English sense for conduct and desire for well-being.

Logic became independent in the hands of Locke, who laid down the fundamental principles of epistemology, or theory of knowledge. Hereby, knowledge for knowledge's sake was set up as an ideal, and a modern tendency was reduced to a system. On until Kant, and from the critical philosophy to the present, the question of the criterion of certainty and its application to the world has been discussed. Separated from objective metaphysics, and with a breach set up between thought and thing, modern epistemology has pursued its own path. Psychology has materialized the soul. In doing this, it has fallen back upon sheer experience, contented itself with phenomena, and aimed simply to give a description of consciousness. This it has considered in the form of conscious life as a process closely connected with the organism.

Novelty has been the result of this differentiation. Modern life has its "new philosophy," "new ethics," "new theology." These are symptoms of emancipation, comparable to the resolute application of " nature " which the Enlightenment made in connection with " natural rights " and " natural religion." In æsthetics, we have art for art's sake ; in religion, worship for worship's sake. It is with such tendencies that we, to-day, have to do ; he who pursues the subject of philosophy must have some synthetic method calculated to reduce these elements to an encyclopædia. This tendency, inaugurated by Bacon and applied by Diderot, must be employed in a worthy manner, which shall consider the sciences as expressions of spiritual life in its various phases.

For religion, this is especially important. This branch of life and culture asserts its own independence, and then endeavours to adjust itself to the comparative phases of philosophy. Let it not be said that in this way we are breaking up the unity of the soul's life. Better is it to lose sight of this for the time being, if, by developing the living content of spiritual life, we may return to the soul. Certainly, we cannot account for the facts of experience by assuming that the soul's nature is like a *res cogitans* or a *tabula rasa;* but from abstraction to introspection our thought must turn. The larger philosophical problem must be solved in connection with a view of all the results which special disciplines have elaborated ; and when philosophy comes to itself again, it may not be so magnificent, but it will be more in keeping with man's life. The special sciences will assume the form of kinds and gradations of a single spiritual life in humanity, which is endeavouring to assert its high character in opposition to merely mechanical existence in the world. This general tendency to ramify and then to return to the source is instructive for religious thought, which is assuming its proper form and undertaking to adjust itself to philosophy in general. The affirmation and limitation of religion is to be regarded as a natural development of thought.

2. *Limitation.* This is a distinct phase of definition. In religion, it consists in marking out the precinct of faith. All phases of thought trace back to some instinct or tendency to react upon life in the world ; each has its own field, and each its phase of reality. Thus it is in the instance of religion, which is now recognized as being able to con-

struct a view of the world and to align a method of life's conduct. When we ask ourselves, under what circumstances does religion arise, and what are the conditions of its normal development, we are on the way toward a solution of the question, What is the religious precinct? Let it be noted, however, that the predicament is one which is not the peculiar fate of religion, but belongs to every genuine philosophical science. Do we not also ask, What is right, and whereby is it sanctioned? What is beauty, and wherein consists its form? And, when we consider the essence of religion, we do not fail to inquire, at the same time, What is knowledge, and what can we know? Everywhere thought is confronted by a *quid facti* and a *quid juris;* as one among many, religion comes within the range of these interrogations.

For more than a generation, limitation in religion has been the cry; to some ears frightful, to others sweet and welcome. But what does limitation really mean? If it expresses the idea that religion is suffering from outside elimination, or that the idea of God is less credible, then we can only look upon it with suspicion. As long as religion permits itself to remain under the domineering influence of intellectualism, it can only complain that logic is not equal to the task of satisfying religious need; and so long as it attempts to cast off this yoke only by the assistance of voluntarism, it will find that the will is not sufficient to produce the desired range of religious activity. Relief must come in the thought that religion is limited *by itself* from *within*, and not by any other function from without. In addition to the idea of the self-limitation of religion, it must be noted that the precinct thereby determined is marked by *qualitative* rather than merely quantitative factors. Limitation consists in the marking out of religion's own precinct, and is brought about by religious consciousness itself. Religion can accomplish only what it is designed to do, and this is to be found within the limits of spiritual life. Since man is fitted with natural trains of ideas, his life need not wait for thought ; and, guided by custom, his actions do not need ever to ask what duty is. Yet logic and ethics are essential. In a similar way, it may be urged that, primary as is the concern for religion, the latter need not be supposed to yield scientific results or industrial benefits. He who makes such demands knows not what he asks.

The self-limitation of religion is no confession that man is unable to find satisfaction in his faith. Suppose it be shown that the Absolute cannot become an object of knowledge ; then it can further be pointed out that the Absolute has no part in the religious life, which long since has found God, in whom it lives and moves and has its being. Suppose we are convinced that an autonomous morality is beyond the reach of man's will ; then we can only be comforted by the thought that autonomous morality is alien to the religious life. In Christian thought there is no lack of satisfactory conceptions of God ; he is the Father of human spirits, and religion is hereby guided in its view. Nor are there wanting sanctions for human conduct ; God has a kingdom which represents the final goal of man's moral activity, and thereby is the ground of religious life made secure. Untainted by an artificial metaphysics and an unnatural ethics, the sound and educated religious consciousness will not find any painful limits within the religious precinct, but will rather find there hidden treasures of thought and life. Accordingly, it is not so necessary to inquire into the grounds of theistic belief, or the sanctions of morality, as it is to indicate the conditions under which human destiny and divine design may be mutually adjusted, and man reconciled to God.

By being self-centred, religion describes the circle of its influence. To it all other phases of culture may be useful, but they are extraneous. Logic does not care so much for the value of its reasoning as for its formal validity ; ethics does not inquire into human inclination or ability, but seeks only to determine norms. Religion has its own field, wherein are included many elements overlooked by other forms of philosophy ; and why should philosophy of religion need to glance toward these other camps, when it possesses its own material and has won its own methods ? There, it is independent, and in its own way it may seek what knowledge is applicable to the needs of the religious conception, and what standard of behaviour is in harmony with spiritual life. Religious ideas are evoked, not by curiosity, but by vital concern ; they are meant to be believed on. Gravitation and natural selection may be universally valid in the realms of matter and life ; but we do not put our trust in these generalizations. Life according to nature, and conduct for the promotion of social health, may have some place in human history, but they are not religious ideals.

Within its own precincts, the religious consciousness has not failed to produce valid ideas and worthy maxims. It is for this reason that the limitation of religion becomes a misconception ; the limitation is qualitative, not quantitative, and is advanced by religion itself. The form of the metaphysical concept is alien to the demands of the religious consciousness, which has its own conceptions. Likewise, the character of the ethical sanction ; here, religion is not inimical, but it does not fail to enjoin its own peculiar commands, unknown in the realm of morality. Upon the lowest stage of religious development, the attitude of the believer is artless ; yet this can only reveal how characteristic is the religious life. Upon the highest stage of religion, the same attitude appears in the form of spiritual freedom and opposition to the letter of legalism. In its progress, religion has guided itself, borrowing no more from philosophy at large than the latter has borrowed from it. For the greater part of modern thought, the attitude of theology has been as that of a judge waiting until all the evidence should come in before he could render decision ; and it is only of late that religion has been regarded as giving its own evidence.

When the internal and qualitative form of the religious precinct is once appreciated, it will appear that the limitation involved is due, not so much to the finitude of man's mind as to the fitness of the subject entertained. For this reason, the idea of a precinct of religion, which is a necessary thought to-day, must not suggest the perverse notion that man cannot know his own mind and that, if he were only super-man he could have a rationale of his own faith, but being all-too-human, he must content himself with agnosticism. If the common notions of human knowledge do not contain the essentials of religious truth, we need not argue against the possibility of religion, which may still exist as an instinct, but may rather question the applicability of the method employed. Suppose that the concepts of the understanding as the percepts of sense do not assert religion, shall we then decide against man's faith? In addition to understanding and experience, there are evidences of truth which may be found in the intuitions of ethical value and æsthetical fitness, and in connection with them religion might still live and perform its function.

Without attempting to carry out the analogy between religion and art, it may here be indicated how the idea of limitation applies to both of these forms of culture. Within the domain of the fine arts, it was the work of Lessing to show that painting and poetry are arts which are mutually exclusive, each having its own sphere. Painting and plastic belong to the realm of space, as poetry belongs to that of time. For this reason, the painter cannot represent motion, nor can the poet portray the several features of beauty. As Edmund Burke also reasoned, Homer does not attempt to delineate the beauty of Helen, for he knows that a face which is seen at once in its entirety cannot be reflected in a series of stages, word upon word and line upon line. That would only confuse the mind which must have the spatial intuitions as a whole, and upon this ground, Burke criticizes Spenser's portrayal of Belphoebe in the same way that Lessing rejects Ariosto's description of

Alcina. On the other hand, the spatial form of beauty as the Laocoon group cannot imitate a cry, and it is fitting in the artist when he covers the mouth of the priest with the lips so close together that Laocoon cannot cry out. Upon the metaphysical distinction between time and space, the mutual limits of plastic and poetry are thus indicated.

In addition to this analysis of religion there may be cited the vast instances of positive religion which arise within the peculiar domain of human worship. Here lie before the investigator strong synthetic judgments developed by the sure instincts of the human race. To appreciate them, we must combine the methods of research and reflection, in the light of which appears the plan of human culture as *phenomenology*, a secure union of contingent and necessary, of sense and reason. It is in connection with religion that the phenomenological most justly exists, history has taught us just what meets the approval of man's religious consciousness, and has established ideals as surely as Greek architecture put forth its Doric, Ionic, and Corinthian. If we but had the proper system and were possessed of sufficient insight, religious ideas of God, blessedness, repentance, non-resentment, and the like would evince the permanency of the objective religious consciousness. Mesopotamia and Palestine, as geographical shadows of the religious precinct, have shown us that religion is at home within the realm of great ideas and strong motives. With these enduring instincts to believe and obey firmly ensconced in our human nature, can we afford, to-day, to be anxious about agnosticism? The religious consciousness is limited, but it has limited itself in order that it may evoke its own peculiar results. But this limitation has not been so narrowly drawn as to exclude the conception of a universal spirit, and world-whole. Unaided by Greek speculation, the Founder of the Christian religion made known the meaning of monotheism in its depths; at the same time, he marked out the limits of the world. And here is another fact, less significant, but more striking for these vast truths : the Palestinian mind was quite ready for, and did not fail to appreciate, the meaning of them. If it is said now that philosophy has its conception of God, and science its theory of the world, it can only be responded that these views are not sufficient unto the demands of the religious life. Philosophy and science have their fatal limitations, but these need not hinder the action of religion in its attempt to relinquish the world and find its home in the realm of spiritual life.

Naturally, we hesitate to ascribe to some single portion of the universe the particular possession of vital knowledge, as though all history had its home along the shores of the Mediterranean. Nevertheless, there are places, as there have been times, in which the full meaning of human life has dawned upon portions of the race, and these have given us our educations with religious life. Not only God and the world, but the soul and human life, have been outlined within the religious precinct, and are hardly to be found within the pale of psychology or ethics. Within the soul's life, the several phases of the religious moment are determined ; and it is on this account that we are continually led to believe in the reality of the religious field and the validity of its limits. What is human life, and wherein consists its significance ? Science and philosophy now have their answers : life consists in knowledge and wisdom. Ethics and politics, too, are ready to contribute their maxims ; life is a form of conduct. But religion has ever had its own answer, and to it men have been ready to listen ; life is no mere knowledge of the world or activity within its boundaries ; but from this knowledge and from this activity a view and a deed enter in to enable man to reach the shores of spiritual life, which his soul has discovered. Hence that otherwise inexplicable behaviour of mankind which is severally styled "sojourn," "exodus," "return from captivity," "crusade," "retreat." These movements symbolize the soul's desire to quit the immediate surrounding for a land which, though unknown, is believed to be the home of spiritual life.

Religion is likewise an attitude. For this reason, we note general views in religious thought; but in addition to them the religious consciousness has manifested the function of judgment. Religious propositions give convincing evidence of the inviolable religious precinct. In both the conception and communication of religion may this fact be noticed. Man expresses religious propositions; that is the simple state of the case; but how easy is it to construe these judgments as though they were obscure intellectual relations, or incomplete moral maxims. Religious judgments relate to God, whose existence they affirm; to the world, whose value they negate; to man, whose nature and character they indicate. Ethics says, Purity is a virtue; religion proclaims, Blessed are the pure in heart. Ethics asks, What ought we to do? Religion demands, What must I do to inherit eternal life? Such statements are vital, and affect the body as well as the mind. This is not to say that religion is a disease, but it is not to deny that religious emotion can bring out symptoms of man's pathological condition.

3. *Interaction.* As a vital phase of human nature, religion is made capable of sustaining relations with all forms of thought. This is not to raise the question, whether the source of science and ethics, of art and rights, is to be found in religion, but only to assert that, in the form of distinct sciences elaborated by calculating thought, religion yet maintains its independent method. It is on this account that a serious study of mankind's religious life, and the religious thought of the western world, must embrace such topics as the following: religion and morality, faith and knowledge, worship and art, revelation and history. What other philosophical discipline makes necessary such a method of investigation? But religion is rich in its relations, and, as long as its independent precinct is emphasized, it can only gain by the use of

E

the comparative method. To keep up this balance between the one and the many is a problem for the present. In its actual history, religion has arisen and developed among these other phases of spiritual life ; and our thought can do justice to the religious problem only as it follows the course of this sentiment among the ramifications of human culture. Greatly is it to be regretted that the intimate nature of religion in individual and race is examined only as though the problem were one of psychology or sociology.

The independence of the religious precinct is seen when religion manifests the tendency to react upon the various parallel sciences. Religion is primarily an art ; its form is æsthetical, consisting of worship, which is nurtured by religious literature. Religion is an art of life and a method of thought. How long have we delayed in our vain endeavour to demonstrate its nature and justify its character ! With its inner and human essence, with its independent power by which it manifests itself in the positive form of culture, with its irrevocable judgments of value and destiny, religion bears fit resemblance to the sense of beauty. Faith and taste are independent attitudes of the mind, making known how definitely a spiritual impulse may create its own precinct. Religion involves knowledge, for it is no blind affirmation of the soul over against the world ; and the essence of that spiritual endeavour, guided by which the mind aspires to gain a complete view of the universe, is something akin to the native religious impulse to find its home in the realm of spirit. To know is a part of man's destiny as a religious subject. But how varied may be the products of human thinking ! Iron is heavy ; God was manifest in the flesh. It is as led by an unerring instinct that religion, turning aside from the logical ideals of clearness and synthetic certainty, seizes hold of that which has value ; and this it includes within its own sacred precinct.

Conduct, individual and social, is involved in that peculiar attempt of soul-affirmation and world-negation which makes up the vital throes of religion. The moral ideal and ethical norm receive life when they are taken up by man in his endeavour to adjust his life to the demands of God. Where religion manifests its positive form, due to the vital influence of history, and further reveals its pessimistic character, acquired by intimacy with a nature all too human, these difficult phases of the spiritual process are toned and idealized by contact with the ethical. The positive becomes moral progress ; the pessimistic prepares the way for a genuine development of human character. In a similar way, the stream of social rights is affected ; and it must be recognized that theology and politics have many points in common. What was Bishop Butler's lament over conscience ? " Had it strength as it has right, had it power as it has manifest authority, it would absolutely govern the world." Here is the dawning of " civic conscience," but, since conscience is not a political guide, the result of endowing it with power would be only persecution. Religion, which works by persuasion and not by might, endeavours to govern the whole world and thus make its precinct universal. Such a hope as this may be found expressed in the idea of the Kingdom of God.

The completion of the religious precinct is, accordingly, to be found in some such conception as the kingdom. Positive religion, which never deals in abstractions, has made use of this idea to show its belief in an order of things at once spiritual and worthy. Religion interacts with the several philosophical sciences, because it sees in them adequate statements of human life and human thought. Where it reacts upon the results and methods of thought, whether in the forms of æsthetic sense or logical intellect, religion is inspired by the hope of finding in these some expression of that spiritual realm toward which its instincts lead it. Logic and art only confess that they are based upon something more than that which perception finds in the world ; and it is this " something more " which religion seeks as its peculiar realm. By virtue of the various speculative sciences, religion is enabled to effect its negation of the world in which it finds itself, but within which it cannot remain. The creative power of art and the categories of thought make it possible for religion, in a rational manner, to turn away from the world; for they very plainly show that the immediate condition of the natural world is not the home of spiritual life. Where individual sciences interact with religion, the latter reacts upon them with the result of transforming their characters.

But in a practical manner as well does this reaction take place, and the positive religious precinct is developed in the light of rights and ethics. Within the kingdom of God, the striving spirit is quickened in its aspirations when it applies the methods of conduct. These make its attempt to affirm itself a justifiable one; and what art and logic have postulated is now more definitely apprehended by the moral will. Right and authority may come from the practical sciences, but strength and power are supplied by the religious instinct. In all this, interacting with other sciences and reacting upon them, religion is itself and remains within its own precinct. There the human and divine may meet. It may be necessary to discourse for a while upon the nature of religion, as a function of the human spirit, just as it may be imperative to discuss the logical grounds of theistic theory; but religion is more than these, and can only be studied when we survey it within its own precinct. There, individual and universal are reconciled.

Thus far, only the form of religious thought has been emphasized, and that with the aim of casting into clear relief the inner nature of religion within the religious precinct. But this is not the complete essence of religion. The religious consciousness fills out the mere form prescribed by consistent thinking, and likewise adds to the actual content of religion itself. Upon the basis of a living consciousness of religion the fundamental religious deed on the part of the soul may be understood. At the outset, religion must be spoken of as a psychological function, and

The Essence of Religion

we must treat the subject in the form of consciousness of religion. But this is not all : spiritual life in man, manifest in his faith, is a deed as well as a consciousness. The soul feels, but it also acts, and hereby it performs a deed unique in its character. For this reason, the precinct of religion, outlined as this is by a sensitive and spontaneous consciousness, is to be differentiated from the world of percepts and phenomena, as also from the world of concepts and noumena, that is, from science and philosophy. Before this can be attempted with any hope of success, the significance of the religious precinct must be felt more directly as a religious consciousness. Then our formal thought shall be invested with a content.

3. *Religious Consciousness*

Consciousness of religion marks off and fills out the precinct of religion ; religion itself is religious consciousness. In discussing the essence of religion, we must continually bear in mind that we are not dealing with a deduction from the understanding, or a production of the will. It is the direct and not the derivative principle which marks the form of religion, and for this reason philosophy of religion must not assume that its foundations consist in the moral maxim of conscience or the metaphysical principle of causality interpreted as divine. The religious problem is one of introspection, and is not invented by reason as a device for elucidating nature, any more than it is designed by the will as one of the supports for morality. Both the psychology of the individual and the history of the race reveal the fact that religion arises in original fashion and manifests itself as something indigenous to human nature.

1. In assuming a psychological standard, philosophy of religion calls attention to the inness of the subject within the religious precinct ; furthermore, the appeal to data of consciousness shows us that religion is neither an influence

nor an ideal. Religion is religious consciousness. It cannot be said that religion consists in reason, for it is not a concept to be explained by philosophy; nor may religion be explained as coming from a revelation to an otherwise non-religious mind. Religion is not a mystery to be explained by theology, but is rather a product of the human soul, and such as can be apprehended directly in introspection. Mankind worships; hence psychology of religion is a fact. Reason has its place, but it takes, as its point of departure, not an indefinite nor an indifferent mind, but a soul pregnant with religious tendencies and impulses. When these are once appreciated, reason may supply an explanation or a ground. Similarly, the idea of revelation is a thinkable one, and when the testimony of the religious consciousness has been recorded, the function of revelation may be seen. Reason and revelation, tendencies to know and to believe, are postulates of the religious consciousness, not premises. They are by no means unimportant; for, unless it culminated in them, religious feeling would be mere subjectivism. But, in all this, the primacy of religious consciousness must be set up as the starting-point in religion; such is the form of religion.

The actual content of religion involves this same thought of an immediate religious experience. Religion manifests itself as an impulse, on the part of the soul, to turn away from the world, where man's immediate life is found, and to reach out after that which is more satisfying. But all this is without meaning, unless it take place in the religious consciousness. It is because the soul is conscious of the vast difference between spirit and matter, inner life and outer existence, that it attempts to find its home elsewhere. And that aspiration, which leads the soul to postulate the existence of some other and more worthy realm, is likewise a psychic phenomenon. All the principles and relations involved are matters of consciousness. The soul awakes to its own characteristic life; then, it perceives its actual condition in the world. As a result of this, there arises the desire to reach out after a spiritual existence. Such a conception as this is not purely logical nor scientific, but it represents a matter of vital concern. The relation of the soul to the world is not an abstract one consisting in thought; it is rather an act performed by a living consciousness. But, as such an act, religion does not consist in sheer effort. All that is done is due to a peculiar consciousness.

The internal quality of religion appears more clearly upon further analysis. To have a philosophy of religion a genuine appreciation of religious consciousness is made necessary, and this is largely because the ever-prevailing tendency is to conceive of religion as though it consisted in something objective, either an abstract concept or a concrete institution. Religion is subjective and does not consist in any external fact which may be perceived or objective relation which may be set up by thought. We cannot say that beauty or utility are qualities which inhere in things as their attributes, but must rather consider beauty as an attitude of the human mind, just as utility pertains to that which is useful, not in itself, but to man. Artistic objects and useful things, as works of art and devices of machinery, are beautiful and useful only in their relation to human intelligence and will. Their qualities are internal. The same inness belongs to religion, and for this reason, the final appeal must be made to religious consciousness which feels the religious value of the relation which the mind sets up within its own domain.

In addition to the testimony which comes from the individual consciousness, there stand out also the crystallized data of positive religion. Just as history separates cult from cult and tries to discover steps in the development of human worship, so the psychology of religion may distinguish the genius of one group of religions from that of another. For European thought, which was the result of Aryan and Semitic elements in combination, nothing can be more illustrative than the obvious difference which obtains between Hindu and Hebrew forms of religion's consciousness. The Indian consciousness was marked by the speculative in the same way that the Israelitish was ever impressed by practical ideals. It was the desire of the Vedic seer to know; it was the aim of Judah's prophet to obey; one tendency was toward consciousness and penetration, the other toward conscience and piety, and the Hellenism and Hebraism, which Matthew Arnold discerns and distinguishes in modern thinking, had their roots in the essentials of the original Aryan and Semite. Thus the religion's consciousness, when thrown upon such a screen as history provides, is distinguishable in forms of cognition and conation.

With direct reference to the Semitic mind, it may further be observed that its religious consciousness has made possible a special science in the form of Biblical Psychology. Rich as sacred literature is in introspective data, there may be traced also certain attempts to isolate the spiritual nature of man, as well as a scheme of division among the functions of mind. In both Old Testament and New we find a trichotomy, consisting of body, soul, and spirit (*lebh, nephesh, ruach,* σῶμα, ψυχή, νοῦς), while the more advanced views of the soul contain a fundamental distinction between mind and body. What is more important than these more empirical phases of Biblical Psychology is found to consist in certain developments of religious consciousness in the form of ideas of the soul, the world, and God. Indeed the testimony of philosophy seems to be that it is from religion and from religion alone that we have obtained just these three all-important ideas of a personal soul, the unity of the world, and the absoluteness of the world-soul. Each of these must be looked at for its own sake.

Whatever may be the explanation of it, the fact seems to remain that it is from religion that our philosophy has received its idea of the soul. While we may finally pay no little tribute to the advanced form of spiritualism which is to be discovered in the literature of Vedanta, it would

The Essence of Religion   57

still seem as though European thinking received and developed the psychological conception from the Christian religion. It was Christianity which separated soul from body in the immortal value-judgment which declared that not the whole world could be given in exchange for the soul. Along with this distinction of mental and bodily comes the idea of inner experience—*sensus interioris hominis*. Christ not only regarded the soul as possessed of an intrinsic principle of spiritual life, but he relegated it entirely to a supersensible realm. It is true that Plato employs the idea of the ἀσώματον; yet the ancient thinker does not conceive of the difference between soul and body to consist of conflict, nor does he elevate one at the expense of the other; his plastic ideals and classic sympathies would permit of no dwindling and deteriorating view of the fine human form.

So obvious is the place of the soul in religious thinking, and so central is this idea to the definition of religion toward which our thought is tending, that no further considerations will be introduced at this time. We must not assume the responsibilities of our second assertion, that religion produces of itself the idea of the world-whole. It seems that such an idea should spring from metaphysics, and we turn naturally toward Aristotle as master of things cosmic, in the same way that we are wont to refer idealistic questions to Plato. Yet the Aristotelian metaphysics fails to yield the idea of unity in the world of phenomenal forms, and the realism of Aristotle leads him to regard the world as limited in space. Ancient philosophy and modern science, while they interpret the noumenal and phenomenal aspects of the universe, fail to represent the unity and entirety of the world. Ritschl goes so far as to assert that it is only in the Christian religion that we find the idea of the world-whole. "*Klar und deutlich aber ist die Vorstellung von dem Weltganzen nur in der christlichen Weltanschauung.*" In Ritschl's mind, this is due to that principle of Christianity which declares that the whole world is not equal in value to the soul. Here, although in a negative way, the significance of the universe is summed up and adjusted to its position in the religious consciousness. To this, science and metaphysics can only approximate ; the religious consciousness, which makes manifest the soul, likewise outlines the limits of the world. Between the two, a sharp line of difference is drawn. This distinction is not based upon an analysis of the nature of these elements, but is brought about by the religious consciousness itself, estimating the respective values of world and soul. The religious consciousness creates the idea of the world, but from this it turns away.

Spiritual religion is always acosmic in its tendencies, so that not only in Christianity, but in Taoism and Vedanta we find a negative attitude toward the external world. It is only within recent years that our thought has been able to feel the force of oriental thought, and even yet we are unable to relate the Chinese conception of the Tao and the Hindu idea of the Self to our own religious thinking. Nevertheless the idea of a world-whole is implicit in the idealistic systems of the Tao-teh king and the Upanishads, just as the medieval notion of ontology and the modern idea of being-for-self are explicit affirmations of the world as one and infinite. From the ontological element in Christianity we have derived our philosophic conception of the world-unity, although in the New Testament the setting of this vast truth is purely practical, and it is thereby asked, " What shall it profit a man if he gain the *whole world* and lose *his own soul ?* " Such a judgment consists not so much in a *contemptus mundi* as in an immortal appreciation of the human soul.

From the religious significance of both the soul and the world it is but a step to the final idea of the world-soul. Kant's critical dialectic found paralogisms in psychology. antinomies in cosmology, and mere ideals in rational theology. Perhaps it is the fate of religion, rather than ethics, for which Kant contended, to supply the demand for soul, world, and world-soul, which ideas can hardly come from metaphysics. To see this result accomplished, the medium of consciousness must be understood in an unusual fashion, and other and more extended views than those which prevail in psychology are possible. We speak of a social consciousness whose ideas are expressed universally in a language, whose volitions are organized in the form of laws; and while the term "consciousness" may be somewhat misleading in such a connection, it indicates something more acceptable than the older view which regarded society as the mechanical result of a social contract among men and with their sovereign. Religion must now be understood as a social and historical consciousness of God, not as a *consensus gentium* with respect to a deity.

Consciousness of God has ever been organic to religion. The actual form of faith may have been crude, and religious ideas may have been dimly apprehended and expressed, but the divine consciousness has not been wanting. Nature worship, naturalistic or spiritistic, as it may have been, sets up some kind of a conscious union between faith and its object. They seem to understand each other. In higher forms of living faith, the same conscious relation holds; of this, prayer and sacrifice are a clear testimonial. The Deity has now some more definite and elevated character, and is thus understood as related to that larger life which man is living. In universal religion, consciousness becomes a more direct relation between the soul and God. This conception of a divine consciousness in man is compatible even with intellects not inclined toward sentiment. Witness the case of Descartes, who based his proof of God's existence upon the ineradicable consciousness which man has of him. In a similar manner, Spinoza, whose philosophy exalts logic and mathematics to a world-system, came to be regarded as the "God-intoxicated man." And if cool science and careful logic do not turn away from this connection with the divine principle, why should common consciousness fail to make room for the presence of the supernatural? Positive religion is the one vast evidence for the soul's consciousness of God. Yet such reasoning does not assert that the idea of God, in the sense of monotheism, has ever been the possession of all mankind, it was here that the thought of man's common assent fell into disrepute; for history was too strongly opposed to such a brilliant theory. But *consciousness*, capable as it is of qualitative variations as well as quantitative distinctions, is more easily maintained than an intellectual *consensus* which substitutes logic for life, theory for experience. Dimly as consciousness looms up out of the unconscious, and indefinitely, as though the idea were too vast for it, mankind has ever seen some phase of the Godhead. And, convinced of the reality of his vision, man has not hesitated to acknowledge the imperfection of his finite mind, which felt that God transcended experience so that the thought of Him was for man too high and unattainable.

When the idea of God is studied as it appears in historical consciousness, the secret of religion is more easily discovered. The peculiar warmth of conscious life is akin to the vital nature of religion, while the range and heterogeneity of immediate experience make possible all the variations which occur in actual human worship. Consciousness is, therefore, a valuable interpreter of religion. Where theory is unsatisfactory, because it fails to account for the given facts of human faith, consciousness comes in to account for these, and adjust them to their proper relation. But to realize the service of religious consciousness, it is necessary to abandon the attempt to interpret it in the light of some one function—thought, volition, affection. Man's spiritual nature, the home of religion, must be considered, and for this, consciousness must be interpreted in a more sufficient manner. Psychology, as the ordinary interpreter of consciousness, is to be transcended by some method of apprehension more worthy of the subject. There is thus a " higher psychology," which is not confined to empirical considerations alone, and nowhere is its presence manifest or its need felt more than in the study of religious consciousness. Such a view of the human mind is a kind of psychognosis, inasmuch as it deals with conscious noumena.

2. Having observed the general psychological form which religion assumes, as well as the three ideas of God, world, and soul which it evinces, we may now proceed to a more intricate study of the content of this consciousness. In considering such a question, care must be taken lest we run to the extreme of mere psychologism, which ends in making religion appear subjective, if not pathological. To turn away from the ground of religion in human reason that we may survey its origin in human nature is a performance not unaccompanied with danger, and while we cannot abide by the older rationalism, we advance with caution into a field which appears to be purely anthropological. Along with its psychological nature, religion is possessed of a transcendental reference; hence, not only its nature, but its character as a world-overcoming principle must be considered. Just as a philosophy of nature starts from the physical facts of experience and endeavours to elaborate a metaphysical view, so philosophy of the human spirit may safely assume as its primary data the phenomena of consciousness, which do not fail to manifest the inness and totality of the mind.

The consistent psychognosis of consciousness must abandon the hope of finding the essence of religion in any isolated feature of the mind. Nor does it seem possible to break up the totality of consciousness or say that religion consists in some one division as cognition, conation, or affection. When we speak of religion as having a psychological form, we must be critical in the employment of the introspective method. Religion, which has ever posed as an ideal formulated by reason, now tends to assume a form indicated by empirical psychology. To make this second type of religious thought possible, no little difficulty must be overcome. Certain conscious processes may be looked upon as having a religious cast, but we are baffled when we attempt to identify, among other elements of conscious life, those which belong to religion. At the inception of the scientific view of religion in the days of Hume, this was clearly pointed out. Hume, who first raised the question as to religion's origin in human nature, did not fail to show that worship could not be regarded as an original possession of the human mind. Religion, so he went on to show, does not arise from any single instinct in man or any direct impression from the outer world. Thus it cannot be put down among such elements as self-love, affection, gratitude, resentment, and the like ; it is rather a secondary and derivative form of consciousness related to the feeling of anxiety for personal life and its needs. Such criticism as this would seem, in the main, to be just. Religion certainly has its seat in human nature, and is manifest in religious consciousness, but it is only as a peculiar form of consciousness that it may be regarded.

Because the religious principle does not adjust itself to the ordinary emotions of the soul, it is easy to see that no rapid definition of religion may be elaborated. We cannot speak of religion as consisting of " fear " or of " wonder," for this would be a species of bad psychology. Whether these descriptions are worthy or unworthy, sufficient or insufficient, is not the first consideration ; it is more decisive to show that these natural instincts arise and develop in independence of the religious sentiment, and that the two can in no wise be identified. The consciousness of religion is complex and highly developed, and cannot be described in terms of simple emotion. It is more consistent with the facts to consider religion in connection with such developments of consciousness as are spoken of by Wundt, who introduces into his psychology the ideas of " value " and "end." These are definite and practical concepts which arise in human experience, and with them the religious principle may be more satisfactorily associated. While these two latter elements of consciousness may not

The Essence of Religion

actually express the inner nature of religion, their psychological force is more direct than that of the elements of fear and wonder. Religion differs from these particular ideas, inasmuch as it is a consciousness in itself; from it to the soul the path is sure and direct.

The current attempts to construct a theory of the soul can learn much from this question of the religious consciousness. When intellectualism and voluntarism seek to explain the ultimate nature of consciousness, they may well be guided by that ideal of the soul which it has been the fate of religious thought to create. At the same time, the religious conception of the soul may gain by coming in contact with a critical psychology. Here are set limits upon the various phases and phenomena of the human mind. When these are appreciated, it is somewhat easier to see why religion should not be spoken of as a feeling or an idea. But intellectualism runs to one extreme, as does voluntarism to another. The one makes of the soul a mere abstraction of thought; the other regards it as an activity comparable to that manifest in lower orders of existence. To neither of these views is religion friendly; these theories of consciousness are not theories of the religious consciousness; for they do not preserve the latter's integrity. They deserve credit for attempting to explain the soul in terms of definite forms of consciousness, and thus avoiding abstractions; but, by the very employment of the ideas, cognition and volition, these theories set for themselves a limit which prevents their getting at the depths of human existence.

As the result of these considerations, it can be seen that the psychological idea of consciousness only partially fulfils the expectations of the religious inquiry. It seems as though the term consciousness, when it is applied to religion, must be understood in a somewhat different manner from the ordinary use of the idea. By adopting it, religion runs near the border of subjectivism, and in making this excursion, it does not gain such insight as leads it to regard the religious consciousness as characterized by some single element. Nor may the religious conception of the soul find any direct support in current formulations of the soul problem. The religious consciousness exists, but in a manner peculiar to itself. Insight into the actual nature of religion may be gained by looking at the latter from the standpoint of the leading features of human consciousness.

While the religious conception of the soul is not one with either intellectualism or voluntarism, it does not fail to regard religion as at once a matter of knowledge and of activity. Religion is in some sense a matter of knowledge, but this is not to say that it consists in concepts of the understanding, or in ideas which arise in the field of sense perception. The method of natural religion, as also that of later speculative religion, does not seem to have expressed the truth of religion's nature. However consistent these ideas may be in themselves, they do not accord with religious consciousness. But in some form or other, the intellectual element in religion must be maintained. This is not to insist upon proof, for the religious consciousness is its own best evidence; neither is it to say that religion shall embrace some particular form of metaphysics. The intellectual element in the religious consciousness is essential, that the latter may exist and remain intact; for here as elsewhere, consciousness is not a swoon, but a kind of knowledge; and, however unsatisfactory is this particular view, when upheld in isolation, it must be carefully guarded. When religious consciousness is interpreted as consisting of feeling, it is but a step to that idea of Feuerbach's, that God represents no definite object in the mind, but only the creation of desire (*Wunschwesen*).

An object is necessary to the religious consciousness; this is given in the form of a representation. In both actual and speculative religion, this is assumed. Myth, tradition, and dogma give evidence that the religious life of a community cannot exist without projecting itself in

The Essence of Religion

the form of an idea. The social consciousness cannot exist at all, unless some common content of belief is set; and, so important is the ideational content esteemed to be, that religious associations are in the habit of insisting, even to persecution, that all men shall think and believe alike. Where religion becomes more spiritual and reflection tempers the mind, intolerance tends to diminish. But in the instance of philosophical religion, where the sentiment of worship is idealized and rendered amenable to the understanding, the ideational element still persists. The idea of God is essential to religion, when the latter is to remain sound and influential. One-sided as may be the view which considers religion to be a matter of intellectual belief, it cannot be corrected by leaving out of religious consciousness the thought of an objective principle of reflection. In all this, the claim which is made is simply that of psychology, where the cognitive element is clearly essential to all religious consciousness.

Religion possesses the faculty of forming ideas and of passing judgments. This fact may be due to the tendency of religion to estimate the value of various things which it perceives, but this very act of value-judgment yields, as a result, something in the way of knowledge. Universal religion inevitably brings with it a world consciousness whereby a definite cosmic idea is framed. In comparison with this is the idea of the soul; this stands in close relation to the religious consciousness. Likewise, the idea of God; if objection is made that this is metaphysical, it can only be said the idea of God is peculiar to the religious consciousness. A purely metaphysical "*deus*" cannot be worshipped, while a mere "lord" of positive religion cannot be thought. Those abstractions which come from philosophy are not readily adjusted to the more concrete ideas which arise in the development of religion. The God who is worshipped and believed in is not the same Being as that which metaphysics seeks to produce. Nevertheless, the idea of God is essential to the higher form of religion;

where worship is in spirit and in truth, it must have as its counterpart the thought that God is spirit.

The religious consciousness has likewise its active side; it is volitional as well as intellectual. Zeal for moralism must not confuse our minds, so that we shall be led to say, religion is simple, ethical activity; nor must a contrary spirit betray us into thinking that religion is mere passivity. Religion is neither energism nor quiescence, but a carefully directed form of doing. Energism is faulty, because it sets up as a standard mere activity and work which are not directed toward any goal. Such energism exalts a hero who can "toil terribly," while mysticism responds by commanding, "Cease your deadly doing." Quietism of this sort is valid only as a corrective of energism. But when the volitional phase of religious consciousness is insisted upon, it is not necessary to interpret this in the extreme form of moralism. Certainly it is necessary to emphasize the conative form, without which consciousness can hardly be explained. Although there may be a term sufficient to express this essential phase of religion, it cannot be denied that where religion lives, it strives and exerts itself in a most significant manner.

Viewed both phenomenally and ideally, religion is related to the conduct of life. Positive religion has ever enjoined upon its subjects various acts of duty, these consisting of rite, ceremony, and the like. Absurd as may be the extreme to which religion may thus go, the active side of the religious consciousness is manifest, and the struggle to purify this central endeavour, so that essential obligation may take the place of extraneous and imaginary duty, reveals the same active impulse in another form. The religious subject conceives that something must be done by him. He perceives the enormous difference between the soul and the world, and believes that there exists a source of life better than that immediately about him. Inner feelings demand actual expression. The world must be abandoned and God be found; the point of departure

The Essence of Religion

is the soul, which must assert itself. It cannot be content to remain in the world, but presses on to some more satisfactory point. This is not as a mere longing, nor is it an act of thought; it is rather a spontaneous act of the will, consciously directed. When, therefore, one like Schleiermacher endeavours to distinguish between religion and morality, by saying that one lays hold of the mind in its passivity, the other in its activity, he makes religious consciousness impossible. The soul must act and affirm its religious feeling; to conceive of it in the form of pure passivity and absolute dependence is a vain undertaking.

Finally, a detailed view of religious consciousness must not omit to note the effect which feeling has upon the religious life. This is easily seen, but not so readily appreciated. Feeling as one characteristic of consciousness stands in close relation to the religious principle in mankind. Its inner and personal character shows how organic the fact of religion really is; for the intimate form of feeling only reflects the inwardness of religion. Perhaps it is as viewed from this formal standpoint that the conscious element of feeling is valuable for the discussion of the religious consciousness. The soul is not merely an intellectual function to be impressed by ideas; nor is it a volitional activity which expresses itself mechanically. The soul is also to be viewed as a feeling, and it is in this connection that the religious consciousness may be understood. But, in more essential points of detail, the affectional form of religion may be shown.

To express the veritable content of religion, feeling must be considered, not in isolation, but in connection with both thought and will. By doing this, gain accrues to religious consciousness in general, inasmuch as it assumes a more natural form. An isolated process of feeling is just as alien to human life as it is to the religious consciousness of mankind. When feeling is related to its companions in consciousness, it may be regarded as making up a judgment and as constituting desire. It is essential to religion that it pass judgment upon the value of what it perceives, and that, in response to its own peculiar impulses, it should desire to have and to attain to that which appeals to it as being worthy. When the religious consciousness is seen to consist, so far as feeling is concerned, of judgment and desire, its nature is more thoroughly understood. Religious feeling is not a mere matter of pleasure and pain to be discussed qualitatively or quantitatively ; it is rather an experience which manifests the peculiar nature of the human mind. The religious consciousness passes judgment upon the world and human life, it does this in a manner peculiar to itself, but with a result no less decisive than that of intellectualistic metaphysics. When philosophy looks for living effects, it can see that religion, with its judgments of feeling, does not err in making a distinction between soul and world. In keeping with such a judgment, religion further emphasizes its position, by expressing a characteristic desire. Religion desires not the world ; in the latter, it can find nothing of value to be given in exchange for the soul. Dissatisfied with its earthly condition, the soul desires that which is more worthy and acceptable. Now, such results as are worked out by man's religious consciousness could not have been produced by a purely subjective feeling. Feeling is not absent from consciousness, but its presence is felt in this act of the soul which is made up of desire and judgment.

So far as we must resign religion to anything like a particular principle in human consciousness, it would seem best to interpret it in terms of *desire*. When man asks, " What may we hope ? " When faith consists in the subtance of things hoped for, the spirit of religion as a fundamental desire is made manifest. The essence of religion as desire, however, does not consist in the mere possession of the wished-for object, nor yet in the sheer pursuit of this ; it is not a having, nor yet a seeking, but a growing and becoming accompanied by the satisfaction of desire. The religious desire is, furthermore, an intelligent process which is directed to no *je ne sais quoi*, and the mind of the *religieuse* is not at all in the condition of Brunhilde—*des Wissen bar, doch des Wunches voll.* He whose religious consciousness is aroused seeks that which is altogether desirable.

Finally, the conception of the human mind which is gradually elaborated in the study of religious consciousness is beyond the domain of empirical psychology, belonging to the realm of spiritual life. It is the totality of the soul which is able to feel that sensitivity which is essential to religious consciousness, because the fact of religion makes necessary the attitude of the soul as integral. The religious sense which seeks to adjust the soul to the world, or which aspires to redeem that soul from the world, is expressive of that unity of spiritual life which religion everywhere postulates. Accordingly we do not first deduce the idea of soul from an abstract view of consciousness and seek then to apply it to religion in the form of freedom or immortality, but we find that characteristic religion has itself produced this idea as self-conscious spiritual life. In the same way, it may be said that the supreme deed of the soul, which arises spontaneously within the depths of consciousness, just as the fact of religion proceeds from man's complete sensitivity, is to be realized and understood only as we regard human consciousness in the form of self-existent spiritual life.

4. *Religion, the Self-Affirmation of the Soul*

Thus far our investigation has confined itself to that formal essence of religion which was the product of the Enlightenment. By means of a qualitative form of limitation, the religious precinct was indicated, not merely as an abstract division, but as a living form of man's spiritual life. The evidence of such a precinct was seen to be manifest in religious consciousness, which puts forth intuitively its own forms of thinking in the form of such notions as the soul, the world, and the world-soul. This establishes a comparison between both science and philosophy, and as religion is distinguished from these and adjusted to its own position in the individual and the world, the way seems prepared, finally, for something like a definition of religion. With its thorough development in modern thinking, and with its clearly outlined province in current speculation, it is expected that the religious idea should assume such a substantial form as to render a definition possible.

Before any attempt at verbal definition can be made, it must be decided just what such a definition is expected to indicate. Do we understand by religion some empirical concept which is formed inductively upon the basis of positive data drawn from various ethnic cults; or, do we look for some logical formulation of the religious ideal as that which should be, but never really is found in orient or occident? Shall we reduce all religious phenomena to naturism, or shall we raise them to rationalism? On the one side, science says, Religion consists of fear; on the other, philosophy proclaims, Religion is the product of reason. Both views cannot be right, and it seems as though both were wrong. A genuine conception of religion must not ignore expirical data, nor must it abandon all claim to rationality; it is not the phenomenal alone, nor the logical by itself, but the *phenomenological* which contains the essence of human religion.

The attitude of thought must be critical, rather than merely empirical or purely rational; it is not the mere fact, or the sheer ideal, but the living act of religion which our philosophy needs. In the parallel case of art, somewhat the same condition obtains. Pausanias' descriptive view of Greek art is as far from the æsthetical as Plato's dialectical treatment of Homer and the drama. Yet it is possible for a thinker like Aristotle or Hegel, like Winckelmann or Lessing, to see as one the empirical datum and the logical deduction which may be made from it. Of the two extremes, neither method may be preferred, because each one presents an abstraction, either an empirical generalization or a rationalistic universal. Far better is it to seek the mysterious union of the positive and reflective, which is a living fact no more difficult to explain than the usual problem of philosophy.

The very essence of religion must now be subjected to scrutiny. No single element in consciousness, no simple point of view in thought, will be sufficient to evince the depth of living religion ; we must seek something at once central and total. In seeking for this, let us observe : (1) The possibilities to be found in the living, conscious, and striving person. Then (2) the self-affirmation of the soul will stand out as the supreme means of which religion may itself. (3) Finally, the result of this self-affirmation will be seen to involve the whole world of human spiritual life.

1. It is necessary to indicate the inner and intrinsic quality which religion possesses. If religion is not science, not philosophy, if it occupy its own precinct and possess its own consciousness, it is because religion belongs to the *sensus interioris hominis*. Thus it may be said, that religion is neither a deduction from the understanding nor a production of the will. Man does not become religious by drawing significant conclusions from the world without, any more than that he raises himself into the realm of spiritual life by summoning various internal impulses. Nor may it be urged that religion is the sum or synthesis of speculative and practical principles in the form of a *tertium quid*. Rather must it ever be assumed that religion is organic ; otherwise the data of positive religion and the elements of religious consciousness remain unexplained. The unity of religion is the correlate of the unity of humanity, and the supremacy of religion over those considerations which involve nature and man's immediate life within her narrow borders, is only the supremacy of spirit over nature. The totality of man far exceeds the limits of phenomena and noumena.

Still another demand must be made when we say that

religion must be regarded as a complete act on the part of the soul, and not as the function of some one particular part. The inness of religion involves its integrity. Logic exercises the understanding, ethics appeals to the will, æsthetics inspires the feelings, but religion arouses the entire man. If this seem too general a qualification to remain intact, or too unwieldy a notion to make headway, let it be remembered that culture stands in about the same position. And, moreover, whole nations in the history of humanity have signalized the integral character of worship in the pursuit of which they have proceeded to elaborate characteristic forms of spiritual life, like Buddhism and Vedanta. These are the outcome of no isolated faculty, but are the outpourings of the soul in its integrity. Religion is not mere thought or action, but the total attitude of the unitary soul. This may be understood as the soul's aspiration toward its own humanity, and where spiritual longing deepens into pathos and pessimism, the sufficient reason and leading motive for these permanent moods may be found in the insufficiency of nature to content mankind.

The key to religion is to be found in the ego. It is this which contains the explanation of our foregoing discussion of religion's essence. The world of religion is not the perceptional world of science, which is based upon naturalism, nor the conceptional world of philosophy, which is founded upon intellectualism, but the world of persons which must be distinguished from the world of things. On the side of life, religion does not consist in the perception of utilities in the world of sense, or in the deduction of values in the world of concepts, but of the soul's destiny in the spiritual world-order. The reason for this is to be found in the self whose affirmation constitutes the ground of religion. In the same way, the religious precinct is nothing more nor less than that which the ego outlines as the sphere of its personal activity. The negation of the world and the affirmation of the soul, indicate the internal and qualitative limits of religion itself. Religious consciousness has the

The Essence of Religion

same source ; it is within the self, and can be described in no other way than in terms of self-consciousness. When the religious consciousness puts forth ideas of soul, world, and world-soul, it exercises the very nature of the self. Thus our analysis of religion centres in the idea of the person.

No extra-psychological analysis is necessary or desirable in the elucidation of the self. Psychological division, which is essential to accurate description or exact experiment, is nevertheless an abstraction, and there is no mental state which is mere cognition, or conation, or affection. Hence we make no substantial progress when we describe the ego in terms of any one of the processes of consciousness. The soul is no simple *cogito*, *sentio*, or *ago*, but a unity of self-conscious life, and it is capable of something more than reflection, passion, and action viewed in their individual capacities. The totality of consciousness which is just as manifest as the particular function, and in the religious deed the whole of this consciousness makes itself manifest. Poetry, law, and other forms of human culture and civilization refer to the person as something whose reality and value need not be doubted ; religion assumes a representative relation toward the soul which it aspires to redeem from nature.

At a more appropriate place, it will be shown how the ego characterizes the most profound forms of actual religion which eastern, central, and western orient produces ; here it is fitting to note the presence of the same principle in typical forms of modern philosophy. First in order may be noted the pioneer work performed by Descartes in the realm of general philosophy. The Cartesian ego possesses logical significance and is not necessarily related to religion. Nevertheless, Descartes himself did not fail to suggest the possible spiritual import with which the ego might be invested. Augustinian ideas mark the beginning, while Anselmic principles indicate the end, of Descartes dialectic. Denying the immediate existence of the world, and doubting also the validity of the idea of God, Descartes sought to eliminate from the soul still another element in the form of the thinker himself. This he found to be an impossibility, inasmuch as doubt involves thought, while thought involves the thinker. Hence, the conclusion to the scepticism : *Cogito, ergo sum ;* which rests upon a fairly convincing rationalism. When the personal ego posits its own being over against the world of phenomena, it strives outward to attain to some other objective principle of knowledge. It has rejected the world ; now it demands God. Descartes here passes from the subjectivism of Augustine to the realism of Anselm and seeks to establish the ontological proof of the divine existence upon the theory that we as humans possess the idea of God *within ourselves*. His proof is more anthropological than theological, as Kuno Fischer has pointed out. The return to nature is indirect ; we conclude the world exists because we have faith in its Creator.

Fichte employs the ego in a fashion more ethical and voluntaristic. While he starts with no sceptical method, Fichte strives to reduce reality to an original positing, or deed-act on the part of the ego. *Das Ich setzt sich selbst.* Such scepticism as is involved in the Fichtean dialectic ends in the atheism peculiar to the earlier doctrine—*erste Lehre*—of this brilliant speculator. The ego, as it posits itself, finds it necessary to apposit the non-ego, or the world. Indeed, Fichte's thought is so self-contained and acosmic that it even declares the non-ego to be a mere creation of the ego itself, which in its ethical calling finds some kind of resistance necessary, and thus the non-ego is called into being that the ego, by overcoming it, may become ethical. The later doctrine—*zweite Lehre*—of Fichte completes the suggestion on an objective ethical world-order which is invested with personal attributes.

Upon the æsthetic side, Schleiermacher's dialectic involves the personal principle in the form of self-consciousness. This is involved in the ideals of religion as intuition and feeling, as sense and taste for the Eternal, as immediate consciousness and pious self-consciousness—*das fromme Selbstbewusstsein*. Schleiermacher negates both the metaphysical and moral orders for the sake of the religious. In the presence of the Infinite, man feels a sense of absolute dependence. Schleiermacher continually emphasizes the passive side of religion, but while this is the conclusion of the whole matter when the self is contrasted with the Absolute, the attitude of the ego is originally conceived in the most active form, by virtue of which the soul negates the criteria of logical rules and ethical maxims. The dependence upon God is so absolute, and the independence of the world so complete, that the self must exercise its peculiar right to affirm and deny. Pure passivity is an impossible psychological condition. With Descartes and Fichte, Schleiermacher centres all religion in the ego, and does not fail to involve the idea of self-affirmation.

The possibility of the integral act of self-affirmation need not be doubted when we face some of the usual achievements of philosophy. Speculative thought sums up the totality of mental life in the form of a judgment, and thereby regards reason as capable of considering the total range of thought without regard to the common relations of "here" and "now," "then" and "there." Practical philosophy evinces conscience or moral judgment, which passes upon the whole life of man and decides accordingly. For religion to exist in the form of an absolute affirmation of the person as a unit, distinct from the manifold external nature, is more than possible. This unity of the soul and the integrity of its deed, however, are not to be assumed as logical premises or deduced as ethical postulates, but must be regarded as living ideals to which humanity strives to attain.

2. Religion itself consists in the self-affirmation of the soul over against the world. Its seat in the person, its nature as organic, its character as intrinsic, forbid that we should dispose of the problem of definition by making religion to consist in a view of the world, or a course of

conduct in the world. Religion is rather a characteristic attribute toward the whole world which leads the person to affirm his own being as something distinct and superior. The reason for this self-affirmation, as an impulse on the part of the soul, consists primarily in the recognition that the essence of the world is alien to that of the soul. To the system of natural forms, the religious consciousness says, " Our kingdom is not of this world ; we must render under spirit the things of spirit, and must not surrender them to the material." Logic distinguishes between ideas, ethics decides between motives, æsthetics shows preference among feelings, religion puts forth one central impulse and sets itself at variance with the world. Not because the world consists of a mere non-ego, to be distinguished mathematically, but because this non-ego is seen to be metaphysically, or qualitatively alien to the soul—such is the first moment of the soul's affirmation.

Still other reasons make necessary the affirmation of the self in opposition to the world. It is the immediate feeling that the course of nature is antipathetic to the interests of the soul's life. The behest of nature, which is so strong and enduring, only serves to convince the soul that its own position in the phenomenal world is only incidental, while the natural world itself seems to stand in no centric, but rather eccentric relation to the personal spirit. Nature and its gifts seem to come in as a by-product or extra effect to be explained only in the light of man's finitude and animal necessities. In the natural order, what is more immediate than facts of interest, pleasure, and desire, and yet what form of idealistic philosophy recognizes these things as paramount ? The ceaseless activity of the will to live, the constant struggle for existence, begin and end with life and existence ; they do not touch the spirit of man, which, by discarding sensuality and self-love, aspires to live in the calm life of contemplation and character. The antagonism of nature and animality reveals the pure and independent character of the person.

It is the fate of the ego to stand in the very presence of both nature and spiritual life, and that in a dignified manner. Religion is possessed of a principle of spontaneity by virtue of which it is able to assert itself as a spiritual force in the world of natural forms. At the same time, there is manifest another trait, that of sensitivity which makes possible the yearning for and approximation toward the spiritual world-order. In face of the perceptive force of the natural phenomena religion spontaneously asserts itself as that which also has a right to exist, and the more real the natural world appears to be, the more vigorous is the negation which the aroused ego puts forth. The force of this denial furthers the ego in its other impulse, which is toward the supersensible. Toward this realm, religion adapts the attitude of receptivity, and with the sensitivity of soul now stripped of the natural, it embraces the spiritual as something of its own kin. To effect the transition from nature to spirit, ego must be both spontaneous and sensitive in its negations and affirmations.

To negate the world is to affirm the world-soul. The self will have an object to contemplate and toward which it may strive, but this object cannot consist in nature; rather is it something self-like. For philosophy of religion to-day it is necessary to urge the personal movement in religious consciousness. Much of traditional speculation has consisted in a mere theology of God, or a mere metaphysics of nature, and these programmes have been so filled with articles about divine attributes and theistic demonstrations that man's religious consciousness has received no attention. The self sets the standard by which the world and God are judged. On the one side, the world is set at naught, because it is alien to the soul with which it cannot compare in value. "What shall it profit a man if he gain the whole world and lose his own soul?" On the other, God is affirmed as that which takes the objective place of the world in the form of the world-soul. The motive which leads to the belief in God is not world-motive, but soul-motive, and arises from no concern for the reality of nature since it is taken up altogether with the desire to secure permanence and progress for the soul.

The act of self-affirmation continues in the midst of the dual work which the religious ego has to perform. On the one side, the negative impulse of the soul in its opposition to nature is the best evidence of the originality and power of the *ego's* act. This constitutes a genuine deed of the soul. It is called forth by no external stimulus; it is the product of no instinct, and while at the outset it does not recognize the meaning of human destiny, the soul is no less aware of the presence of spiritual ends than the body is conscious of the impulses which work the will to live. The call from nature may be strong, but it is not clear, while man's higher vocation makes its presence felt as a constant factor in the midst of material issues. The primitive man interprets disease and disaster in a manner which expresses concern for the soul as well as for the body, and fears lest some inimical power may cast both into destruction. Life and death are subject to no mere physical consideration, but are made the subjects of superstitious regard. The characteristic deed of the personal soul involves the total range of spiritual life.

3. In completing the deed by virtue of which the soul becomes religious, the ego affirms the existence of the spiritual world-order. Here its form of self-affirmation, which has no longer an antipathetic nature to negate, is mildly affirmative and consists chiefly of consciousness, or active recognition. Humanity's struggle against nature and animality seem to mark its most characteristic work in the world, whereas its recognition and acceptance of culture and spiritual life, while accompanied by no such stress and strain, really constitute its own essence. To be conscious of God is to affirm His being, and this affirmation is more in keeping with the soul than was the all-engrossing conflict with nature. For this reason, all forms of religious consciousness like renunciation, quiescence, and feeling

The Essence of Religion

of dependence are affirmative in the midst of man's seeming passivity; they consist in the pure positing of the soul's existence after the work of negation has been done.

The meaning of religion is to be found in the idea of life, absolute life. This must not be deemed a vague and general principle which does not belong to religion in particular, and which religion is not sufficient to handle, for the whole trend of religious activity is directed toward strengthening and sharpening of this central conception. Universal forms of positive religion, like Taoism, Vedanta, Buddhism, and Christianity, handle the question of life with an ease which is calculated to surprise the logician and moralist. Furthermore, when it is remembered how unconscious and inert the natural man is to the obvious fact of death, the function of religion as a reminder of mortality will appear more clearly. The thought of the seer scours the complete horizon of human existence, and makes life and death subjects which are discussed with no great difficulty. Logic clarifies thought, ethics fortifies the will, art beautifies the soul, but religion invests and informs the whole life with an absolute significance.

While the notion of the soul's self-affirmation may seem vague and incompetent, its meaning will further appear when we add to it an idea, no less mysterious, but more usual, that of human destiny. The study of nature, as carried on to-day, provokes such a question just as it suggests that the natural world cannot fitly provide a goal for the human race. It is the destiny of the ego to be, that is, to affirm its genuine existence as something more than, and better than, the natural world, as seen through the body which is a significant part of it. Destiny must remain an incomplete idea until it is attained; yet its vagueness may turn out to be due to the fact that the thought lies at the very depths of man's nature to be realized only in an exalted and exceptional moment. Religious destiny, like human culture, is an idea which penetrates to the life of the soul, which informs the man that no immediate satisfaction will content the spirit, which is aware of a spiritual calling. Religion arises with the consciousness of destiny and attempts to solve the problem thereby proposed.

The motives for the soul's self-affirmation are to be found in the self rather than in the world. Philosophy everywhere must see that its problem arises when man perceives that he belongs to a double order of things ; the natural, where his position is final, the spiritual, where his part is that of a novitiate. To adjust these realms, and to effect the transition from one to the other, is the one human problem. Religion seizes man in the moment when he seeks to pass from the lower to the higher. In nature, man feels that his position is only incidental, consisting of the actual, but not partaking of the ideal. If he were mere animal, he would remain content in the immediate world of perception ; if he were sheer spirit, he would need no self-assertion, but being man, he has his own destiny to achieve. Nature seems to prescribe too narrow limits for him, whose industrial sciences seek to improve it, while his fine arts aim to perfect it. At the same time, man's life in nature is such as leads to surprise, which is worse than actual pain, so that he soon conceives of his life as something more than natural.

Various vital concerns continue to apprise man of the fact that his relation to the world should not be that of acquiescence, but of opposition. The human spirit desires freedom, and the mechanism of the sensible world defeats this dream. Man's satisfaction can consist of no experience which nature can arrange for him, when his human interests demand something more substantial than bodily well-being or conscious pleasure. Hence the systematic opposition of man to the world, which he cannot accept as the genuine correlate of his own being. The religious act has as its motive the desire to set man over and against the world ; above it because its nature is alien to his own, against it because his own naturalness and animality do

The Essence of Religion

not yield immediately, upon the perception of the metaphysical difference, but must be worked up practically to a condition of interest and excitement. Such ideal excitement is provided for by the various forms of worship which belong to the religious life.

The conception which has been developing in the midst of these ideas is strongly marked by humanistic elements. Of the three elements discovered in the religious consciousness, the soul seems to stand out as the mean between the extremes of nature and God. It is the usual mode in philosophy of religion to effect the union of these two by postulating the immanence of God in a world toward which man assumes merely the attitude of spectator. And if, as the new Theism declares, we have made a mistake in relegating the Deity to a position without the universe, it may be replied that now we commit another error when we force humanity to vacate the world of nature to which he most obviously belongs. As the half-gods go, the gods come in. For this reason, it is advisable to emphasize the human side of religion, even though, for the time being, the scheme appears to be all-too-human in its anthropological character. Man, not the world or the world-soul, is the necessary point of departure in consistent religious thinking.

The humanism, which we see no reason to deny, makes necessary, as its correlate, the idea of pessimism. For religion, which seeks the ideal in the midst of the actual, this is inevitable. The world of nature is negated, both within and without, not because of any mere logical distinction which human reason would make, but because of the conflict which man carries on within the world of immediate experience. Psychology and cosmology need raise no question of value in their study of the forms of nature and consciousness, but religion must somehow feel that the world is ill-adapted to man's nature and unprepared for his human career, which itself is carried on in moments of sorrow and sin. World-pessimism and life-pessimism alike are peculiar to ethnic religion, although, in the western world of Judaism and Christianity, the cosmic and eudaemonistic features of the question are not as marked as the historical and ethical ones. It is when man enters upon the scene, or when he awakens to his human destiny, that the perplexity and pain arise. In this way all religion is humanistic.

PART II

THE CHARACTER OF RELIGION

THAT religion has a character peculiar to itself cannot be doubted any more easily than the fact that it has an independent existence in human nature. Viewed philosophically, as a subject for thought, considered psychologically, as a fact of experience, the religious affirmation of the soul cannot be esteemed less real or less worthy than any other product of spiritual life. But this is not all; the mere fact of religion, which proclaims that the latter is no abstraction, could not account for the influence of faith in human life. Religion is also a factor on a par with other functions of human nature. The precinct of religion is marked by boundaries which are contiguous with cultivated philosophical fields, and, for this reason, a second step is necessary in developing the religious principle, and this involves the character of religion. Compared with philosophy and science in general, and adjusted to its place among the various philosophical sciences, the religious precinct, which contains the essence of religion, is established. Thus located as one among several forms of culture, and by its own nature rendered independent of every one of them, religion begins to assert its own character.

By virtue of this comparison, religion shows its intrinsic character. At the same time, its behaviour is peculiar, and is likely to surprise one who has thought upon the subject in a traditional manner only. Religion is not philosophy, nor is it a combination of speculative and practical views; its character is such as to transform it into a subject more like art and law than logic and ethics. Alien to speculative philosophy, religion turns away from purely metaphysical and moral implications; allied with historical life, it assumes an æsthetical and juristic character. This is not the usual view, perhaps; and yet, is it not more than a century since Schleiermacher called attention to the truth that religion is no mixture of metaphysics and morality? It remains to be shown how genuine religion is inclined toward the positive and institutional sciences of æsthetics and rights. Religion is consciousness and deed, not demonstration and conduct; religious consciousness is æsthetical and is expressed in worship; religious activity is juristic, being evinced in commandment and custom.

The assertion of characteristic religion will necessitate the same independent attitude as appeared in the contrast set up between the essence of religion and the fields of science and philosophy. To-day it is the fashion to negate the metaphysical, and, with added emphasis, to affirm the moral side of religion, as something demanded by an age which, since Kant, has distrusted speculation and then sought to compensate for this by reaffirming its belief in practice. Such an ethical philosophy of religion, which now reigns supreme in Germany, is cynical in its attitude toward metaphysics, just as it is bitter in its hatred of speculative affairs in general. This view is suggestive of a half-truth; we must indeed affirm that religion is not metaphysics, but we shall not say, therefore, that it is morality; for, in reality, it is neither one nor the other. To believe in the validity of the religious precinct is to see that religion is not speculation, any more than it is action, and a consistent view involves a negation of both speculative and practical views of an independent form of spiritual life and human culture. Nevertheless, we feel that we do no harm to either morality or metaphysics when we say that of them religion is wholly independent.

A. THE RELIGIOUS VIEW OF THE WORLD

To consider the essence of religion, as a form of spiritual life limited by itself alone and conscious of its self-affirmation, is to calculate that such religion must adjust itself to the world and to the soul. The first adjustment arouses the problem concerning religion and knowledge ; the second pertains to the question of religion and conduct. In itself a problem, knowledge is often regarded as a constant principle in contrast with which religion varies in its approximation to what men are pleased to call truth ; but more consistent reflection will show that we are just as sure of our beliefs as of our theories, so that, in the face of the infinite world no particular discipline can claim any preeminence, but can only indicate how consistent thinking is to be carried on in its own province. So far as religion itself is here concerned, it may be said that we need only assure ourselves that religion is intelligible, and after that it can be pointed out that its character is not so much that of metaphysics as of æsthetics.

1. *Religion as Knowledge*

The character of religion is such as to differentiate it sharply from the field of logic, at the same time, religion itself is more pronounced than art, morality, or jurisprudence in its claim upon the process of knowledge. Religion need not be ratiocinative, but it must be true, and it possesses truth in a manner unknown to the other practical disciplines which have been mentioned. We must therefore assume that there is such a thing as religious knowledge, although this may consist in æsthetical intuition rather than in logical inference. In order to elaborate the relation which obtains between religion and knowledge, we must (1) observe the parallel development of theory of knowledge and philosophy of religion in modern thought. Without the latter, the former would never have arisen.

(2) The essential connection between the religious and reflective functions of the human spirit must then be deduced and (3) the positive interaction of the two realms must be deciphered in the progress of ethnic religion. The modern man is now conscious of a problem which has always existed in the faith of mankind.

1. Modern logic, as expressed by Kant, differs from the antique logic of Aristotle chiefly in this : the modern feels that reason and reality are separated by a wellnigh impassable chasm ; the ancient assumed that thought and thing were one. If ancient philosophy had not been so profound we might style it naive ; if its spirit had not been so lofty, we would call it dogmatic. And so with modern logic ; if it were not so healthy in its origin and so strong in its growth, we might speak of it as sceptical. At any rate, some such distinction must be made between classic and Christian speculation, for their attitudes toward the world are very different. By virtue of this tendency on the part of our modern thought to detach itself from nature, there is made possible the analogy with religion, which consists in the endeavour made by the soul to emancipate itself from the world. In the scepticism of Descartes and the criticism of Kant, theoretical antipathy to the world of things is coupled with a decidedly religious tendency ; modern logic and modern religion have in common the belief in spirit and the distrust of matter. Knowledge and religion are equally problematical ; therefore, we may not claim that logic is perfect and religion imperfect ; but must assume that they meet upon a common level. Knowledge, in its nature and validity, is as much of a problem as religion ; in each, we must avoid the danger of dogmatism. As moderns, when we consider how sceptical and critical has been the spirit of our thought, shall we vainly assume that the present condition of formal logic is such as to be wholly satisfactory to its promoters ? From the standpoint of current thought, it may safely be asserted that modern thought, in reforming scholastic

logic, has been no more successful than modern philosophy of religion has been in regenerating medieval theology.

It is by slow steps that we reach the present; the path is through the past. But in this regressus and return, the field is that of modern thought alone; ancient and medievalist, were not worried by the problem of knowledge and religion, but confidently proceeded in their construction of metaphysics and theology. Arising in the seventeenth century, the questions of knowledge and religion were, not only contemporary, but inwardly connected. This appears in Herbert and Spinoza, in Locke and Hume. During the Enlightenment, and by virtue of these modern thinkers, a great work of emancipation was carried on; in the course of this, knowledge and religion became forms of study in independence of metaphysics and theology. Was it only a matter of coincidence that these two forms of human culture should at the same time manifest their independence and their tendency to outline a new course of development? History of philosophy does not proceed in that way, however. Logic and religion were united in the new "religion of reason."

Rights afforded the means, but logic the method, by which religion was made an independent object of study. The first contribution to deism was Herbert of Cherbury's work on truth, "De Veritate"; at the same time, this book was one of the earliest writings on epistemology. The logical value of Herbert's work is now being appreciated, as, for example, by Gunther, whereas a generation ago Herbert was only the traditional founder of natural religion. Just as modern ethics sprang from natural rights, so logic, in the sense of epistemology, traces back to natural religion. Here, we note the peculiar influence of Grotius; there, of his friend Herbert. The aim of Herbert was to discover the ultimate ground of religion and, in working out the problem thus presented, he made use of a theory of knowledge. Just as Kant, inspired by ethical earnestness, endeavoured, in a system of criticism, to lay down the fundamental principle of life and conduct; so Herbert advanced from logic to a philosophy of religion. In his work, Herbert considers the problems of truth, of blessedness, and of worship, deducing the principles of these from the *instinctus naturalis* and *communis consensus* of mankind. As a conclusion, he lays down five articles of universal religion, which are at once speculative, ethical, and theological. In all this, natural knowledge and natural religion are unified; in each is found the common idea of truth. Such was the origin of modern logic and religion.

The development of natural religion was not as smooth as the complacent system of Herbert might have given reason to expect; but where turbulence entered in, it was due to the influence of natural rights and the accompanying revolutionary spirit. But the guiding-star of deism was reason, in the sense of the new theory of knowledge. By aid of the principle of reason, the universality of religion was pointed out, and herein consisted one of the chief services of the period of natural religion. But English thought, which has ever been empirical, was not critical in its application of knowledge to religion; from Herbert to Hume, it was assumed that religion is a reasonable thing, and that among the innate ideas of the mind are the principles of natural religion. This tendency was not corrected by Hobbes or Locke; indeed they were deeply interested in that which was as alien to their theories of knowledge as the religion of nature. But this was due to their interest in the problem of government and the corresponding juristic nature of English Deism. Hume was more critical and consistent. His scepticism was epoch-making for modern logic, while it was the means by which natural religion was destroyed. According to Hume, knowledge is so constituted that it does not give us the ideas of substance or of causality; in the same manner, religion fails to prove the ultimate grounds of religion, in God and the soul.

Hume, however, explains knowledge as a function of consciousness, just as he deduces religion from the history of humanity. Thought is guided by association or the natural train of ideas; and "custom," to use Hume's very language, "is the great guide of human life." Such is, likewise, the spirit of Hume's religious thought: there, he abandons the ground in human reason for the origin in human nature, and concludes that religion is seated, not in reason, but in some phase of emotion. In the development of the race, we do not observe that natural religion was an original possession of the human mind, but that man's earliest form of faith consisted in a low kind of worship, directed toward the objects of nature. Hume, in changing the point of view from reason to experience, was effecting the transition from natural religion to the religion of nature, and when he emphasized the psychological element in logic, he did not fail to make this supreme in religion. If a critical theory of knowledge was awakened by Hume's scepticism, a science of positive religion was made possible when he applied this scepticism to natural religion of reason. Throughout the progress of natural religion, from Herbert to Hume, the peculiar interaction of logic and religion cannot fail to be noted.

To speak of knowledge in connection with religion is to refer to Kant. Yet the philosophical personality of Kant is perhaps larger than we may imagine, and his system need not be included under the head of *neo*-Kantianism in philosophy or Ritschlianism in theology. If Kant's influence was nugatory, how shall we account for the bold speculations of Fichte, Schelling, Hegel, Schopenhauer? The Jena-movement in philosophy accepted the method of Kant, but did not adopt his results, while Schopenhauer was a Kantian who felt none of the suffocations supposed to attend metaphysics. Our own view of the matter is that Kant does not deny too much, but too little. Religion is not logical, he claims, nor is it ethical either, he might have added. Kant's attitude is that of a defeated and disappointed man; he had trusted reason, yet found that it could not yield knowledge of soul, world, or World-Soul, but like the Stoical Roman who fell upon his sword and exclaimed, "Oh, virtue, I have followed thee and found thee but a shade," he might have abandoned not only the category of causality, but the categorical imperative. Indeed Kant's own philosophy of religion is almost as critical in its treatment of morality as his "Critique of Pure Reason" is of metaphysics. What is to be regretted is that Kant should seem disappointed when he finds that religion does not consist in knowledge as he might have discovered also that it does not consist in action. It is here that Schleiermacher shows his more perfect insight when he affirms that religion consists in neither knowing nor doing. Each of these questions must be taken up for its own sake.

To show that piety does not consist in knowledge is to perform a service for both logic and philosophy of religion. Knowledge as a logical product springs from experience without and understanding within, and as long as we are human, and yet not merely animal, we shall need both sources of certainty. To examine the source and the form of knowledge is to see that it cannot be identified with religious consciousness. It is natural to assume that thought, which follows the method judgment founded upon the concept and finished in inference, should be either empirical or rational. Yet there are certain ideas which come neither from the logic of experience nor that of understanding. No one has seen and shown this more clearly than Kant, in his discussion of the æsthetic and the complementary form of this, which appears in the first two antinomies. We should say of space and time, as well as of the world within space and time, that our knowledge came from either experience or understanding. Yet space and time, which are intuitions, are likewise units which are not built up at particular times and spaces, which do not and cannot exist in the manifold, are not empirical generalizations. On the other hand, these self-styled forms of thinking are not deduced from anything higher than they, as the idea of man is derivable from the

The Character of Religion

concept anumal, but are formed at once as something *sui generis*.

Why may we not carry this logic of the transcendental æsthetic into the plan of the cosmological antinomies, for surely they are parts of the same idea? By doing this we may conclude, as Kant did not see fit to do, that not only are the units called space and time formed intuitively, but the unity of the world-whole can never be demonstrated by appeal to any data of experience or any categories of the understanding, but must be formed intuitively in a single act of thought. Kant himself believes in such an ethical world-order, and the æsthetical ideas of his "Critique of Judgment" might have inclined him to postulate also an æsthetic world-whole as a given and yet thinkable principle of the larger human reason. This is a defensible view of Kant's system, as we may see when we note that the essentials of the "Critique of Judgment" are founded upon that which is fundamental to the "Critique of Pure Reason": namely, intuitive thinking. Like space and time, beauty and taste represent "the universal without the concept." This æsthetical conception contains the very heart of the logical transcendental æsthetic. The world-whole, abandoned by Kant in his destructive dialectic, may be interpreted thus as a universal arrived at by means of no induction or deduction in the way of concepts, but apprehended at once by means of intuition. As we have already pointed out, the intuitive consciousness of religion can and does arrive at the idea of unity in soul, world, and World-Soul, and that by no logical or scientific means. Over and above the facts of experience and the necessities of thought there stand out the rational criteria of æsthetic fitness and ethical necessity. Reason is justified of these her children. Yet here the ethical is not as important as the æsthetical.

While Kant's "Critique of Pure Reason" ever tends toward the enhancement of the ethical, it is just as markedly in opposition to theology of the speculative sort, and where

Kant's work ends in a transition to moral philosophy, it begins with a withdrawal from the ideas of God, freedom, and immortality. Likewise the transcendental æsthetic which, in its elaboration of space and time as intuitions, seems to be devoted to mathematics, was evidently prompted by the antinomies of God and the world, which arise as soon as thought regards space and time as realities. It is not because Kant is inclined toward the subjectivity of space and time, but because the objective view of these is wrecked upon the further question of the finitude or infinitude of the world. Thus do the transcendental æsthetic and transcendental dialectic unite in demanding a new view of the temporo-spatial world. In all this, Kant's aim seems to be to show that the understanding, which is adapted to knowledge of appearance, cannot grasp reality, just as our common axioms and logical laws often fail when applied to the infinite. We say that the whole is greater than a part, and a part is less than the whole. What can be more obvious? Yet look at the following arithmetical series which we relate and the geometrical one below it:

$$2 \quad 4 \quad 6 \quad 8 \quad 10 \quad 12 \quad 14 \quad 16 \ldots$$
$$2 \quad 4 \quad 8 \quad 16 \quad 32 \quad 64 \quad 128 \quad 256 \ldots$$

The first series contains all of the second one, which is a part of it, yet there is no limitation in the second which goes on to infinity; part and whole are alike infinite. As Galileo pointed out, our axioms are in vain when we deal with the infinite, and Kant, who was fond of likening himself to Copernicus, reaffirms Galileo's position when he shows that common logic can neither affirm nor deny when dealing with infinitude in the form of the world-whole. Yet what is condemned is not the subject, but the method, and if logic cannot evince the world unity, it is not because this does not exist, but because it is here insufficient. Religion which springs from the unitary soul is able to intuit the corresponding unity of the World-Soul.

2. The essence of religion may receive various deter-

minations, but no satisfactory view may be developed unless the element of knowledge is admitted as an abiding feature. From the religious consciousness, where feeling and will are emphasized, the process of cognition cannot be eliminated. Religion may not be perfect, but it is not blind ; worship may not be calculated to instruct in dialectics, but it does not fail to develop essential ideas. Being chiefly an impulse, religion manifests itself in the form of a deed on the part of the individual, and an achievement of the race. Thus, it is so immediate in man that it may be spoken of as an instinct, which traces back to the spontaneity of human consciousness. Owing to the perverse tendency to consider religion as a result rather than a cause, and as having clear, logical form and an ethical nature, it is necessary again and again to emphasize the fact that religion is advanced for religion's sake, and is produced by the originality of our human consciousness. Religion is a cause, and at the same time would seem to be prior, logically, and perhaps chronologically, to the other phases of spiritual life which make up our culture. At any rate, the originality of religion may safely be affirmed when worship and logic are being compared.

Yet, we cannot run the risk of setting up the ideal of irrationalism ; religion is cognitive, and it makes possible consistent reflection. What must be avoided is the substitution of abstractions for living ideas ; and the reason for this is that such principles of mere logic are not religious. Cosmology may strive to rehabilitate the world in the form of substances ; but religion finds nature alien to its demands. Metaphysics aims at causality ; faith aspires toward freedom. Ontology succeeds according as it works out a perfect system of related Being ; the religious life reposes in the unconditioned, in which it believes. Religion, therefore, does not consist in demonstrable theism ; and the substance of things hoped for is not to be found in the world-ground. On this account, we must avoid the fallacy of the *argumentum ad deum*. The proper programme for philosophy of religion may be outlined, when reflection apprehends those ideas which are put forth naturally by religion itself, and ignores the empty deductions of the understanding. When we return to the one question, What is religion ? we shall see that religion is something which, by its very nature, creates ideas and, in its development, makes necessary a consistent train of thought. But the cognitive moment is peculiar to religion, so that it is not to be regarded as a branch of metaphysics, or a mere sketch of formal logic.

Religion, however, is not blind. Agnosticism is not the best form of expression which will occur to the consistent religious thinker, who does not claim to possess all knowledge. Positive religion does not hesitate to regard God as transcending human knowledge ; so divine is He that man cannot know Him perfectly. At the same time, the Apostle of Christianity conceived of this divine knowledge as a possession which man, who is very human, might lose, and the foolish heart might become darkened by sin. There are still other ways in which apostle and prophet have shown the disparity maintaining between God and man. St. Paul concludes that now we know in part, because we see through a glass darkly. Such is his merognosticism. But the point at which religious knowledge differs from knowledge about religion is found in the qualitative difference, rather than the merely quantitative relation of more and less, the whole and a part. Granted that certain metaphysical assumptions concerning substance cannot be demonstrated, that does not affect belief in the living God ; and it is this latter with which religion has to do.

Owing to its peculiar nature as a deed on the part of the soul, which instinctively strives to affirm its character in distinction from the world, religion represents knowledge as well as the other functions of the human spirit, as an achievement, which results from cumulative effort. In that supreme act of the soul, by virtue of which it manifests its spiritual character and seeks its own peculiar goal,

The Character of Religion

there are involved several elements of human life. As an impulse to declare oneself a citizen of the Kingdom of God, religion offers no very imperfect analogy to the principle of rights. In the characteristic representation of itself as an instinct, worship expresses itself in the same direct and genuine manner as art. With its peculiar estimate of humanity, and in the method which it follows in satisfying the demands of this, the religious life is very like ethical conduct. But religion is not without its bearing upon knowledge. To know is an essential part of the religious achievement. The soul knows itself, and perceives how alien to its own peculiar nature is the world; in the endeavour to free itself from mere existence in nature to spiritual life in the religious realm, the soul postulates the idea of God. Yet God is more than an idea; His existence is postulated for no mere logical reason. Because the soul, in its attempt to become itself by passing from the natural to the spiritual, feels its need of aid from some extra-source, God is believed on.

The idea of God, however, is peculiar to religion. The deity of theism has about as much to do with the God of Christianity as Plato's Republic with the Kingdom of God. From the religious point of view, it is not a question of the demonstration or non-demonstration of the existence of God; it is not an either-or which says, "God either is, or He is not," but it is a vital question which asks how far is God known to us? So important is this interrogation, and so peculiar to the essence of religion, that the problem of speculative agnosticism is comparatively unimportant.

Positive religion is not wanting in the idea of God. But what does this fact signify for philosophy of religion? It does not mean that primitive religion was monotheistic; extremes do not thus meet in history. The ideas of the Deity which nature-people have entertained have been correspondingly as imperfect as their actual religion. Even upon the higher plane of national religion, the peculiar character of God as an only Being was not manifest in any more perfect form than the conception of mankind's unity.

In universal religion, as in the case of Christianity, the view of the world as a unity, and of mankind as one, made possible the transition to monotheism in its perfect and spiritual form. Living faith in this God thus arose in a manner peculiar to religion and foreign to logic. And with what result? Not the agnostic question, whether we know or do not know God, but the religious question of how thoroughly God is known to us. From this second point of view, it may be said that monotheism, which is a conception reached only after a continuous conflict on the part of human faith, is only partially entertained to-day, in the twentieth century of the Christian religion. While far removed from anything like the unitarian conception of God, monotheism has never been adjusted to the doctrine of the Trinity; and, in still other ways, it shows that it is an idea far beyond the communication and even the conception of our religious thinking. God is; but we hardly know Him.

Much the same may be said of another conception, organic to religion, namely, the soul, which affirms God. Religion does not wait for intellectualism or voluntarism, for monism or dualism, in order to deliver the soul of man from agnosticism. Early animistic reasoning did not penetrate to the depths of the spirit, and, in the progress of religious belief, it was not until the dawning of spiritual religion that the unity of nature, spiritual character and immortal destiny of the soul were conceived. In turning away from agnosticism, shall we say that we know the soul in its perfection? We are as ignorant of the soul as we are of God; yet religion dealing with them in their mutual relation does not hesitate to treat them as realities. Agnosticism, if it have any relation to metaphysics, certainly does not belong in philosophy of religion, which can easily account for the human limitation and imperfection of our knowledge.

So far as the world is concerned, non-religious logic has ever felt sure of itself, and has made use of this assurance

The Character of Religion

to point how imperfect is our knowledge of things spiritual. But do we know the world so perfectly after all? And do our cosmic philosophies satisfy? Take the case of monism, which is a theory relating, not only to the world, but to mind, both human and divine. According to this theory, there is one substance which in the human appears as the unity of mind and body; in the divine, as the community of God and the world. The ambition of this theory is in strange contrast to the halting attitude of agnosticism; yet, there is a kind of connection between them, inasmuch as monism declares that the common element in mind and body, God and the world, is unknowable. Within the precinct of the religious consciousness, these elements of God, the soul, and the world, play a part quite different from that of agnostic logic. The soul knows itself well enough to perceive that, for it, the goal of life is not to be found in the world, but in God, wherein it may live and move and have its genuine being.

From the course of positive religion, and especially from the culmination of this in Christianity, it may be concluded that religion possesses some kind and degree of knowledge of those things which pertain most directly to it. Knowledge is therefore essential to the deed of faith. That which provokes it is not curiosity; that which promotes it is no mere matter of scholastic method. Knowledge relates to life as well as to logic; and hence it cannot remain indifferent to that great factor in life which we call religion. There, to know becomes a necessary step in the religious achievement, just as cognition is an essential part of the religious consciousness. At the same time, the religious impulse offers a peculiar spring to the function of knowledge, inasmuch as it supplies the latter with an intrinsic feeling for knowledge and an interest in its pursuit. Logic does not arouse our thought, nor do we reflect for the sake of being consistent; behind the thought is some greater interest which is making use of logic as a method. That interest, which is expressed as a desire to know, is the source of man's destiny and, accordingly, it is easily associated with religion. Religion may be said to be the source of our thought about the soul, God and the world-whole. In these problems, as such, logic has no direct interest. By the aid of the faculty of judgment we may say, " This is the soul ; God is infinite ; the world is one," but we are not gaining any content for our knowledge. Religion, which is *infra*-logical, supplies the living content with which logic may deal.

When we advance into the essence of religion, we see that it is, at least, a cognitive process within, and an intelligible act on the part of the human spirit. By the aid of religion, we learn to appreciate the value of knowledge, and to estimate its bearing upon human life. Psychological thought in the field of religion has failed to note that the intellectual moment cannot remain unemphasized. Religion contains ideas which indeed have had an historical origin, and now appear in the form of representations rather than concepts ; but they express knowledge and have a kind of necessity and universality. Formal logic cannot remain so secure in its divisions, now that evolutionary science has redefined some of our most essential ideas—animal, life, man ; these are not so clear-cut, but seem rather to shade off into other definitions. For this reason, we cannot be so sure of our concepts as we were fifty years ago. Positive concepts (*Inbegriffe*), are found everywhere in religion, as Hegel has shown ; and it is with these realistic ideas that religion has to do. Knowledge then becomes a living process. Thought is not the ultimate principle in thinking, and knowledge ends in that which is *supra*-logical.

Not only the essence of religion, when it is analysed, but the expression of religion in human life, is fraught with elements of knowledge. Truth appears, not as a relation among ideas or a result from their combination, but as a demand made by the awakened spirit. The soul needs knowledge; and after this it aspires. For this reason, the worshipper exclaims, " Oh, that I knew where I might find Him!" "That I may know Him, and the power of His resurrection!" In all this, nothing save knowledge is asked, yet it is the desire of desires. "This is the life eternal, that they might know Thee!" Knowledge, when it is thus viewed and estimated, becomes a duty, imposed upon the religious subject, who must also discover what kind of knowledge is of the most religious worth. It was in this spirit that the Apostle Paul compared ancient σωφία with Christian μωρία, with the end of condemning them that by wisdom knew not God. In this, there is some irony, due to the personality of the Apostle, but there is also a serious statement of the difference between knowledge which is religious and that which is not. When the soul makes use of thought, to assist it in emancipating itself, it does so in a manner peculiar to itself and its religion.

In the light of positive religion, knowledge is a natural tendency. This will be seen in the origin, development, and culmination of more than one ethnic faith. The conception of religion on the part of its adherents need not, however, be expressed in a logical form; it is more likely to be æsthetical. Doctrine enters in to emphasize the logical moment, but it finds art already ensconced. When the soul, feeling the religious desire, seeks expression for its faith, it naturally turns toward something concrete and immediate, because its own feeling is intense and unarrested by culture. For this reason, it is more natural for primitive religion to assume the æsthetical than the logical form. The fetish appeals to the crude religious consciousness because it may be apprehended, as thought cannot be. But the fetish, if we may accept the explanations of Tiele and Tylor, also appeals to the vague religious desires because it is "neat" and "well-made." The æsthetical moment in this early condition of religious culture is further emphasized by the idea of magic, so common to crude beliefs. Nature worship, whether minor or major, further reveals the fact that man, in contemplating the world, is not struck with the scientific idea of uniformity, but rather with the æsthetical idea of attractiveness. From this, worship naturally follows, and perception leads to æsthetical, rather than logical judgment.

Likewise, the development of ethnic faith; thereby is brought about the transition from religion of the tribe to that of the nation. In this advanced condition, the tendency is still in the direction of the æsthetical rather than the logical. In India, Greece, and Rome, the peculiar union of faith and art is manifest, appearing especially in architecture and literature. These æsthetico-religionis productions are extremely national and correspondingly limited in their significance. Even with Judah's repugnance to religious art, the æsthetical is not wanting, but is simply kept within appropriate bounds, which shall exclude idolatry and mythology. In this attempt on the part of Israel, there was a marked degree of success, which may be seen when we reflect upon the psalms and the temple of the monarchical period. The purely æsthetical is not emphasized; but the logical is not mentioned. In the culmination of faith in universal religion, art still maintains and offers rivalry to the now-awakening understanding with its logic. Christianity has both archæology and theology; its Christ has been a principle of reason and a model for art. Whence the transition to the logical, or pure thought? It is due to development.

Upon the side of both Hindu and Hebrew forms of religion the development of the intellectual appears. When Vedism loses its hold upon the Aryan consciousness, the Brahmanism which follows has recourse to the Vedic principles of the Upanishads, and in the transition, the poetical conceptions of Agni, Indra, and Soma give way before the rationalistic notions of the self, the soul, and the Person. Yet it was this intellectual development, which makes of Veda the Vedanta, that made Brahmanism a religion more nearly universal. Israel's local and traditional ideas were also destined to give way before more pure and per-

The Character of Religion

fect conceptions, after the return from captivity. To come from Egypt gave Israel the impetus and content of its worship, while to return from Babylon was to invest that religion with a form approximating to world-religion. As Brahmanism develops the idea of self, Judaism reveals the idea of God. When religion comes to itself, which it does by means of no rationalistic method, it shows that it is possessed of significance as well as force. It may not be metaphysics or theology, but the intelligible side of this phase of human life does not fail to appear.

The communication of religion, in addition to its conception, makes necessary the intelligible. True it is, that, even here, the æsthetical element is of value as an educational method which the Roman Church does not fail to employ; but to "teach all nations" the essentials of spiritual religion is a task beyond the effort put forth by patriarch in guiding the clan, or the monarch in instructing his people. Universal religion can be communicated only as concepts take the place of figures. The temple is abandoned as the only seat of worship, the symbol of God's presence gives way to a spiritual conception. The worship is now in spirit and in truth. Christianity is capable of reflection, in a manner unknown with Pagan and Jewish faiths, whose content was so alien to thought that the mind could not rest upon it. A universal religion like Christianity must be put in a substantial form, and this is supplied by logic. Christ's conception of the Father thus received a metaphysical determination, while His own personality was taken out of history and regarded in the eternal form of thought. When, to-day, evangelical theology desires to rid itself of ancient metaphysics, it must observe that, in the natural development of Christianity, this logical moment would enter in; and when we strive to adjust historical religion to speculative logic, we must not fail to note that the latter can never be more than indirect in its bearing upon faith.

Faith is thus the form in which the intellectual element

in religion is expressed. To determine the nature of faith, it is not sufficient to regard it as a magical faculty of knowledge; but, because it supplies the worshipper with an object, it may be said to have a quasi-intellectual function. The method which faith employs, however, is more æsthetical than logical. This will appear when we observe how immediate is the relation between the belief and that which is believed in. Faith is spontaneous, being prompted by some inner condition of man's spiritual life; it is put forth for religious purposes, and not for the sake of vying with an indirect logic. Competition has had the effect of warping both religion and philosophy from their true positions. Faith's point of departure is religion and not logic; the explanation of faith is psychological and educational, not logical and metaphysical. We have religion and this we seek to express; among the various methods is that of faith, which objectifies the inner experience. The determinant of faith's soundness is to be found in the idea of value, which is so practical as to offer support to the rise and development of religion. Faith is the substance of things valuable, and religion consists in the belief that that which is desirable is also real.

Yet the intelligible side of religion which appears in spite of sceptical criticism is little more than a possibility, and where we cannot deny we cannot affirm. Some other method than that of abstract knowing must come in to make religion a secure process of cognition. What is needed to serve such a conception is, first of all, an inner and intuitive method of intellectual apprehension which shall realize the immediacy of religion within its own precinct. At the same time, the obviously positive or historical form of human religion must be represented in a manner more consistent than the critical yet non-creative method of logic. This must come from art; and the æsthetical method of treating human worship has this advantage over the logical one: it reveals the inner and historical character of human religion.

2 Religion as Æsthetic Intuition

The result of the speculative study of religion has been to show that while the character of religion is significant, and intelligible, it is not by reason of any logical form which human worship possesses. Religion demands a living form of apprehension which is at once internal and positive, and this is supplied by the æsthetical moment which it contains. For itself, art may arise within in response to a play-activity, just as it may be called forth by desire for ideal pleasure, yet art is not so superficial as to content itself with these simple elements of consciousness. It is more worthy to consider art as play of spirit, *jeu d'esprit*, as though nature could not quite contain man, nor animality satisfy his humanity. Like religion, art possesses an internal and profound character, which is wholly independent of logical deductions and ethical duties, and both the religious and artistic functions of the human spirit possess a spontaneity without and a sensitivity within which enable them to project their respective characters upon the objective world of humanity. Both forms of human consciousness agree in setting aside the purely practical, yet neither relinquishes reality. Art and religion manifest a characteristic reconciliation of the real and the ideal, and make possible a spiritualism which is based upon life. Each apprehends the concrete; yet only regards it as the symbol of the spiritual fact. The ancient found this reconciliation in the æsthetic alone, where logic and life, form and matter, were unified; the modern finds it in the religious, whereby the breach between matter and spirit, life and thought, may be overcome. Religion is no theory of the world, or of human life; it is itself a world-life, characterized by social events and individual deeds. These, however, must be idealized. How this reconciliation is to be effected may be seen in the case of æsthetics which unites inner and outer forms of life, in the individual and the world. Art and religion represent not merely an analogy, but an interaction ; this will appear when we examine (1) the career of modern religion and romanticism ; (2) the substantial bond between æsthetics and spiritual life, as well as (3) the commingling of the living forms of art and worship.

1. Ancient æsthetics was as far from a just appreciation of its own art as its philosophy was from spiritual life. That which seems to have clouded the mind of such thinkers as Plato and Aristotle was the presumption that art must be imitative and useful. Such metaphysical and moral presuppositions were not calculated to interpret the fine arts, and it is well known that Plato failed to appreciate poetry and the drama. Where art is delivered from the formal principles of philosophy it is further put upon a religious basis ; that is, in the dialectic of Plotinus. With Platonic ideals and Gnostic prejudices, Plotinus was still able to view beauty in independence of morality, just as he came to regard art as symbolic of the internal spirit rather than imitative of the external form. At heart, Plotinus was a religionist and a romanticist and his insight further reveals the intimate spirit of Christianity. Beauty consists in the ecstatic contemplation of the hyper-real and hyper-rational shining through the various forms of its own emanations, while art retraces the superior steps of the beautiful and signalizes the supremacy of spirit over matter. Plotinus' theory accounts for the difference between Phidias in Athens and Angelo in Florence ; the Christian consciousness represents the subject as suffering and as putting forth effort. Ancient art was passive and optimistic, and could not evince any inclination for spiritual religion.

Where art is the product of spiritual endeavour, it associates with the religious life ; and where there is a spiritual interpretation in æsthetics, this affiliation is capable of clear expression. Art and religion unite, because they are related ; happiness and devotion go hand in hand. Christianity consists essentially in a spiritual view of life and its conduct, and hereby Christianity receives its crown and glory. But this same religion has ever been friendly to art, and as a competitor of classicism, it has produced romanticism, a combination of Christianity and chivalry. In its medieval and modern forms, romanticism has emphasized elements at once religious and Christian. Ancient art was a combination of ethics and æsthetics, and Plato was both moralist and artist. With the dawn of Christianity, religion displaced ethics and joined itself with art ; such was the method of medievalism. In spite of the maxim, "Art for art's sake," modern æsthetics evince some connection with the religious life.

What shall be thought of medievalism ? Enough has been said about scholasticism and the Dark Ages ; let it be remembered that the period which developed Christianity also produced chivalry ; if there was darkness, it was the magnificent gloom of Gothic architecture. Gothicism and scholasticism are sometimes compared, and the analogy between them is based upon the common elements of finesse and infinite detail, which are coupled with rigid adherence to system. The scholastic theologian never ceases in his discriminations, yet he never departs from his central idea. In a Gothic cathedral, the *more geometrico* is glorified. In the side aisles, the vaulting is built upon the four points of a square ; that of the nave rests upon the corners of a rectangle, whose area is equal to the sum of these squares. All kinds of ornamentation may be reduced to forms which are geometrical or plant-like. The portals shelter groups of various figures ; but these uniformly consist of saints, of Christ, or of the judgment. In all this, the most elaborate form of architecture is made possible by rigid adherence to a self-contained plan. Medieval thought and life, which produced these two systems, have shown the possibilities in the combination of religion and art. If we have no Gothic architecture it is because we have no faith ; if no Raphael paints the Transfiguration, it is because we do not believe.

Without there being any inherent connection there was an implicit and substantial bond between Plotinus and scholasticism as well as between medievalism and romanticism. It was by means of religion that Neo-Platonism interpreted art, that Gothicism grew up in the Middle Ages, that romanticism formulated our philosophy of religion. This last service was performed by Schleiermacher, who felt the self-consciousness of religion and perceived the universal life of the world. Its political views developed by the personality of Napoleon, its poetry masked by the superiority of Goethe's verses, its philosophy awed by the criticism of Kant, it was chiefly in theology that it attained to anything like greatness. Romanticism inculcated religion when it pointed out the sufficiency of insight, as well as the attractiveness of a remote interest in life, and by virtue of the internal ground of reality and the ultimate goal of human existence it made a religion of art, just as it found the true art of religion. To look within, while foregoing demonstration, to aspire beyond, while ignoring the ordinary demands of life, was a romantic method peculiar to religion and worthy of Christianity.

2. The inner and essential connection between art and religion is due to the common spiritual character which these two functions disclose. This character, when analysed, consists of a synthesis of sense and spirit, of real and ideal in the form of *pathos* and *ethos*. Art possesses a metaphysical basis revealed in the intuitions of space and time, and, no matter how lofty its character, it never becomes imperceptible. Like religion, beauty is marked by limitations which are qualitative and self-imposed. To be beautiful a sentiment must pass through the senses so serenely that it suffer no crass means of enjoyment to absorb the mind; nevertheless, beauty must appeal to the warm intuitions of humanity in such a convincing fashion that the subject shall forget the particularity of the spectacle, while not yielding to abstraction. Furthermore, it is the holy vocation of art to touch the humanity

The Character of Religion

of man so lightly that it leave no stain of finitude on his soul. Religion, which labours with its ideals and reveals the aspiration of man in the bloody sweat upon his brow, profits by this serener method of attaining to the ideal, and no wonder that human worship is made as artistic as is convenient.

The religious significance of art is further seen in the complete unity which the æsthetical attitude involves. When the subject beholds the beautiful object, he empties himself of his interests and partialities and, as a complete personality, he is pervaded by pure contemplation. That which confronts him is neither the particular nor the general, but the one, and in the landscape he sees the world, in the statue, humanity, in poetry, the total life of mankind. Pure object is intuited by pure subject as "Aldeberan and Orion glance forever." It is just this attitude of complete contemplation which fills the soul with a religious significance. Man is somewhat more than himself, while the world is no longer his, but belongs to the Infinite. Here, the attitude of art and religion is one; both exchange humanity for man, and spiritual life for nature. The conduct of art and religion is here alien to that of speculation, which advances by means of abstraction and generalization, and the spiritual nature of humanity penetrates at once to the oneness and inness of the universe. The result of artistic and religious intuition cannot be questioned after it is observed that universality and necessity follow in the path of such insight. For logic, abstraction is a necessary step in the development of the concepts' marks, while generalization comes in to complete the work by grouping together the various examples of the concept; the first process discovers the necessary, while the second unfolds universality. Intuition arrives at these essentials directly and in less secure a fashion does reveal human knowledge.

Religion and art never contradict logic; they only exceed its limits, for both of them contain the infra-rational and the supra-rational, in the peculiar dualism of sense and spirit. The æsthetic and religious are never unperceptible and abstract, and yet they maintain their proper characters in the midst of sensuous elements. Clothed and clothed upon with the positive, religion descends to the level of nature and seizes hold of man as he is, while it is still able to maintain the ideal. On the speculative side, it is art and religion alone which are able to bring about a synthesis of such extremes as sensation and spiritual life, and the artistic festival, which is commemorated by frieze or canvas, and the Paschal meal, which has become a sacrament, show how serenely this may be done. Could eating and drinking elsewhere be glorified?

The æsthetic attitude is none the less apparent in the supra-rational form which art assumes. Logic varies from general to particular, from particular to general; here its thought is abstract, there it is concrete. Art seizes neither of these extremes, but finds the unity of spiritual life. It is now well known that æsthetic intuition must be viewed, just as it itself must be formed, apart from the concept, whose universality and necessity ever imply generalization and abstraction; nevertheless, this absence of the concept further implies the presence of the percept, which art invests with an extra-significance. Intuition is not only introverted in its nature, but it is unified in its form. Under its gaze, the individual becomes a type, nature assumes the forms of a world-order, history traces an ideal course. Where æsthetic contemplation is purest and artistic creation is perfect, the mind of man is able to discover the unity which of necessity belongs to the soul, and to the world; from these overcome standpoints, the æsthetic attitude is adjusted to the fact of the World-Soul.

Not only the æsthetic attitude, but the artistic deed on the part of mankind evinces that significance which is peculiar to religion. Already, we have described religion as an attempt on the part of the soul to affirm itself over against the world, because the latter is as alien as it is antagonistic to the soul's nature. If we have any doubt of the reality of this performance, we may turn to the case of art, which in its way manifests a view of the human spirit's independence which is simply convincing. Art seems to imitate nature, whereas in reality it improves upon it, as though the two were in competition; and art becomes art just as soon as it abandons nature. In the same way, the animality of man is negated by his triumphant humanity, where he learns to crave ideal excitement for his own spirit and to find satisfaction in a pleasure which is not related to the practical interests of his life. Art thus perfects nature and human nature and redeems man from all that is crass and ordinary; religion assumes the same task, except that religion carries on its work with a peculiar vehemence, which is due to consciousness of human destiny.

Particular examples of the artistic evince the triumphant nature of the creative spirit. Landscape painting, which reveals the spirit of the world and shows wherein man is related to nature, unfolds before the contemplating spirit, not what nature is, but what she might be. The full humanity of man cannot abide by the real world alone, but demands the extra beauty of art. In the same way sculpture cannot rest content with the living forms of actual animal life, but must go on to perfection. The plastic artist sees what nature has tried to do, and, accepting the hint from these cases of arrested development, he perfects humanity. Thus, when Mignon disclosed to Wilhelm Meister the glories of the land of laurel and myrtle, with its palace and pillars, she points to the statues, which in their plastic perfection seem to speak for the creative sculptor:

> There marble statues stand and look at me,
> And say, poor child, what have they done to thee?

And everywhere poetry and plastic serenely triumph over the highest in the world of natural forms.

Where art is interpreted in the larger sense of culture,

it betrays the same holy affinity for spiritual religion. Culture, which often calls upon the soul for sacrifice, is pledged to the most remote aim in human life, so that the immediate interest of man is constantly denied in the spirit of *Kunst ohne Gunst*. While man seems to belong to the natural series, and is actually engrossed with the objects of his immediate environment, there is something within him which cannot remain content until some ultimate conception becomes an aim in life. Herein does culture depart from mere improvement and assumes the form of the imperative. Within its shining domain, man has a vocation which calls forth his highest efforts and causes him to withdraw from the world.

Religion and art are functions of the human spirit, which are at once intimately related to human nature and pragmatically expressed in human life. In them, man has an interest, which he has not failed to express in a living way. As a result, each of these phases represents a positive creation, which cannot fail to be recognized. But, with all this, the religious and æsthetical sources in human nature are so internal that they might perhaps be viewed as extra-human; without them life and its utilities might still be conducted. For this reason, worship and art seem supererogatory; necessity does not demand them; but they are evoked by freedom. With thought and action the situation is far different, for these tendencies must be developed. The world at once provokes thought, and hereby philosophy and science are rendered inevitable; life cannot help inaugurating some kind of conduct, and ethical custom follows as the natural issue of life. Apart from some scheme of knowledge and some rule of conduct, we can hardly conceive of man as existing. But, with art and religion, this is not so. To be sure, these institutions are an organic part of humanity and a veritable creation of history, so that their reality and might cannot be doubted. It is when we seek to explain the sufficient cause of these that appeal must be made to some other form of spiritual behaviour, some unwonted sensitivity on the part of humanity. Man worships and creates art, not because these tendencies are necessary or useful, but because of some inner demand which his own spirit makes upon him.

The common source of art and religion is to be found in spiritual freedom, which causes the beautiful and the august to arise spontaneously. Art may be extreme in romance or rococo, religion may be absurd in its ceremony and superstition, yet these aberrations of artistic and religious consciousness only emphasize the independence of the human spirit. Yet these fine sentiments are not lost in subjectivity. Just as the artistic instinct must objectify itself in some tangible form, so the religious desire can satisfy itself only as it goes forth toward external phase of expression. Such objectification may be considered as the Church as an institution of worship, revelation as a means of religious instruction, architecture as the visible sign of worship, and poetry as the form of religious truth. Where the utilitarian view of life predominates, it is difficult to see the value of the æsthetico-religious, yet the excess of spirit over matter provides for progress in the realm of human culture. The power of religion and art may be seen in the building of the pyramids, whose existence may be explained in part by referring to their functions as tombs for royal personalities, but whose final significance appears as a belief, on the part of the Coptic consciousness, in the immortality of the soul. Viewed as purely architectural works, the pyramids may indeed be among the seven wonders of the world, yet the religious impulse which produces them is an obvious element in human consciousness.

3. As religion and art develop side by side in man's consciousness, so they express themselves in a common positive form. It is for this reason that the two are speculative forms of human culture which are quite independent of any logical consideration. In distinction from the method of the understanding, art and religion possess a dual form

of conception marked here by inner beauty, there by outer art, here by subjective religion, there by objective worship. Logic is a purely formal discipline which exercises, not a creative, but only a critical function in human reason. The complete view of religion must include an analysis of an internal instinct and also a survey of an external institution, just as æsthetics possesses a psychology of beauty and a history of art. It is just this binocular method of art and religion which produces a stereoscopic effect in man's contemplation, while the logical view of the world as well as the ethical view of life are capable of only superficial vision. Logic, in its normative capacity, is called upon to recognize the psychological train of ideas which, as a given principle in the human mind, can generalize in the field of colour-sensation, but can never produce a tint from red to blue, from white to black. In the spiritual realm of religion and art there is also something given in the form of intuitions which logic strives to rationalize, and just as thought cannot produce redness or sweetness among our sensations, so it fails to create beauty and love. Religion is made up of the vast, yet particular synthetic judgments of history, like the migration of the Aryans and the Exodus of Israel, the teaching of Jesus and the renunciation of Gautama.

It is in the furtherance of religion that art finds one of its characteristic tasks, and the masterpiece may thus become an object of worship. Religion has feelings which seek consistent expression, and this can hardly be brought about apart from art ; the eye longs for colouring, the ear listens for tone. It is the function of art to define the sensation and to indicate its proper limits, and the service of the æsthetic is called in to train the religionist to respond to the proper incitement, and to believe in the reality of its desired object, as Angelo saw in Ghiberti's bronze doors the very gates of Paradise. Where religion itself is an effort on the part of the soul to affirm its being in opposition to the world, art may be said to prefigure this impulse in the creative work which it performs, and the value of the religious performance is made more actual to the subject when he sees what can be done in an allied precinct. To realize the aim of religion the soul must be able to feel ideal excitement directed toward a remote object in the spiritual world, and it is for the training of this that art is peculiarly adapted. As man is confronted by life, so the artist is greeted by the raw material of his work; in both religion and art gigantic effort must be directed toward a fine spiritual aim.

The original form of the soul's self-affirmation is expressed in architecture, whose leading motive is the opposition to gravitation on the part of the selected and fashioned material of the architect. The pyramid solves this problem in a laborious fashion, but in accordance with a simple plan, which involves no freedom of construction. Columnar architecture exercises more intellect and less will, while the arched form of construction, which attempts the greatest task, accomplishes this by using small stones, as in the Romanesque arch, and a peculiar device in the case of the striving system of the Gothic. The Gothic architect, with his failures at Beauvais and his successes at Amiens, encounters a difficulty which belongs not only to his material but to the inherent form of his projected edifice. He aspires to raise a high and heavy ceiling which rests upon no palpable wall for its support, and to overcome this mechanical impossibility he throws out flying arch, strung buttress and minaret. Yet all architectural forms, pyramidal, columnar, and arched, manifest the religious principle of striving against the world of dull matter.

Sculpture presents the religious motive for self-affirmation when it shows how hardly does the human body contain the spirit which invests and informs it. Christian sculpture, like that of Michel Angelo, reveals the attitude of man toward his existence. A classicist may portray humanity at ease in the world, but a romanticist is anxious to deliver man from the body of death. Angelo assumed this tempestuous form of conception, although he taxed the possibilities of marble in perfecting it. " Moses " at the tomb of Julius the Second, the figures of " Day " and " Night," " Dawn " and " Evening " are pained and perplexed statues which seem to say, " We can strive and we can suffer." In the study of Lorenzo of Medici the head is so crowned by a ponderous helmet, and so pitched forward as it rests upon the hand, that a marked shadow is thrown across the face, only to enhance the gloom which envelops the whole figure. Even the younger studies of Angelo, like " Giovanni " and the youthful " David," as well as the frescoed medallion-bearers of the Sistine Chapel, reveal the same troubled attitude toward life, and nowhere in the Florentine's studio do we witness that sense of relief from earthly care which invests the classic Apollo Belvedere.

Such striving involves suffering, and the whole creation groaneth in world-sorrow upon the self-affirmation of the soul. No bodily resonance can give expression to such a condition, and the seer feels constrained to say, " Some god gave me power to paint how I suffer." Nature finds in the artist a medium for expressing infinite pain. Leonardo da Vinci was fitted by nature and talent to display the pathetic side of human life. La Gioconda is the classic example of facial expression, and her countenance lights up the *grande gallerie* of the Louvre. The beholder cannot discern the spirit of the smile, which is there portrayed; but its mystery is no more and no less than that which human life everywhere reveals. But Leonardo has shown something more than the possibilities of pure pleasure; he has also revealed the tendencies toward pain. In the face of Christ, as He sits at the table in the " Last Supper," the same magic of expression may be found; here, the features are religious, and express a sorrow of unfathomable depth. Dürer has had similar triumphs. His canvas of " Christ on the Cross " (1506) is a small picture, but how many are they who love it! The finely-moulded body suggests the possibility of pain, which is expressed in the face. Death in the Christ is made more tragic by life in nature. A strong wind tosses the hair of the quiet sufferer, while it throws into exquisite folds the cloth about His loins. Upon Him settles the darkness, while the background of the picture is lighted up to reveal a hill and several trees by the river. Art and religion are here reconciled.

The spontaneous and sensitive quality of religious art further appears in poetry. Religion is by its very nature a literary matter, for the realities and intensities of human worship must have the direct form of poetic expression rather than the reflective and discursive forms of speculation. Language is an organic thing, and in warm qualities of its development it follows a matter in keeping with the religious precinct. Isaiah was no dreary deist, but a prophet who beheld the glory of God in the form of seraphims with six wings. Ezekiel's vision disclosed four-winged beasts, and his God, instead of being clad in royal garments and seated on a throne, was entirely wrapped in flames. Amos and Micah differ, in that one is royal, the other rural, in his method of theistic representation. These prophets do not infer but intuit, as their deliverances will show, and no calculating systems can explain, much less explain away, the Vedic, the Homeric, or the Judaic, which are indigenous to humanity. If life has no transcendental vanishing point, and man has no destiny, then these plays of spirit are fantastic and vain, but if spiritual life is real and of world-power, then the seer deserves the immortal credit for his discovery.

In the midst of these intuitive forms the truth of religion still persists, and we need not be alarmed when we find that propositions of immediate evidence are not concluded by means of logical inference on the part of the critical understanding. Religion creates because it is possessed of life; thought criticizes the given product of humanity with its religious consciousness. And this view of life need not dwindle in significance, when it is said that religious ideas may possess a "poetic truth." It is genuine truth which we desire, and when it has been obtained we need not be anxious over the particular method of its apprehension. Intuition, which has a certain metaphysical form peculiar to itself, supplies the mind with universal and necessary ideas, and we may depend upon these, even though they are not produced by means of abstraction and generalization. With respect to historical religions, it may be added that Christianity is the most æsthetical, since it represents not mere sense or sheer spirit, but a triumphant unity of outer and inner functions. At the same time, Christianity is as intelligible as it is artistic.

B. THE RELIGIOUS INTERPRETATION OF LIFE

In the same way that religion constructs, and itself consists of, a view of the world, it also furnishes a characteristic interpretation of human life. As we seek to unfold the practical portion of religious character, we must again remind ourselves that we are dealing with a subject which occupies an independent province in the human spirit just as we should see that, with a nature *sui generis*, it is likely to assume representative relation to human life. Furthermore, the self-centred and creative form of religion, which makes it consist of art rather than knowledge, will here exert an influence which is calculated to demonstrate that religion is not so much an ethical consideration of the ideal, as it is a juristic production of a positive form of life. Toward ethical science our attitude must be critical, although it should appear that religion, which is a worthy form of existence, is not inimical to morality, although it is ever inclined to adapt itself to the principles of law.

1. *Religion and Ethics*

It would seem as though our thought must move more cautiously in suggesting any invidious contrast between religion and ethics. With Hume and Kant behind us, with the atmosphere of positivism about us, we are almost willing to say that religion, like other forms of spiritual life, need not have a metaphysical basis consisting of substantial and causal categories; but, when we survey the ethical, we are not so prone to deny and to say that the same non-logical religion may further assert its independence of morality. But why should we hesitate? If non-rational religion may still be as intelligible as the intuitive discipline of art, so non-ethical religion may still be good in the puristic sense. Not all of truth is logical, not all of goodness is ethical, art and law still have their views and their claims, and with them as bulwarks, religion may assert the independence of its precinct in apposition to both metaphysics and morality. The present age has learned half of this lesson, and has accepted a part of the truth; it means now to render religion independent of ethics as well as of logic.

In adjusting religion to ethics we must settle accounts with Kant, who puts morality upon the independent metaphysical basis of freedom, and then subsumes religion under it. As a philosopher and ethical personality Kant holds a unique position among modern thinkers. His transcendental logic, expressed in the " Critique of Pure Reason," acts as a final arbiter between the empiricism of Locke and the rationalism of Leibnitz, while his æsthetical " Critique of Judgment " is also imperious in its attitude toward the sensualism of Burke and the formalism of Baumgarten. Combining experience and sense with understanding and thought, Kant creates an epoch in speculative philosophy, on the side of logic and æsthetics. But the " Critique of Practical Reason," with all its practical import, does not assume an attitude parallel to the other two critiques ; it assumes no magisterial position, combines no schools of hedonism and rationalism, but follows the usual trend of intuitionism. We cannot say, of course, that Kant imitates Adam Smith and Butler, who anticipate him in several ways, nor can we say, on the other hand, that he deals with these representatives of heteronomy and autonomy as he had elsewhere adjusted school to school. Kant's misoneism is expressed again in " Philosophy of Rights," which refuses to abandon the artificiality of the school of natural rights, even when this was engulfed by the French Revolution; and the founder of the critical system is as conservative in dealing with life-problems as he is destructive in the realm of thinking. The strength of his philosophy is its moralism, but this is also its weakness, and if he flouts logic for the sake of ethics, it may be said that Hegel ignores ethics in behalf of logic, while Schleiermacher casts both from the province of religion. If, therefore, we have tried to show that religion, while intelligent and intuitive, is not logical, we must now complete our work by pointing out that religion, while it embraces the idea of piety, does not consist of ethics.

This should not sound strange in the ears of those who believe in the intrinsic quality and imperative significance of the moral principle, for we desire merely to show that religion also exists. Where modern æsthetics, in distinction from the ancient, regards art as having a basis independent of morality and metaphysics, so that it is necessary for us to evaluate it in ideas other than those of utility and imitation, so religion may be said to have a precinct of its own, wherein it elaborates values other than those of virtue and the good, conscience and duty. And we have no more sufficient reason for saying that religion is not metaphysics than we have for affirming, as we here do, that it is not morality. The immediate identification of religion and morality is an incestuous union, and it is only when the ties of consanguinity are broken that thought may celebrate the mystic marriage of these two children of spiritual life. What is here attempted is a formal separation of distinct phases of culture, and that upon the basis of an intimate conception of each in its genius and philosophic status. Our present line of inquiry is thus to find out what is the essential difference between the ethical and the religious. Then the real point of contact may more readily be found.

The discussion of this twofold problem must do justice to the various phases of the subject. First of all it must be shown where the essential form of religion differs from that of ethics. In this way a clear distinction between the two sciences is made possible, and that in a manner which is just to each. When once this distinction has been pointed out the problem of connecting the two is more readily apprehended. Secondly, an examination of the conditions of positive religion will show that there is an actual connection between human worship and human conduct. The extent and substantial character of this relation must then be fully examined. Here the real problem arises. Distinct phases of human speculation evince an association which may turn out to be only circumstantial and contingent. Then, in the third place, it must be asked: How may the union of religion and morality be effected? Why must religion be essentially moral in order to carry out what it claims to be and do? Such a question can be answered only when these two distinct provinces are related philosophically. Trespass and incursion will then give way to an amicable and satisfactory settlement of the claims of two adjacent fields. How shall this be done, unless there be found some common concept which shall overcome the breach between these forms of culture?

1. The distinction between religion and morality will appear as soon as we develop the idea that religion is in its nature *positive* and in its character *pessimistic,* while ethics is ever normative science based upon the ideal which is discussed in an optimistic manner. To ignore particular ethical theories, for a while, and to investigate the nature

of ethics itself, we see how purely regulative and how merely influential the moral is.

Manifold as are the meanings which may centre in the ethical idea, a sufficient classification of them may, perhaps, be made by saying, the ethical signifies (1) a general concept; (2) a theory or science; and (3) a form of life, which may be called common-sense morality. Apprehended in the form of a *concept*, studied in its manifestation in a moral *consciousness*, and represented in variations of social *custom*, the idea of the ethical may be fairly well understood. Then the demands of ethical science and the possibilities of ethical culture may be appreciated. In order to make headway in the philosophic treatment of the practical reason and its problems it becomes necessary to identify these three forms of study and to correlate them. Thus, the general principle of morality must be related to a more or less definite ethical theory, which latter must sustain some vital connection with morality, as given in the life of man in society. Various have been the relations which ethical science and ethical culture have sustained to the ethical principle in general, but the necessary form of the connection has not always been considered. What is the ethical? When we answer this question, saying that it is a form of reason which surveys the world *sub specie boni*, we may ask whether our ethical formulations are subtended by corresponding facts and differences in the world of reality. The moment we endeavour to philosophize on the ethical, we see how intensely theoretical is its essential nature, and we despair of finding any basis in reality. And behold! what a phantom is morality! How shall thought apprehend it? As a science ethics is not constitutive; as an idea the ethical is dependent upon a theory. We cannot content ourselves with a purely philological treatment of the problem where the natural history of the idea may be represented, nor is much to be gained from any set definition which may, after all, mask some favourite theory. The ethical remains as an unsolved problem. Call it practical philosophy, regard it as a science of life, treat it in the form of a particular theory, and still the inner quality of the concept eludes us. That the ethical is a theoretical product seems to be the conclusion reached when the nature of the science and character of the concept have been examined. Apart from theory we cannot say what the ethical may mean, nor may we conclude that it has an independent existence. Certainly modern thought, which has aspired to give us a science of ethics, has confined its attention to the theoretical nature of the problem. As a science ethics is formal, and cannot be compared with religion; rather is it to be likened to what in speculative thought we esteem logic to be.

The ethical may further be expressed by a series of definite concepts which could in no wise apply to religion. Here, the analogy between logic and ethics becomes patent. Each is a normative science, supreme in its own field. The validity of thought in general, or in the particular field of religious speculation, is to be found in logic with its concepts and judgments. In the same manner, the standards of religion must finally be brought under the surveillance of ethics; here the sanction is to be found. Whether ethical judgments are *a priori*, or depend upon experience with pleasure and pain, is a question whose solution depends upon the interpretation of this or that theory. The ethical principle is present, and assumes its place as supreme in the conduct of life, as logic is ultimate in thought. But just this position prescribes a peculiar limitation to the ethical; for, being formal and regulative, it does not correspond to any phase of reality. Life, action, and progress come from some other source. Ethics may arouse conscience, and pass judgment upon actions which have been done; but the spring of action is not to be found in morality itself. We do not think for the sake of being logical; nor do we act for the sake of being ethical. All this would be scholastic and perfunctory. Ethics is thus normative and suggestive in its nature; we are to understand it as a "method." To fill it out and make it a living process, recourse must be had to that which is real and constructive. All this may be found in the religious experience of mankind; there, though it may have been blind, a living fact has developed.

In addition to this, the ethical is a theory, being the product of the practical reason. Hereby it assumes its own peculiar character, just as it wields a sway over the subject of religion. The theoretical nature of ethics makes the latter what it is destined to be, just as it constitutes its relation to religion. Psychological considerations tend to show wherein the essence of religion consists. Logic points out the truth of religion and the validity of a religious form of speculation. It remains for ethics to investigate the value of religion for human life. When fragments of human faith, which may appear in the form of primitive religion, are encountered, there can be no doubt that the ethical quality of these is a matter of question. An immoral cult may exist. But what of universal religion, which represents the best we know of the religious consciousness? The practical power and the logical consistency of such a religion as Christianity cannot be set aside; nor may we speak carelessly of the value of religion in this universal and spiritual form. Yet the question remains, and it can be answered only by appealing to ethical principles. Though ethics may lack in executive power, it makes up for this in judicial authority. To such, all phases of religion are amenable; and this is because ethics is the theory of life. The limits of its nature may be indicated by terms whose significance we have thus analysed: subjective, formal, theoretical.

In strident contrast to the normative and influential nature of the ethical stands out the positive form of human religion. As a result of this, religion assumes a dual capacity, so that we have, first, the religious *instinct*, consisting, perhaps, of feeling or desire, and, secondly, the religious *institution*, called either Church, Synagogue,

The Character of Religion

or Samgha. Among the most ideal of human sentiments, it is one of the most real of historical forces, and although it is transcendental in its character, it is positive in its essential nature. When benediction is pronounced upon the pure in heart and the poor in spirit, the beatitude is sincere, and unto them belongs the Kingdom of Heaven ; where men are meek they also inherit the earth. Religion is thus seen to consist of a complete and stereoscopic view of the world, because it is possessed of a twofold form of apprehension. If psychology says that religion consists of knowledge, or action, or feeling, history completes the view by showing how living religion is made up of cults like Confucianism, Brahmanism, Christianity, and hereby we are apprised of the positive and actual nature of the religious sentiment. The ethical, however, is a formal discipline whose real significance pertains to the metaphysical world of concepts, and does not participate in the historical world of humanity.

But this dual and positive form of religion may be found in another discipline of practical philosophy, the philosophy of rights. This theory of human activity consists of two essential parts : *jus* and *lex*, which relate to opposed conceptions of humanity, called nature and culture. Grotius, Locke, and Rousseau, like the ancient Sophists, Cynics, and Stoics, exalt the principles of nature and rights to such a degree that law and civilization stand out in unfavourable contrast, while others, like Puffendorf, Vico, and Montesquieu, may be more inclined to temper the abstractions and impulses of natural rights with ideas drawn from the history of civilization. Yet there ever remains the dualistic form of jurisprudence, which shows that an internal sentiment may objectify itself in an institutional fashion, and while law may be inferior to rights, and culture may appear pale in contrast with nature, the fact and the value of the external form can never be denied. In modern times, if not among the ancients too, rights and ethics arose and developed together, yet the ethical has nowhere succeeded in becoming an institution comparable to positive religion and established law.

Both religion and rights signalize their impulses to objectify their respective natures, when they resort to the common æsthetical tendency to be observed in the temple of worship and the forum of justice. These provide motive for the creative artist, who employs his talents with the result of producing characteristic works of art and architecture. Religion and rights have their respective symbols in figures of "Justice" and in forms of saints, while they have also appropriate structures in which to carry on their own works. Ethics and logic, while they are no less germane to the human spirit, are so constituted that no objectification in either civilization or culture is even thought of, and these normative disciplines of life and thought content themselves with performing a function purely critical. The human mind, in reacting upon life in the world, elaborates a science of rights and the practice of law, just as it also develops a philosophy of religion and a science of ethnic cults ; in logic and ethics, the case is in no wise parallel, for here the situation demands only the abstract correctness of the speculative principle and the ideal sufficiency of the practical maxim.

Religion, as a form of philosophy which is distinct from ethics, is historical or it is nothing. To religion, in distinction from ethics, there belongs a definite and positive form which is due to various ethnic faiths. It is just this positive form which is wanting in ethics ; for it has never had a history. Moral customs may vary and expand ; ethical ideas may assume different degrees of clearness and scientific cogency ; but the constructive development which is found in religion is never encountered. Religion, which is social and historical, has no general form which may exist apart from different cults. Where religion *per se* may be a useful idea for philosophy, it is only as an abstraction that it may be treated. For this reason, all attempts to deduce a so-called "natural religion," independent of, yet common to, all forms of positive religion, can end only in words. Natural religion is a pure *nihil*. The philosophy of religion, assuming the religious sentiment as a general characteristic of human life, does not commit the error of regarding this idea of religion as a reality. It rather finds the actual life of religion to consist in various forms of living faith, and these appear, not as purely subjective principles, but as historical realities. True or false, good or bad, religion exists in itself, and has behind it a history, which shows what its actual career has been.

The essentially positive form, which religion likewise evinces, shows how realistic the latter's nature is and must be. Being positive, religion is highly differentiated; and, in the midst of a manifold array of phenomena, the unity of the religious concept may be lost to view. So distinct is the emphasis laid upon the particular, that no such thing as religion in general is conceived of as existing. Where the age of "Enlightenment" sought this in a rational deduction from the static conception of nature, the nineteenth century has pursued somewhat the same method in dealing with the various phenomena of an evolving religion of nature. The method may be different, but the error is the same. The *consensus gentium* applied with the hope of verifying a rationalistic conception of religion, is just as vain as the generalization now being put forth by the science of "comparative religion." The moment that the idea of religion in general is applied to the features of all cults taken together, the glory of the religious sentiment has departed. Religion, as such, is not to be found by the aid of a logical concept or an empirical generalization. But universal religion is recognized by science as constituting a definite type of worship; call it Buddhism or Christianity. Such universal faith fulfils the demands of the logical concept, while it also represents an actual phase of positive worship. To exist, religion must be positive and characteristic.

In still another way does religion detach itself from

any lingering connection with ethical theory; with its painful adherence to the positive, it assumes a character which is essentially *pessimistic*, while ethics pursues the ideal in an optimistic manner. The spirit of religion which broods over the melancholy facts of human history is marked by a sincere desire to conserve the ideal, and this necessitates a negative and critical attitude toward the realities of the actual world. At the same time, religion does not disdain to survey, or to lay hold upon, the sorrow and sin which seem to constitute the long moments of human life. Among oriental systems, the form of this pessimism is cosmic and eudemonistic, whereupon it is concluded that the world is not fit for man, whose life therein fails to evince any amelioration or improvement. On the western side of the world, where humanism is more prevalent, pessimism assumes the historical and ethical forms, and accordingly it is declared that, while nature may not be at fault, history fails to fulfil the hopes of the human spirit, which itself is to be blamed, inasmuch as it inclines toward the bad in its love of darkness. Of these distressing views of the eastern and western worlds respectively Buddhism and Christianity are representative.

The practical attitude of spiritual religion thus becomes nihilistic, although the denial of reality in the world or in human life is often due to the perception of unworthiness rather than of illusion. Taoism cynically expounds a negative view of being, and exalts the ideal of " doing nothing." Vedanta distrusts all phenomenal existence, and retires within to the Self. The Avesta fulfils the pessimism inherent in Aryan culture, by creating a dualism of light and darkness, of good and bad. In the presence of these sombre conceptions, man is admonished to retrench his natural activities and follow the path of renunciation. Such a negation of immediate existence finds its most extreme form in the Buddhist programme of annihilation which belongs to Nirvana, nor is it wanting in the Christian conception of self-denial. Buddhism invites a complete annihilation which consists, not of bodily destruction, which in the face of transmigration would be useless, but of spiritual nihilism. Christianity negates in order to affirm, and declares not only that to love life is to lose it, but to hate it is to find it, while to die is to live again. Far removed from the painful actualities of the living world, ethics follows the serene course of theory, and serves mankind *au distance*.

The secret of ethics is to be found with ethical theories. In ancient thought this was true; modern philosophic attention has made it more evident. With his intellect the antique thinker sought to fathom the depths of the *good*; the modern, energized by will, undertakes to perform an imperative *duty*. So far as the present is concerned, current ethical tendencies may perhaps be summed up by saying the activities of the human spirit are ordered by desire or duty. In each case there is a struggle to express the quality of the ethical, and to endue such an interpretation with sufficient moral power that it may live. The ethical is thus an ideal which is not attained in theory any more than it is realized in conduct. At the same time the theoretical form of the ethical is surcharged upon the features of common-sense morality; as a result the moral life is expressed in the form of a generalization. The manifold of impulses, ideas, and affections, which make human activity what it is seen to be, is reduced to a unitary form of expression called hedonism or intuitionism. As a concept the ethical equals desire, or it is equivalent to duty. But here arises a question: Does the theory conserve the quality of the ethical? To answer this question particular theories must be examined.

Under the hand of the psychological function of desire hedonist ethics became a fairly consistent view of life, only it lacked depth. Hedonism has had many a method of treating the problem, but its ideas of pleasure and desire, of happiness and health, of prudence and benevolence, are all incomplete. Where the theory gains in naturalness it loses in ethical quality. Does hedonism represent that which the ethical in human experience is felt to contain? In answering this question we are at the very heart of our inquiry. It matters not how adequate may be the psychological analysis of the hedonist method, or how consistent the theory as such may be. The one essential is this: Is the ethical found therein? Hedonism, with its heteronomy, with its psychological calculus of pleasure, with its purely social construction, ever falls below the plane of ethical truth. Utility and sociability are not part and parcel of the ethical; nowhere within the circle of them is absolute character to be found. Spiritual life cannot thus fall a prey to organic impulses and social schemes; a "man's a man for a' that," and his qualities must not be reduced to characterless living.

Guided by a theory of duty, the ethical has had a meritorious interpretation, yet the secret of the former has not been solved. Intuitionism has proceeded from the moral life in the same way that hedonism has departed from the natural or psychological consciousness. By means of the intuitional view the ethical has been dignified and infused with practical force; the problem has been presented, but this is almost the limit of intuitionism's service. The ethical theory of duty involves a circle, while the practical result of the principle is to create a labyrinth. No goal is presented; no result is attained. To make duty teleological would be to defeat its own peculiar aim; to temper it with life and love would seem to make it "pathological." Such was the judgment of one like Kant. More recent advocates of the doctrine have not failed to see and to acknowledge this difficulty. Thus T. H. Green was wont to admit that ethical principles were only "formative and influential." Here consists the condemnation of intuitionism. As a theory it leads nowhere, produces no fruit, accomplishes no result. We blame the Jesuit for his ethical maxim: "The end justifies the means"; we should similarly blame the intuitionist for his continual tendency to let the means take the place of the end. Teleology and resultfulness are just demands of the human spirit, and the latter cannot be confined in a mystic maze of endless avenues, and enjoined to walk well therein. Let the theory of the ethical, whatever that theory may be, interpret its problem so that life shall have a goal for human endeavour and a response to human aspiration. Man cannot remain content with an interpretation which is only, after all, a tendency in the object and an attitude in the subject. To do justice to the ethical, something more than a tendency is necessary. Thus far intuitionism has contented itself with adjusting its compass needle, but has done little to discover the pole toward which it points.

The controversy over the ethical is not yet over, and no one can say when it will end. Evolution enters in to offer the intuitionist an explanation of the origin of conscience and the development of common-sense morality, and to correct the aggregating and hedonistic idea of utilitarianism by supplying a new principle in the form of " social health." In a similar way, eudemonistic ideals and theories of value serve to unite the oppositions of intuitionism and hedonism, and yet it remains a fact that the ethical is a theory of a life whose supporting pillars are either puristic or religious.

When we return to the problem of actual religion, we discover that the positive and pessimistic does not prevent the incoming of a very different ideal—that of eudemonism. The natural condition of the human spirit may be wretched and unworthy; but religion provides a scene of things where these elements are displaced by what is satisfying and meritorious. It must never be forgotten that religion is a living fact; being such, it is of necessity grim and severe. In all this, however, the religious instinct does not lie dormant; nor does it merely react, in a mechanical way, upon the given circumstances of the world. Religion presses onward to some better condition of life, found upon a higher plane of existence. This is a state of blessedness; it is attained by religion only after conflict. Religion is thus destined to work out something as a result; living and historical as it is, it must develop and then achieve some definite purpose. In so doing religion is far removed from any ethical system which, if it be intuitional, cannot consistently have regard for the results of morality; or which, in the hedonist form, cannot construe these results as anything more than some immediate and earthly advantage. The completion of the religious problem consists in the real passage from woe to weal, from the lower to the higher. If, in the judgment of religion, all is here in vain, there is another scene of things where positive gain may be found. In all this the religious consciousness feels that a gift is being bestowed upon it; true, it may strive, and it does this; but from above the power of man and from beyond his ken come the visions and the benefits.

When religion is thus compared with morality, it turns out to be at once *infra* and *supra* ethical. All this is due to the fact that religion takes as its point of departure human life; for this it provides a goal. Without such a destiny in sight, religion cannot exist; provided with it, faith passes on, far beyond the realm of morality. Where ethics attempts to supply an object for man's activity this end is either purely subjective or narrowly objective in its nature. Duty done gives personal satisfaction; benevolence exercised contributes to human happiness. But from either point of view, nothing more than some immediate object is presented; and thus great achievement is made impossible. When it is once clearly seen and appreciated that ethics is subjective and normative, while religion is historical and positive, the distinction between them may be made. In the light of this distinction, religion is seen to be positive and pessimistic, and, at the same time, eudemonistic and teleological. These characterizations are native to religion, as they are alien to ethics. As forms of speculation they may thus be separated; but how far may this be carried on? To answer such a question we must examine the actual connection between religion and morality, and inquire whether there be any living connection between forms of culture which, as alien as the mental and the bodily, seem to be in introaction.

2. The actual connection of religion with morality is to be found in the former's history. Worship, in the various stages of its development, evinces an ever-increasing inclination toward the ethical; while universal religion, in the particular form of Christianity, has elaborated a distinct conception of righteousness. In the complete history of religion, wide differences may be noted. It is not impossible to indicate cults which are capable of the immoral, and that under religious sanction. On the other hand, certain forms of ethnic faith have so thoroughly entertained the idea of morality as to exclude that transcendental element which belongs to worship. But these extremes do not represent an " either-or," as though religion were called upon to decide either for or against morality. The more satisfactory view represents religion and morality as developing side by side, each aiding the other. A naive form of religion naturally entails primitive conceptions of the world and human life. God is represented as being an arbitrary being; to please Him, various non-essential acts of devotion—offering, sacrifice, and the like—must be performed. When a higher stage of worship is reached, as in rational religion, ideas and duties are more perfectly represented. God is not arbitrary, but He is sovereign. His will is law. A higher type of morality now enters in; it is obedience. In the fulfilment of it conduct has its point of departure in national life. But a new view of God and a third stage of religion enter in to present new duties. God is one; He is spirit, infinite and eternal. The soul is self-centred, and has more value than all the sum of the world. To such ideas the soul responds. Man must love God with a whole heart; his brother he must love as his own soul. In this larger view the folk-morality of the tribe, as well as the legal ethics of the national code, are lost sight of. With universal religion the ethical life has

begun. This is not to affirm that religion has been the source of morality, or vice versa ; it is rather to demonstrate that imperfect morality and undeveloped worship go hand-in-hand. The chief point of interest consists in the observation that such a religion as Christianity has had the fate to create a definite type of morality.

By observing the correlated development of religion and morality this peculiar fact will appear, that, when religion becomes spiritual and universal, morality finds its own independence, and that for the first time. So long as religion remains upon the plane of the national and ethnic, morality can be viewed only in an imperfect and unworthy manner. Socrates and Christ are esteemed as teachers who have made possible, for the occidental world, a pure ethics and a spiritual religion ; and in various ways the parallel between these souls may be instituted. The final testimony, however, can only reveal the infinite difference between them. The distinction between morality and religion appears more clearly when we survey it in this definite personal manner. Socrates created an intrinsic ethics ; Christ revealed spiritual religion. By the world each was rejected and condemned. The four centuries before Christ, in which the Socratic ethics flourished, were indeed significant for western morality. Yet it was in Christianity that we first found our true ethical and religious views ; in each we are Christian. From Christ, ethics thus received, among other things, the following ideas : the distinction between good and bad ; the difference between inner and outer ; the sense of obligation to do right, and the value of this performance. Now, Socrates felt none of these things. His reference to the soul was only an intellectual one, while his adherence to virtue was only eudemonistic. Hence, our thought to-day, dealing with duty and right, benevolence and value, returns, not to Socrates, but to Christ, as its true source.

The veritable founder of ethics, Christ, was likewise the creator of spiritual, universal religion. His twofold position thus becomes intensely significant for our problem. Spiritual religion brings with it pure morality; this it emancipates. Was this brought about by means of a smooth evolution? The facts of history seem hardly to warrant such an assumption. Christianity, in enlarging the world and expanding the soul, made the moral life over anew. Christ's teaching effected a complete transvaluation; geocentrism in ethics, narrow, limited, and immediate as it had been, became heliocentrism. The Founder of Christianity was not breaking away from the ethical, but only from what he considered a false view of conduct. His soul was inspired by the idea of creating such a view of the religious life that it might content the profoundest aspirations of humanity, and, at the same time, assume a divine character. In effecting this, he produced an ethical doctrine which was in every sense philosophical. By citing this case of universal religion in the person of its Founder, we may see how similar are the paths of worship and of conduct.

But there is perhaps a more fundamental connection in the soul of man between the two series which are parallel in the history of the race. Association in thought and parallelism in history are not the most substantial *vinculum* between worship and duty, and in the presence of such a sharp distinction as may be made between them, something more satisfactory must be found. For, the history of humanity has associated religion with other phases of man's life, and the case of ethics may be only one of such instances. But here it may be said that religion has elaborated a distinct .type of life-conduct, which possesses a character at once ethical and religious; this fusion has assumed various names, as holiness and righteousness, and these all manifest the definitely ethical character of religion. And such conceptions as these naturally appear in the precinct of religion.

In the religious consciousness, conduct is represented as being at once specific in its nature, sacred in its character, and serious in its final significance. Piety, as this sentiment may be called, has its point of departure in a divine order of things. Not as determined by the state or by society, nor by the individual acting in response to motives of desire and duty, but from another point of view must the religious life be determined. Religion is life, rather than a course of conduct. Centred in man's very nature, it manifests a peculiar tendency; it is looked upon as making its subject acceptable to a Divine Being. Christ, as the true type of this life, was spoken of as one who was in favour with man; he was also said to be well-pleasing unto God. The relation to the divine order implies a peculiar obligation; man feels that " he ought to obey God rather than men." And thus a peculiar dualism may be set up in the soul; where common duty to man opposes itself to this higher sense of obligation. In literature, profane as well as sacred, this appears. Take, for example, the four lines from Racine's drama " Athalie," which so appealed to Boileau that he spoke of them as possessing all the attributes of the sublime. They are the words of Jehoida:

> Celui qui met un frein à la fureur des flots
> Sait aussi des mechants arrêter les complots.
> Soumis avec respect à sa volonté sainte,
> Je crains Dieu, cher Abner, et n'ai point d'autre crainte.

It is the last one of these lines which brings out that significance of religion which we are examining; and it was such a sentiment as this which so appealed to Bismarck that he spoke of the Germans as those who fear God but fear no one else. To fear God does not imply the fear of man; indeed, this attitude of mind may make one all the more resolute. This is due to the specific nature of righteousness, and, hereby, the contrite soul is led to confess: " Against thee, thee only, have I sinned, and done this evil in thy sight."

Religious morality likewise points out the sacred character of the ethical. Ordinarily conduct may be judged as being right, or it may be appreciated by society as being helpful. May it also be said to possess sanctity? Religious conduct assumes just this character, for it aims to unite man with God. As a result, the moral law no longer assumes the unattractive character of rigoristic, blind duty; nor does it appear in the secular form of utility and social service. The law is loved, because it is of God. To the subject righteous judgments seem more valuable than gold, more pleasant than is honey to the lips. In such a law man may delight. At the same time, God is represented as being pleased with man's actions; at least, this is the ideal goal which is presented to the heart of the religious subject. Where conduct arouses the interest of man, to whom it appeals as being the highest and the best, where it seems pleasing unto God Himself, it is far removed from the ordinary thought of morality.

When thus viewed, religious conduct presents a serious problem; its specific nature and sacred character conspire to make the accomplishment of it a task to which man's powers are unequal. Without dwelling directly upon the pessimistic attitude which religion seems to assume toward human life, it can be seen that the effort which religious activity may make is insufficient to work out that which righteousness demands. Conduct of life is not merely normal desire or imperative duty; it is man's destiny. For this reason, the philosophy of religion can only look with distrust upon any system which, like the ethical scheme, works out its method with such ease and complacency. Where thought was ruled by such a method as that of the ancient formalism, this near-sighted view may be understood; but modern dynamic conceptions, which represent life as a matter of conflict, can hardly be justified in making of human existence a subject of optimistic regard. The religious life, alive to its true goal, and painfully aware of its actual condition, demands redemption from the world. To make this possible, appeal must be made to some new source of life; this is found in

God. If human activity is to be interpreted in the light of the divine; if human character, to be what it ought to be, must please God, then, the problem becomes so serious that God Himself must aid man in solving it.

3. Distinct as concepts, yet parallel in their actual career, religion and morality must finally be conceived of as evincing some relation more satisfactory than either of these. The interrelation of the forms of spiritual life composes a problem as distinct as that of mental-bodily interaction. Thus far, in our discussion, the case of the religious and moral stands in abeyance. Logic demands the separation of them; but in life they are not divided. To overcome the difficulty which is here presented, some new view of both religion and morality is made necessary. It is the privilege of religion to indicate the true service of morality. Whatever may be the proper explanation of the moral life, or however the development of this is to be carried out, there yet remains the question as to the worth of this life: What is the final ground for doing right? To answer this question, appeal is made to religion. Conduct becomes the means to a higher end. Religion is primarily concerned with man's salvation from the world, and the redemption of his earthly life; when the soul denies the world, it affirms itself in its own true existence. But, to accomplish this peculiar task of religion, something more than mere power of effort or intensity of life is made necessary. The only true means is that of ethical force and character. To overcome the world, there is demanded an act of the moral will working in the interest of the good. Thus to turn away from the earthly life in nature, and to find the life of the soul in some higher realm, necessitates an ethical activity, without which religion is impossible. Where religion seeks to accomplish that which it was manifestly designed to do, morality has an essential part to play.

Let us revert once more to the original spring of religion, which consists in the self-positing of the human soul. Man is moved by a peculiar yearning after that which is not of this world; dissatisfaction with the present unworthy condition of his existence leads him to hope for that which is more satisfactory and substantial. But how shall man attain unto this, without something like an ethical performance? To turn away from immediate existence in the world, and to reach out after an eternal life, is no physical act on the part of the body, or purely psychological deed performed by the mind. This fundamental religious performance is throughout ethical. The world is denied, because conscience judges it to be unworthy; the other world is affirmed in response to a desire which would be inconceivable if it were not expressed by a moral being. Religion is an act of the soul; as such it is performed after the manner of ethics. And from still another point of view may this essentially ethical moment in religion be expressed. Religion brings with it a certain benefit conceived of as coming from some supra-mundane source; in this sense, eternal life is styled " the gift of God." What is the result of this? Man feels within him a certain sense of gratitude, and he is led to ask: "What shall I render unto the Lord for all His benefits?" Where religion rises above naturalism and nationalism it proclaims that genuine gratitude is expressible, not in offering or sacrifice, but in contrition and righteousness. Privileges imply duties; by righteousness man may hope to please God. This attempt is successful only as it is saturated with the ethical, and the soul can affirm itself by no means so well as those of moral motive.

Religion, then, points out the true value of morality; by coming in contact with it, ethical principle can only be the gainer. No harm can come to the idea of morality, when it is shown that it is of service in human life. Exercised in the interest of such a religious idea as the redemption of mankind, ethics assumes a superior character. No longer does the sense of right result in the mere feeling of self-approbation; no longer does morality assume the simple guise of a helpmate for society ; but the ethical is raised and transfigured to the dignity of providing for the soul a means of realizing its destiny. In this way the religious view of the service of morality shows wherein the latter's true value consists. And it is just this idea of which ethics seems to stand in need. An intuitional view of morality, relying upon the purely formal considerations which it employs, does not and cannot regard that morality as bearing any fruit ; while the hedonist method, which has always been opposed to this, can supply as the content of ethics only that which is immediate and unworthy. We still believe that morality is resultful and valuable ; but our faith rests upon what is more than ethical ; it is a hope, founded upon religious aspiration.

For this reason morality becomes a sacred consideration. Man sees that by righteousness he is exalted, while sin is for ever invalid and in vain. Profound religious spirits have at times been led to doubt this value which should attach itself to righteousness. Self-approbation may be present, and social merit bestowed ; but something more than this is demanded. " Can a man be profitable unto God ? " Where the good is realized, is it sufficient unto this end ? " Is it pleasure to the Almighty that thou art righteous ? " Here is a question the answering of which is by no means easy, yet there appears " the fine innuendo by which the soul makes its enormous claim." It appears in a more serious form when the soul, following the principle of righteousness, feels that after all it has been in vain. " Verily I have cleansed my heart in vain and washed my hands in innocency." It is here that religion, which points out the vanity of evil, must step in to manifest the essential value of righteousness ; yet not in this conception alone, but in the further idea of the conservation of value. Religion, which alone appreciates the intrinsic worth of morality, shows wherein the service of the latter consists. This is done by the aid of an idea well known in universal religion : that of the religious world-order. At the same time the religious character of morality appears even more definitely when the soul is related to the idea of God. Where religion regards righteousness as being well-pleasing to God, it must avoid doing it in a manner likely to suggest anything arbitrary in the divine will. If religion, with its idea of righteousness, makes possible the realization of human destiny, it must not fail to construe this as of divine design. God is no longer to be surveyed as the leader, who makes a covenant with his tribe ; nor yet as a sovereign, legislating for his peculiar people ; He is rather to be looked on as the life and spirit of the kingdom of righteousness in which religion lives and moves and has its being. Such a realm, wherein religious value is conserved, is the common goal of God's sovereign power and man's free activity. Righteousness is not merely an ideal or a means of making this life bearable ; it is in itself real ; and man, by following it, is not to be defeated or suffered to remain content with temporary satisfaction. The soul of man attains to a blessedness which is not of morality, but which cannot exist apart from this, and a man may be profitable even unto God ; for it is pleasure to the Almighty that He is righteous.

To realize the inherent possibilities of religion, recourse must be had to something more vital and convincing than theoretical ethics with its critical aims. In philosophy of rights we discover a practical discipline which, like religion, descends to a plane *infra* ethical in order that it may rise to the *supra* ethical, which it does in promulgating the ideal of non-resentment.

2. *Religion and Rights*

To survey the practical side of religion is to perceive the seriousness of the religious problem. Thought may consider being and non-being, but religion is confronted by life and death. In its endeavour to emancipate the soul from the slime of the earth, religion has wrestled with spiritual wickedness, and has witnessed upheavals and downfalls among the nations of mankind, wherein the acutest nerves of humanity have been touched. Shall we seek then to solve these problems and allay these alarms by turning to theory or the elaboration of an ideal ? The moralistic view of religion is as far from the history of humanity as the metaphysical view of things is from nature. Religion demands scrutiny most serious, and, for this reason, we relegate to the positive and pessimistic forms of treatment that which properly belongs to jurisprudence. The connection between religion and rights is no contingent one which depends upon the mere fortunes of the human race, but is rather an essential nexus which obtains between these parallel forms of human striving. Together they constitute an ineradicable impulse toward the affirmation of humanity, contrasted with which the formal and influential principles appear for ever invalid and vain. It is from such a view of the life-problem that we relate law and theology just as we have separated morality and religion. The unity of rights is like the unity of religion, and when men postulate a common good in which all participate, they do not fail to indicate a single destiny which religion seeks to achieve.

1. However alien the realms of rights and religion may seem to be, we cannot deny that the actual history of religious thought in modern times was originally contained in and conditioned by the career of juristic speculation. There was thus a unity of natural rights and natural religion of which deism was the outcome, and our modern philosophy of religion was primarily a philosophy of rights, which latter was due to the work of Hugo Grotius. It is true that the author of " The Rights of War and Peace " went so far in his exaltation of *jus naturale* as to say that it would hold *non esse deum*, an atheistic view of the problem which was not accepted by the deists in England, who proceeded to elaborate a rational conception of God and religion. More consistent within and more signifi-

cant without, deism employed the rationalistic conception of rights with the aim of inaugurating a system of natural religion, while in reality it was preparing the way for systematic philosophy of religion. From rights to free-thinking, from free-thought to the toleration, it was but a step to rational Christianity and natural religion as the eternal gospel of the universe. In itself the deistic movement was due to the new spirit of freedom, yet the theory of natural rights was destined to relate itself to the scheme of natural religion, not only as a *causa efficiens*, but as *causa formalis*. As Grotius had appealed to reason to evince the validity of natural rights, and had then sought to corroborate his theory by an appeal to existing codes, so Herbert turned to the understanding of man for the explanation of natural religion, and then appealed to the history of mankind for justification. Accordingly, the inherent logic of *jus naturale* and *religio naturalis* was at heart the same.

Upon religion the effect of natural rights was indirect and exemplary, and both forms of culture were united in their weakness rather than in their strength. The jurist of the day did not explain society or justify its laws, while the contemporary religionist, guided by the equivocal principle of "nature," could not account for religion any better than he could indicate its character. In a practical manner, however, the apostle of natural rights emancipated human nature while the deist went on to outline the inner character of religion. Such important work could never have been done had the modern adhered to the ideas of authority and tradition; when he wrested himself free from them, he inaugurated a struggle whose traces can be discerned all the way from Hobbes to Kant. Did not even the great Königsberger justify his own rationalist treatment of Christianity by publishing his philosophy of rights, that he might set himself aright in the eyes of the Prussian magistracy? Here the order was reversed; first came the free treatment of religion, then the demand for speculative rights. In seventeenth-century England the numerous tracts on the " reasonableness of Christianity," the " true Gospel of Christ," " Christianity not Mysterious," and the " Naked Gospel," were but signs of that political tendency expressed in the " Letters of Toleration," " Discourse of Free-thinking," " The Rights of Mankind "; while in America a noted revolutionist and free-thinker coupled the political and religious in his popular writings called " The Rights of Man " and " The Age of Reason." Such were the tendencies, and, in view of them, we should not be surprised to find that theology should have followed a political method. Indeed, so far as actual religion is concerned, it is not too much to say that rights has, in modern times, been more effective in advancing a consistent view than either ethics or metaphysics. This honour it shares with æsthetics.

But, with the passing of natural rights, the end of natural religion was nigh. This was at the close of the eighteenth century. Nineteenth and twentieth centuries discuss problems of human life upon a very different basis. Nature, as an idea, may still have influence; but by this term we understand an empirical thing whose general content is filled out by biological data. Accordingly, rights and religion are put upon a basis which is not static, but evolutionary; nevertheless, the parallel still maintains. Religion has interests so vast and crises so great that it cannot express itself without touching the field of law; and, for this reason, the crimes of man and the bad condition of society become objects of study with a theology which aims to help, not only the individual in his conduct, but society in its condition. The individual, however, is not lost in this stream, nor is his responsibility swallowed up in its vortices. With consistency may religion take up the task of helping mankind universally; for religion is by its very nature an historical factor. If the American consciousness can see that there is something better than novelty, can see that the history of religion is not mere matter of paleography, then it may feel some sympathy for the Mesopotamian consciousness of mystery and striving.

Past and present in religious thought have witnessed the transition to the historical method. Logic and ethics, as represented by Locke and Hobbes, did not suffer so keenly from the artificial system of nature, as had natural rights and natural religions. Apart from history, these two forms of human life amount to very little. Jurisprudence has abandoned the rationalistic method for the historical one ; the same may be said of most of our religious thought. Here it is more than important that the historical perspective should be measured, lest we lapse into mere archæology. Comparative religion, social evolution, and the psychology of religion, show how extreme such tendencies may become, and how far beyond a theological position they may press. When we consider the importance of Southern Asia and Northern Africa in the development of human faith, can we ever be led to believe that the trim views of the present represent essential religion ? We have found the historical method ; we should not betray it by any assuming optimism or naive adventurousness.

2. Modern thinking has had its own methods ; in religion they have indeed been peculiar. And here we notice a rather remarkable condition of speculative affairs ; whereas dogmatic thinking has endeavoured to connect religion with logic and ethics, and thus make it at once a rationale and morale of life, a critical examination of the actual source of the thinking Protestant spirit can only show that rights and æsthetics have been the guiding stars of our philosophy of religion. This we see in the history of four centuries' reflection, and especially so in the case of juristic influences. So far as the development of positive religion is concerned, the same leaning may be observed ; for primitive worship and for national religion the function of legislation was paralleled only by the power of art. Worship seizes hold of man while yet in his primitive

condition; then he cannot be logical or ethical, in the sense of one like Socrates. But, imperfect and naive, he yet perceives the æsthetical and feels the power of law; and is not this but a natural tendency? Æsthetical perception is instinctive; logical thought is an indirect method demanding time for development. Obedience to authority is well adapted to an unemancipated spirit; while intrinsic morality can come only after painful development. Religion, which is the first spiritual instinct, is so human that it need not wait for man to find himself; indeed it is by virtue of this function that man's spiritual education begins. Accordingly, the peculiar intimacy of religion with law and art may be accounted for by observing that these realistic and positive forms of human thought are fitted to touch humanity in its primitive condition.

Is the origin of law to be found in religion? Let anthropology answer this, but let it do so consistently. Certainly the priest has been a person of authority, and may have been man's primitive judge; even in an advanced stage of religion the priest may dictate to the sovereign. Perhaps science in the form of myth, and ethics in the guise of ceremonial custom, had their origin in worship; and the case of jurisprudence is just as likely. To-day law is less accustomed to ignore religion than is morality, and why should not primitive man have felt the divine character of his rudimentary code? When Locke contended for toleration, he reached a point where he hesitated; that was the idea of atheism. Upon such a basis, he argued, how could government maintain? "The taking away of God dissolves all." Without the thought of God an oath could not be taken. And does not popular thought feel that God is the conserver of justice?

The interaction of the social and religious consciousness is native to the development of worship. In the case of legalistic cults this is strikingly true. And shall it be deemed strange that faith affiliates with politics? The social contract which the social consciousness spontaneously produces has vast resources. Hereby, the virtue of justice, which demands a plurality of men, is made possible. But the common life of men is such as to evoke ideas more vital than those of utility and progress; destiny, individual as it may be, is yet emphasized by the thought that what it does and suffers is for all men. Herein the religious moment is manifested.

Among various ethnic faiths Roman and Jewish religions stand out as evincing a peculiar phase of theology and law. In each case there was a national consciousness, which was the dominating factor. The religion and the rights were, here, Roman; there, Jewish; morality and metaphysics have never had such social colouring. For Israel, how essential was the political bond, not only among the people, but with God! " Ye shall be My people, and I will be your God" was a promise vouchsafed to Israel as a people near God. Such a theocracy was but the most perfect union of religion and rights, as it was the reconciliation of law and prophets.

Realism in religion makes possible the affiliation of spiritual religion even with an objective law; the same is true of art. Indeed, at the other extreme of mere nature religion the same relation maintains. This may also be due to the social-historical element in religion, and where men are naturally bound together it is inevitable that law should come in as the firm expression of such union. In Abrahamitic worship the social element figures in the form of a clan; the patriarch was influenced by the promise that he should become the leader of a people in covenant relations with God. At the other extreme is Christianity; but here as well the religious does not cast off the juristic. Christ gave His disciples commandments selected from the law; He founded a Kingdom over which He ruled; among the believers He assumed the position of judge. In the case of the Apostle Paul the same element may be discerned. Paul's opposition to Mosaism was but the opposition of rights to law, and the whole tenor of the apostle's Galatian and Roman epistles is juristic. The peculiar apologetic of this great epistolary writer was wrought according to what method ? There are touches of metaphysics and of morality, but they are only touches ; St. Paul's method in introducing Christianity was that of jurisprudence. Just as Christ in His career elected the interest and also opposition of the lawyers, so the chief apostle makes manifest his one great desire by employing the philosophy of law.

But to return to the gospels, where we may find constructive legislation in religion. Man, as Aristotle said, is a " political animal " ; and we know that man, in distinction from the animals, is a creature who worships. Here he regards his neighbour, there his God ; and from the mass of pentateuchal legislation Christ selected two appropriate commandments. From Deuteronomy He chose this one as supreme : " Thou shalt love the Lord thy God " ; from Leviticus another : " Thou shalt love thy neighbour as thyself." Who is the neighbour and who is God ? God is universal spirit, the neighbour is mankind. But Christ had other laws as given in the Sermon on the Mount, and these, likewise, were revisions of ancient legislation. These new commandments were a kind of pentalogue, and by referring to them we may see how superior was the religion of Christ. For Tolstoi they are all-important ; because, in his mind, they set at naught the common order of things and inaugurate a reign of non-resentment. But, whatever may be the interpretation in fine, the juristic moment cannot fail to be noticed ; a religion, perfect in spiritual conceptions and sanctions, may still hold fast to the principle of rights.

This affinity between two different phases of the soul's activity may explain certain peculiarities of our theology. Take the case of Calvinism, and you may wonder how a vigorous and healthy mind could set at naught human freedom and the issues of human life. The leading spirit is juristic ; this is the explanation. Saturated with the thought of divine sovereignty. Calvin could find in the destiny of the individual very little value. But, as Ritchie, in his "Natural Rights," suggests, Calvin was a jurist arguing the claims of the Christian against the domination of the pope. The salvation of man is no affair for the priest to decide; for it is a matter which the Almighty determined before the foundations of the world were laid, when the destiny of each individual, from the youngest to the oldest, was ordained. With the number of the elect thus foreordained, no power on earth could avail against the soul, which was put under one form of bondage to be emancipated from another and lower one.

3. Yet there is something more substantial in the bond between rights and religion than their community in the life of humanity, or their parallel development in modern philosophy. This may be found in the psychological and metaphysical realism which pervades them. At once it may be seen that rights and religion represent the idea of necessity, for they show that man must obey, he must believe. On this account politics and theology do not represent culture so much as conflict; not evolution, but catastrophe. Strenuous is the path which each has followed, and thus it was that Bismarck said, " I made the German nation out of blood and iron." Logic may be ignored, formal thought despised, and irrationalism may thus exert its influence. Ethics may be set aside as casuistry or moralism, and mere force may take its place; while æsthetics may be deemed mere sentimentality. Law and worship, however, cannot so easily be overcome; anarchy and atheism, being brutal attempts to negate the strong affirmations of the soul, only illustrate how unconquerable are our theologica-political tendencies. For more than a century our logic has been confronted with the question of the possibility of metaphysics, while our ethics has studied the origin of conscience. Rights and religion do not wait for theoretical possibilities or introspective identifications, but find in human life, as it is, a fertile field for insight and system. Thereby universality

and necessity are evinced as principles native to rights and religion.

Religion is rarely metaphysical, but is sometimes metapolitical. It is not an individual attitude, but a social type, which is reflected in religion. It is a vain view which regards religion as a matter of taste, to be cultivated or not according to one's desire, and without any responsibilities being entailed. Man may or may not study music; but he must cultivate God. Religion means, not desire, but destiny; toward this law urges man on. Positive religion is only logical in its development and reasonable in its demand when it enjoins a code. In the conduct of life this must be obeyed. By virtue of the apprehension of religion a new fact has been revealed and a new life unfolded. What is the result? Something must be done, and done by all. The satisfaction of religion cannot be found in contemplation, but must be created in activity. This must be everywhere apparent, and not confined here and there to isolated individuals. Hence the prayerful desire, " Thy kingdom come; Thy will be done."

Psychological analysis of the religious consciousness cannot fail to reveal the latter's metapolitical character. Religion is an impulse; law is volitional. In each case there is a distinct phase of self-affirmation; in the one case as member of a body politic, in the other as citizen of the heavenly kingdom. Living in the world among men, the individual sees how his *dignity* is guarded by the institution of law; while within the higher realm of social, spiritual life, he finds in religion the safeguard of *destiny*. Both of these branches of human life have a social and psychological colouring unknown to metaphysics and ethics. Thought is guided by interest; conduct leads to that which is desirable. Law and religion do not depend upon postulates or ideals, but fall back upon the actual, and find therein their field. Very human considerations are included in the practice of law, which makes use of the appeal *ad hominem*. Let any one follow the progress of a trial, and he will be surprised to observe how many personal elements enter in to constitute a motive—pride, fear, love between the sexes, religious sentiments ; these are urged by attorney, allowed by judge, and weighed by jury. By reason of its intimacy with human nature, and because of its concern for life's interests, law can fitly sympathize with religion. Logic and ethics are singularly indifferent to our desires, which they regard as pathological ; law and theology regard them as normal conditions, which also represent valid arguments.

The ethical estimation of rights and religion may now come in after the philosophical and psychological elements have been analysed. If we may regard morality as being midway between legislation and theology, we can better see how these extreme views of human nature may be reconciled. In the case of Bentham we have an attempt to reconcile morality and legislation, and his jurisprudence is as unpractical as his hedonism was unethical. Kant represents the alienation of law from ethics, and accordingly he is led to speak of action objectively right as being "merely legislative," but Kant's views on ethics were rigoristic, as his idea of rights was artificial. Ethics does not make law either unnecessary or unworthy ; nor does it make invalid worship for worship's sake. Life consists, not in the functioning of an unqualified will, but in such a richness of living as is suggested by practical legislation and vital religion. In its nature, and with regard to its aim, religion is like rights, inasmuch as both are extra-ethical. We do not live *a priori*, but in a manner altogether human. The true function of the ethical is normative and critical.

4. The inherent realism of rights appears now in a sense more metaphysical. Among more than one moralist may be noted the lack of metamoral, as well as the lament over the emptiness of the ideal. Of conscience, Butler finely says, " Had it strength, as it has rights ; had it power, as it has manifest authority, it would absolutely govern the

world," while Kant calls upon mere man to " act so that the maxim of conduct may become a universal law." Among heteronomists Mill approximates to the ideal by postulating, not happiness, but the greatest happiness of the greatest number, while Spencer prophesies the evolution from " relative morality " to " absolute morality." The purely moral is necessarily empty. As a realist Hegel expresses the ethical in the form of a " *Rechtsphilosophie*," reminding us of Plato's " Republic." Hegel's " Philosophy of Rights " calls upon the mind to observe the actual existence of the ethical relation. Thus it is with a purpose that Hegel uses the term " rights " to express the historical idealism of practical life. Rights is a constitutive affair, revealed in history in independence of an idealized will. And is it not so with religion ? This branch of human life exists, not by courtesy of philosophy, but by its own right, and does not depend upon transcendentalism. Its character is realistic. In the field of religion we are not advised, but are called upon to behold that which is given and which goes on in independence of our infinitesimal strivings ; at the same time the realm of religion is built upon cause and effect, rather than upon ideals, and we can only perceive the substance of the things hoped for. To appreciate the self-constructive character of man's religious life is one great need in the present which is wavering in its faith ; to do this, nothing can be more instructive than to note the analogy of rights and religion.

Mutually adjusted as they now are, politics and theology may fairly stand as the pillars of human life. Ethics looks from right to left toward these supports. The departments of rights and religion contribute content to life, and hereby reflective ethics is made possible. Law and worship live by virtue of institution and tradition, which also add continuity. Guarding the interest of morality, law makes possible some kind of conduct even among imperfect men. By a different method, religion works toward the same end ; it regards goodness as the one thing needful, hence conduct follows as a natural consequence. In humanity's culture these two tendencies have been the impulses toward conduct ; we may wish to make sheer conscience and blind imperatives the sanctions of life, but obedience and reverence are the real motives. Men act to serve one another, or to please God. In everyday life we may make use of any sane influence for the promotion of the good and the prevention of the bad ; while doing this we need not stop to inquire what may be the final sanction of every act. But in reflection it can be seen that sheer moralism, which ignores both inclination and consequence, is both blind and empty. Religion and rights must come to guide and to give content to the conduct of life ; then morality becomes possible.

In the complete study of the problem, where we correlate and contrast the several phases of political and religious realms, we may further note the common form of these. It is the form of positivism, yet in the most general sense of that much-abused term. Among all the philosophic disciplines, law and religion are the only ones which are firmly ensconced in actual history. Logic and ethics are intuitions, but not institutions. They are monocular in their view of human life, and accordingly lack the third dimension. Æsthetics, which is expressed in art, is more nearly akin to the first pair than to the second ; but art has not those grim features of necessity which rights and religion reveal. Rights is no subjective or non-essential tendency, confined to individual opinion and taste ; it is an indispensable system objectified in code and court. Religion is similarly positive in its form, having historical documents and organized societies as its basis. Legislation and ecclesiasticism thus objectify rights and religion, and they do this in a manner unknown among other phases of science and philosophy.

With their firm hold upon human life rights and religion make manifest a spirit internal with each and common to both. It is the spirit of pessimism, yet the broadest kind of pessimism. Law makes room for crime; religion for sin and misery. Shall it be said that, by such an interpretation, we are encouraging vice, and that it were far better to hold up the positive good rather than the negative bad? This arrangement will not do for men. Religion indeed has its holy sanctions, and these supply an ideal higher than that of ethics; and thus religion says, be holy and sin not. But religion does not content itself with the unrealized precept; for, it goes on to say, if any man sin, we have with God a righteous advocate. This completes the affair, and makes of faith no chimera, but a realizable fact. In a similar manner law, which is built upon peace and justice, handles crime for which it is ever prepared. When, therefore, the ideals of holiness and justice fail, religion and law are not thwarted; it is then that they apply their most characteristic methods and accomplish their most valuable results. Non-religion and socialism may perhaps be ushered in when man becomes universally upright.

Yet it is for just such a condition of human affairs that religion especially strives. And this is the idea expressed in the phrase "Kingdom of God." Herein, along with religion, a juristic ideal is contained; the Kingdom is a condition of peace where everywhere one has attained unto his destined end. Likewise that which is realized, when religion reaches its goal, is justice—a matter of interest, not only for the human, but for the divine as well. Justice, however, is no easy ideal to promote; to arrive at it religion and law must join hands. How pathetic was Plato's treatment of the problem! For this æsthetical and ethical genius it was not difficult to construct an ideal republic, which should embrace departments consonant with the forms of nature, and adapted to the faculties of man. Then mankind could readily be divided into classes of workers, warriors, and rulers, having the respective virtues of temperance, courage, and wisdom. But justice—what of it? In Plato's cosmos there was no source for this virtue;

it was not found in man, and no class of individuals could be found to administer it. Justice has, therefore, no anchorage in the ideal republic. In the New Testament the conservatism of justice is surrendered to God, and having thus given way to wrath, man need not avenge himself.

The common climax of rights and religion is found in the ideal of non-resentment, whose metaphysical basis we shall discuss in the latter part of this work; here we need examine only the motive which is calculated to inspire non-requital of evil. Schopenhauer involves this ideal in his discussion concerning the "denial of the will to live," which is the proper destiny of man. In the negative atmosphere of renunciation, where one denies self and mortifies the flesh, we need feel no sense of injury when we suffer at the hands of others, for they only advance us along the path of suffering and denial which we must necessarily pursue. Such a view is somewhat grim and not wanting in the amusing, as we notice in the cruel and yet comic figure of Richard III :

> *Anne.* Didst thou not kill the king?
> *Gloucester.* I grant ye.
> *Anne.* O, he was gentle, mild and virtuous.
> *Gloucester.* The fitter for the King of heaven, that hath him.
> *Anne.* He is in heaven, where thou shalt never come.
> *Gloucester.* Let him thank me, that holp to send him thither;
> For he was fitter for that place than earth.

Mirabeau was able to eliminate resentment from his ferocious nature, because his mind was unable to retain the memory of injury done him, and the Spanish Duke was similarly capacitated to forgive, for when upon his deathbed he was exhorted to forgive his enemies, he said: "Enemies? I have none, for I have killed them all!" Tolstoi pursues non-resistance in a sincere fashion, and while he admits that without civil and national defences we should thereby suffer, our sufferings would not be as great as they are now, under the auspices of enmity and militarism.

The course of human history may be understood to prophesy a condition which is at present Utopian, and although this paradise is still separated from us by a remote future, it may safely be inferred that, at the present rate of progress in our culture and civilization, humanity is just as likely to realize the practical ideal of justice as the human understanding is to solve the speculative problem of truth. Life is as swift and as sure as thought, if philosophy feels confident of itself, religion need not despair of reaching the Kingdom of God where prevail peace on earth and goodwill to men. When man learns to think correctly, he will also live without harbouring revenge in his heart.

PART III

THE REALITY OF RELIGION

TO perceive the independent essence of religion, as this is manifest in consciousness, is to estimate its intrinsic character in the form of sensitivity and spontaneity which do not arise in thinking or acting; both of these points of view involve a third question which concerns the reality of religion, as also a fourth which will inquire into the possibility of construing historical religion into a world-order. One half of the work proposed has thus been accomplished, and, having discovered the independent nature and self-constituted character of the religious consciousness, we must now proceed to inquire concerning the universality and necessity of these religious sentiments. Religion asserts itself as a form of culture which is distinct from both science and philosophy, and does not fail to differentiate its inner nature from logic and ethics; in doing this, religion assumes the validity of its ideas of a spiritual world-order and a realm of positive religious life in humanity. May these ideas be regarded as partaking of truth? Such is the question which lies before us. To answer it we must investigate the world-order of humanity, and see whether the world of persons can appear as real as the world of things.

Religion proclaims its universality in manifesting its history. The term "world" is to be understood in a dual sense, in which, not only external nature, but the particular nature of humanity, is the determining factor, and it is in this second sense that we employ the expression " history of the world" to indicate the systematic development of humanity. It is in this sense that we refer to the reality and world-order of religion, and, thus understood, the precinct of religion reveals the unity of religion and history in humanity. To believe in the world-order of humanity would not be difficult for our Anglo-American speculation, had not the history of our thought, which traces back to the physics and ethics of Butler, and the "causality and conscience" of Martineau, been educated upon purely mechanical lines. At any rate, religion which ever culminates in the idea of an independent realm, as "Tao," the "World of Brahman," or the "Kingdom of God," cannot attain completeness until finally it assume the form of a world-order.

From the employment of such terms as "reality," "world-order," and the like, it must not be imagined that we vainly attempt to create the corresponding ideas, for the sole purpose of this part of our work consists in making intelligible certain facts which are given in the history of humanity. The understanding, possessing as it does certain categories, does not refrain from taking its concrete data from the domain of sense, and while it realizes that sensation can never speak for anything beyond itself, just as sense-experience can reveal actualities only and not necessities, it finds external elements essential to the content of human knowledge. In the same way thought may carry out its own reasonable programme, and yet involve the data of mankind's history, and just as the immortal soul participates in time, so the religious view of the world need not refrain from employing the elements of positive occurrence. The eternal verities need not lose their sufficient character when they are interpreted in the living form of Buddhism and Christianity, and the essence and character of spiritual religion may be maintained in the midst of the positive.

The problem proposed by the positive must now be set in a clearer light. As a sheer fact religion is a positive

The Reality of Religion

affair, and in no sense does it consist of eternal verities which come directly from the understanding. To see this one need only glance through the volumes of the "Sacred Books of the East," which are saturated with the positive elements, incident upon language, custom, history. Nevertheless, the purely positive cannot suffice to render religion valuable, and it is apparent that the data of history are not in themselves convincing. We appeal to the positive fact in history, not because it is a matter which emphasizes time, place, and circumstance, but because the fact is an event of peculiar significance in the life of humanity. The renunciatory decision of Gautama is a merely biographical fact in itself, but it shapes the destiny of millions in the Orient, and the advent of Jesus is of magisterial significance for the Occident. The ideal event is native to religion, the inclusive influence of which is able to elevate simple facts to sovereign principles. Religion does not forbid revelation, but, as in the case of Persian dualism, it takes the purely historical fact of the division of the Aryans and transfigures it into a doctrine.

To reach the idea of a world-order is to realize religion itself. That which threatens religion is subjectivity and humanism, and that which must now come in to correct this tendency is the thought that religion has a world-meaning; accordingly, we ask, is the precinct of religion subtended by any world-principle? Traditional theism asks whether its idea of God demonstrates His existence, and in the same spirit it is now inquired whether subjective religion possesses any objective significance, or any theological realm. To satisfy the demands of such a question we must consider the objective side of religion as it appears in history. There it must be asked whether the positive sustains the character of a revelation, and if, finally, such religion has an ontological significance. Thus, rather than select a category of the understanding, like substance or causality, and try to raise it to the rank of ontological verity, we follow the intuitions of living, characteristic religion with the hope that they may reveal an eternal life.

The ideas of ontosophy, to use Clauberg's term, tend ever to relate the total life of humanity to the supersensible world, and not only in the alert and skilful thinking of the dialectician, but in the dreaming consciousness of artist and religionist, does the Absolute appear. True art, true life, and true religion contain more than innuendoes of the circumambient One who is life and truth. The Deity is not a citadel which we attack in vain, but a home which we possess in security, and we need not strive to enter into the inaccessible, for we can live in the presence of the supreme God. It is not by searching analysis, but by a vast synthesis, which humanity has long been developing, that we arrive at the Godhead, so that, at last, philosophy of religion has not to create but to contemplate. Now, the positive nature of religion makes necessary a beginning in human history, and it is this argument from beginnings which must be reduced to philosophy.

1. *The Origin of Religion*

The reality of religion is found in history. To fathom the precise meaning of religion is to indicate the lines of its historical progress, and this involves, not only questions of fact and problems of relation, but another form of inquiry which seeks to render thinkable the communion of historical humanity with God. Readers of the Kantian "Kritik" cannot fail to notice the striking interrogations which were put forth by the arbiter between expiricism and rationalism, especially the one which raises the whole problem of knowledge when it asks, "How are synthetic judgments possible *a priori?*" In the larger sense this question asks, How may the actual be regarded as necessary, or how may the temporal become the eternal? Such is the general nature of the problem before us. Not satisfied with the phenomenal connection of things, our thought presses on to indicate the noumenal order, and thus ascends from explanation to justification. History is the path from nature to spirit, and the problem which it proposes, while it resembles the logical inquiry of Kant, is not unlike the metaphysical investigation which Descartes carried on in the spirit of dualism. The facts in the present case include the origin, development, and culmination of religion. Of these three, the second is the most obvious one, since we are as far from an explanation of the beginning of religion as we are from a prophecy as to its end. What here concerns us is the feeling that what is so excellent as religion should be without beginning or end of days.

The *argumentum a tergo* is neither fallacious nor convincing; in itself it represents one of the problems which the new logic must take up, since constructive thinking is now making use of it, while its value as a canon of thought remains undetermined. Questions of origin were among the latest to arrive in a philosophic world, which had long pursued questions of ground, and we need not Nietzsche's suggestion, that it was democratic prejudice which exerted the retarding influence, to see that this is so. The fallacy of origins, like the fallacy of etymology, is often suggestive, and the logic of the future must learn how to connect the natural development of an idea with its rational deduction, just as human culture must be trained to respect the validity and value of that which has been explained. Scientific evolution, as a theory, has been our possession for a half-century, but it has not as yet been assimilated, and the repugnance which we feel is a psychological fact which, thus far, we cannot gainsay. When we suspect that art, law, and religion have sprung from the dust, we fear lest their sanctity be lost to us.

What we explain, however, we do not explain away, and to see the beginning is not to see the end. Therefore, we shall continue to regard religion *a fronte*, while we glance backward toward ideas *a tergo*. It is startling to note the way in which Lotze declares that the question concerning the origin of space ideas has no bearing upon the metaphysical status of Euclidian space, and it occurs to the reader, who feels that there must be some connection between origin and ground, that the author of the theory of "local signs" was just the one to indicate the substantial bond between the two. The condition obtains in the case of conscience, whose appeals do not seem to be so fearful when biology and sociology have done their awful work of explanation. Nevertheless, there must be some root for the remorse which we feel, and an idealist like Schopenhauer is able to discover the same. It would seem, then, that it is not the mere idea of origin which offends us, but the further suggestion that this origin was brought about in an occasional, if not unworthy, manner. To retrace the steps of religion to its beginning is an undertaking which should be fraught with satisfactions, and we may then see the totality of human faith, surveyed *von vorne herein.*

From our own point of view, whereby we seek to indicate the religious precinct, it may be assumed that religion did have a genuine beginning, while we may leave undiscussed what that beginning may have been. "Beware of beginnings" is a maxim which may be heeded in theory as well as in practical life, yet philosophy may strive to reduce the idea of a *terminus a quo* to consistency. The myth of Prometheus is advanced to account for the origin of fire, while law is said to arise upon an angel's having deposited the sacred scroll in a convenient cave. Art has its inception in the crude form of play-activity by which the animal and primitive man consume their surplus energy. Conscience arises socially as a sense of shame, while duty traces back to the relation of debtor and creditor. Yet it is a long way from those supposed beginnings to our ideals of justice, beauty, and goodness, and it is here that we feel the lack of both data and methods to indicate the connection between that which arises in time and passes on in succession, and that which inwardly unfolds and deepens according to a plan.

The Reality of Religion

To be convinced that religion did have a beginning, and that it has had a development, is no small gain in a philosophy which regards time as subjective, and we have only begun to see what these genetic principles mean. At this point we may express the conviction that, like art and law, religion has had a normal beginning. To conceive of it as circumstantial is intolerable, in view of what religion has become, and to regard it as something pathological will offend every serious-minded person who appreciates the character which human religion has assumed. The insane may produce interesting examples of art, but masterpieces come from the genius. As we noted in speaking of the religious consciousness that religion does not consist in any one, simple passion, so we may here point out that pathological explanations of religion have this difficulty in addition to their only clinical problems. Thus we need not pay serious attention to the ancient view that religion consists of fear, still less need we accept additional suggestion of one like Feuerbach, namely, that human faith is the product of morbid desire. Like other forms of human culture, religion may have had a naive origin, but it could not have grown to the immense proportions of Buddhism and Christianity had it arisen in some unhappy circumstance of human existence.

False, but well-meaning views appear in the forms of supernaturalism and rationalism, views which coincide in ignoring essential religion, but disagree when it comes to showing how non-religious humanity learned its principles of faith. Supernaturalism confuses the purpose of religion with the question concerning its origin, just as it involves the unhappy idea that the man of nature was originally an atheist. From such primitive atheism to primitive non-atheism there is a change which would have shocked the consciousness of the early man, just as thoroughly as it astounds our thoughts in contemplating its impossibilities, and the theory which demands such extremes is painfully lacking in any psychological appreciation

M

of the human soul. Supernaturalism expresses the valuable and defensible idea that there is a real and supreme worth to religion, but it is unsound in its method when it strives to read these theological profundities into the mind of the nature-man.

Rationalism is as impotent to construct religion in the ideal as it is to account for the existence of religion in the actual. As a view, it takes as its point of departure, not the religious consciousness with its warm, though undefined content, but the cool and rigid categories of the human understanding. Like supernaturalism, which it affected to despise, rationalism was forced to assume that no real progress was made throughout the history of the race, and that the only change made was a decline from the perfect religion of nature to an unworthy form of priestcraft. Yet neither the perfect religion of nature nor the authoritative religion of revelation could account for the actualities of positive religion, and if the ideal in religion presses upon us for solution and justification, these must be found in some other manner than the dubious one indicated by the rational and supernatural views, neither one of which indicates a genuine and normal beginning for religion. It is possible for the primitive man to apprehend something like religion, and to do this in a manner consistent with his own mental condition, and for this reason we maintain that religion has a natural, or genuine, origin in the mind of man.

2. Thus far we have contented ourselves with the thought that religion did have a beginning, and this is an admission which the older philosophy of religion was hardly willing to make. In the eyes of a self-constituted science of religion, which assumes much for the primitive man and correspondingly little for the modern, our result will seem meagre indeed; but the anthropologist can afford to be less scrupulous in his care than we, since his metaphysical responsibilities extend only to the conditions which prevail in the savage mind, while the precinct of religion has

The Reality of Religion

a second boundary line in the spiritual religion of humanity. With the philosophic ideals of the value of religion we may still cherish the feeling that, having originated in the consciousness of man, religion is possessed of organic nature and intrinsic character, just as we may pass to examine its significance as an interpretation of the world. To be reassured of the tenability of the fact of origin and the argument therefrom, we must continue this examination long enough to establish, or to indicate, a second phase of the argument from origin. This should reveal the likely fact that not only is the source of religion natural, but it is also humanistic, since it arises in connection with the affairs of human nature.

To refer to the current attempts which are made to explain the origin of religion, we may say that the difference between naturism and spiritism is largely a difference of emphasis, because neither can be excluded from the interpretation of a primitive which, as yet, has made no sharp separation between subject and object. Fetishism arises within the soul of man, but is immediately invested with material significance, while the more philosophical tendency represented by animism is not without its naturistic implications. Even the highest forms of human faith can hardly exist without glancing at the natural world, so fruitful as it is, not only in itself, but in the poetic and parabolic mind, and why should we expect the nature-man to be wholly devoid of attachment? Nevertheless, the psychological moment is uppermost, just as it is likewise fundamental; nature displays herself in vain where the human mind is absent, and the glory of the celestial body, the warmth of the earthly one, are appreciated only by a sensitive nature, and man is logical, though chronologically, prior to the world in which he lives. Where our conception of religion consists in the soul's attempt to emancipate itself from nature, we can only be gratified at observing that the origin of religion is not wholly alien to the ideal.

In addition to the assumption just made, namely, that

human religion arises in a humanistic fashion, there is the more definite truth that the data of primitive worship may come from consciousness just as well as nature. The savage mind, incompetent as it is to handle either physical or psychical problems as such, makes just as much progress when directed toward self as when busy with natural objects. Thus arises an animistic regime under which mental processes, instead of entering by means of sensory and passing out through motor channels, seem to pause in the mind where they are scanned as though they were ends in themselves, and not mere instincts. Dreams, which are necessarily without relation to the external world, possess an extra-spiritistic value, for when the senses are no longer the avenues of perception, and the muscles cease from their activities, the brain is enabled to devote some time to itself and the extravagant products which come forth are deemed to be of more importance than the whole train of normal, waking ideas. An unscientific mind is more subject to hallucinations and illusions, and, having no standard of genuine perception, the primitive mind becomes a prey to fears which assume religious significance.

The same humanistic quality is made manifest by the several forms of naturism. On the side of naturism in general, the worshipper seems to ally himself with some external object which, as he surveys it anthropopathically, serves as a support and mirror for his own fleeting feelings. Such natural powers as may be selected by the primitive man are further conceived as being either friendly or inimical to him. In the particular view of fetishism the mingling of physical and psychical further appears. Here the natural object, which may be of minor or major proportions, is adopted as the residence of some spiritual being, which, after the manner of animistic thinking, had been hovering in half-reality. The mythological conception, which is indicative of something less primitive, involves feelings freer and more ideal than the crass reasoning of animism would permit. Such a view regards man in an

The Reality of Religion

artistic light, when it sees that the primitive man, besides investing a natural object with human properties, further considered him as following a quasi-human career. What is significant in such immature attempts at religious thinking is the inevitable tendency on the part of man to assert his own being and to establish human values in the midst of environment apparently of nature alone. The fact that the mind still clings to the natural object does not demonstrate that his feelings are purely naturistic, but rather reveals an element of contrast and competition, whereby the soul puts itself upon the proper plane. In the same way that art seems to imitate nature, while it is really transcending and perfecting the several natural elements of landscape, human body, and historical event, so does religion surpass nature by meeting her upon her own ground.

Religion is secure in the hands of the primitive man because he is poetical. Philosophy and science may be far removed from his considerations, because the age of humanism has not yet dawned upon him, but his mind is able to see into nature and into himself, and the free treatment which physical and psychical facts receive only reveals the spontaneity of a soul which is aware of its transcendent position in the world of immediacy. No logic of abstraction or ethics of the ideal can participate in this naive condition of the nature-man, but poetry adapts itself to his spiritual needs, which it satisfies only to awaken vaster desires. An age, like the present, whose positivism seems to relate it to nature, can express but the letter of the primeval, and it is only in history that we may now secure its inimitable poetry. Where modern barbarism fancies it is exercising a "healthy animality," it is only exhibiting its own decadence, while the egoism of the "blond beast" possesses none of the redeeming elements of naturism. Still less in our virtues do we moderns rehabilitate the primitive traits of religion, and to speak of a revelation made to an age of "blood-iron," whose language is the stridency of modern English, is another symptom of degeneration.

The savage, as such, is less and more than science imagines him to have been. Whatever may be the result of anthropological investigations, it may be assumed that the primitive still reacts upon the world in a human fashion, and assumes a standpoint which, instead of possessing the centric and commanding position of the man of culture, is rather eccentric and characteristic. Upon the side of both naturism and spiritism it seems to be the extraordinary which calls for recognition, and which makes excessive demands upon the human soul, and in the childhood of the race it is safe to say with Goethe, " The miracle is the dearest child of faith." Yet even this Goethe, whose scientific sympathies and poetic insights should have ever inclined him toward the highest view of the phenomenal universe, shared with Voltaire, himself a believer in the orderly world of Newton and Shaftesbury, an instinctive horror of the Lisbon earthquake. Regularity in the natural order, and smoothness in the course of human events, are not calculated to elicit the peculiar sense of divinity in the world about mankind, so that the grounds of theism are not the sources of religion. Nevertheless, what should be emphasized, at this juncture, is not the bizarre or catastrophic, in the form of an earthquake or a fit of madness, but the striking effect which this has upon the naive spirit of man. The startling occurrence in nature, or the alarming condition of some member of the tribe, makes its dread appeal to a consciousness otherwise stolid. Man, who stands in need of just such shocks, if he is to become himself and assume his humanity, thus sees that the world of immediacy, without and within, is subject to such uncertainties and surprises, whence he learns that nature cannot contain the soul, whose genuine life must be found elsewhere. A pessimistic regard toward nature in the world and in man has the effect of indicating the path to that which is of intrinsic worth and world-significance.

The Reality of Religion

By such peculiar means the primitive man realizes himself and distinguishes his being from that of the external world. The man of culture transcends nature by aligning an ideal unity of the total universe, while with the primitive man such an assertion of independence comes only when the fantastic and exceptional seem to violate the order of things physical and psychical. Yet it may be assumed that even the primitive man has secured for himself an *a priori* principle of belief, inasmuch as his mind is now depending upon something which is beyond experience. The unwonted in nature here takes the place of that "natural supernaturalism" which philosophy discusses under the head of the noumenon, and the extraordinary event assumes the form of *causa occasionalis* before the entirety of nature can become the *causa formalis* of cultured theology. In the consciousness of the nature-man, the view of nature is not wholly æsthetical, because it is put forth in a utilitarian spirit, nor is it logical, since it argues from the concrete and exceptional; nevertheless it is human, and has in it the possibilities of development, and we may safely assume that religion has had a genuine beginning in the midst of the fantastic elements which enter in to characterize the worshipper's mind.

In the career of human religion the positive element must receive recognition, just as the actual origin of religion must be reckoned with as one of the factors in religious thinking. But such a concession to history implies a limitation which must not be transgressed; hence the scientific thought of the day, which has recently espoused the cause of religion, must see that its share in the work is confined to the phenomenalistic realm. True it is that the externals of religion have a symptomatic value, inasmuch as they reveal the internal condition of human consciousness; yet their evidence can never be convincing in itself, any more than the origin of religion, while highly suggestive of the end of human faith, can prove anything concerning its ground. The age of the Enlightenment, in its zeal for static " nature," set all history at naught, and thereby precipitated the problem of culture; shall the age of culture repeat this well-known error, and thus idealize the primitive man, and search for vestiges of primitive faith in the religion of the present? Freely let us admit that we live in an age of degeneration, but why should we desecrate our thinking by a form of religious thinking which seeks to retain all the elements of barbarism which are at all possible, and aspire, in theory, to return to the distressing conditions of the primitive man? Far wiser is it to make the man of culture the standard, and thus employ the positive in religion, not at its inception, but at its culmination, in the forms of world-religion. Before our philosophy may reap the benefits of living, universal religion, we must raise and consider another question which, like the argument from origins, concerns the very character of religion; it is the problem of progress, in the form of development in religion.

2. *The Development of Religion*

Having found it possible to interpret spiritual religion in terms of positive phenomena, and having seen, moreover, that the actual beginning of religion, where that is found to consist in the extraordinary, is compatible with philosophy, which is necessarily timeless, we may now assume the problem of progress in religion. Modern thinking has never handled this question satisfactorily. First there was a tendency to distrust anything which stood in need of development, and the static speculation of the seventeenth and eighteenth centuries postulated an immovable *natura*. Then, after suitable reaction contemporary with the social changes of the late eighteenth century, there followed a genetic form of philosophy which has never failed to emphasize the merely temporal passage from a primitive condition to one more perfect. To one who cannot abide by the mechanical views of Newton and Spinoza, and who has metaphysical scruples against the evolutionary formulations of Hegel and Darwin, the situation becomes acute, just as the philosophic spirit engendered becomes intense, since it tinctures more than one phase of speculation.

1. The theory of development does not fail to arouse questions concerning the validity of fundamental principles of thought. For logic to exist and exert its proper influence, it is necessary to assume the validity of the concept whose meaning shall be fixed, and without such a principle of identity thought can hardly be conceived of as obtaining. The theory of the concept thus involves something permanent in such terms as "plant" and "animal," "man" and "brute." Yet this point of view seems to be askance in contrast with the theory of "transmutation of species," and where Darwinism does not wholly disturb the poise of our conceptual reasoning, the Hegelian dialectic participates with the result of wearing away what seem to be fundamental differences among our ideas. And just as the validity of logic seems to suffer at the hands of genetic philosophics, so the value of ethics appears to share the same fate, and the permanence of conscience, as a moral criterion, is as badly threatened as is the essence of the concept. Logic and ethics, which upon other considerations will find it necessary to change their traditional forms of expression, are not exempt from the problem of development which is so keenly felt by religion.

With art and law, the heraldic figures which reinforce religion laterally, the same question of time-passage and essential progress arises, and yet it does this without arousing any undue alarms. In the school and forum progress is to be expected, and with all the native love of tradition and precedent, there is no great shock occasioned when departures enter in. These forms of culture are so closely bound up with our most human ties that movement and variation are not so startling as is the case with philosophic disciplines, which, by a process of idealization, have been raised to the stars. We shrink from the suggestion that law and art have arisen and developed in a manner which should indicate no metaphysical or moral responsibility, yet we are ready to accept theories which point out genuine progress upon successive stages of evolution. It could hardly be otherwise in the case of culture and civilization, and when we remember that the significance of man's existence consists in his self-affirmation in opposition to nature, we expect to witness degrees of spiritual emancipation in which the vestiges of nature only gradually disappear. Law and art have developed, and, not in spite of this plan, but by means of it, have they become what they are to-day—living expressions of humanity.

In religion the situation is not unlike that which appears in the realm of æsthetics and jurisprudence, hence the problem of progress assumes a form not wholly unsatisfactory. Where a phase of culture is abstract, the result to be achieved can appear at once, and in an instant a Socrates can found the science of ethics, just as an Aristotle creates logic. Art, law, and religion, however, are more dependent upon history, which can do very little for theories of thought and practice, while it contains the possibilities of positive forms of culture. Having determined the character of religion upon the basis of the positive element which the latter contains, we may now pass on to observe that, over and above the mere fact of the positive, there is something akin to philosophic necessity, which makes the connection between religion and history appear as a substantial one. Religion has a certain affinity for history, and the instinct which leads man to react upon nature and affirm another form of existence is only a consciousness of that power which, in the guise of history, is making its way from nature to spirit. Just as the positive is symbolic of the presence of religion, so the idea of progress is suggestive of its innate activity.

Faith in the positive, which was able to save the character of religion from abstraction, involves increase of faith in historical progress. Where history is nothing, as was the case in the Enlightenment, and where history is almost everything, as it is to-day, it is scarcely possible to secure a convincing idea of its function. The transitional period, which witnessed the fall of rationalism and the rise of the age of culture, was not wanting in attempts to use history, and that in an appropriate manner. None have conceived of history more worthily than Vico and Herder, and even a sceptical Hume and a cynical Voltaire admitted the vast influence of custom in the life of humanity. In the midst of these more systematic forms of treatment, Kant and Schiller, in their discussion of the ethical problem, involved a distinct conception of the historical, which is by no means wanting in insight. Kant's memorable formulation of the moral problem was so severe that, having projected it, he was forced to admit that it was only under the auspices of immortality that the soul could fulfil the demands of the categorical imperative. Meanwhile, so it was argued, man must make use of certain aids to strengthen as motive within, that which is perfect as maxim without, and these are supplied by religion, with its doctrines of sin and redemption. Man adopts religion in order that he may become moral.

Hegel's connection with history is more systematic, just as his treatment of religion is more lingering; yet Hegel does not recognize the precinct of religion in all its independence. It is by no whim that this centre of German idealism entitles his leading work "Logik," for while the dialectical system departs altogether from the prejudice that the concept is supreme. Memorials of art and traditions of religion are only introductory to the principles of philosophy, and that inner evolution of the human spirit reveals a transition from the æsthetical *image* to the religious *idea*, whence the way to the *concept* is safe. Yet this treatment of religion, to say nothing of the flagrancy involved in the low position accorded to art, is insinuating, since it can only suggest that worship is but an exoteric and diluted form of speculation, and the situation is calculated to become worse when the genetic function of the system comes in to suggest that the entrance of philosophy is the exit of religion. First we are artistic, then we become religious, and finally our taste and our faith blend in the concepts of philosophy.

The sacred use of history which religion thus makes is far removed from the metaphysical and moralistic views which upon all sides must be rejected. It is plain to be seen that Kant reveres history merely because it happens to contain those events which have peculiar moral significance for man, but as for any faith in the historical idea, there is found in Kant no trace. The event is exemplary, nothing more. From the antipodal standpoint of Hegel's logic much the same may be said, and the dialectic of the genial idealist merely tolerates the contingent truth of history, or of nature. It is to the perpetual credit of Hegel that he strives to unite fact and theory in the form of a magnificent " phenomenology of spirit," but the carrying out of this process only results in a playing with the data of human history. The actual plan which Hegel's dialectic pursues relegates Brahmanism and Buddhism to the lowest plane of human worship, while it raises the Persian branch of Aryan religion to the next stage of development, where it stands in close connection with the religions of Egypt.

History is not the mere vehicle of human religion, but its living form. The relation obtaining between the two is substantial, not circumstantial. Both rationalism and empiricism, like moralism and intellectualism, must recognize this sterling fact. The older view, with its supreme confidence in the human understanding, could regard the history of humanity as only the mere copy of eternal reason with its necessary ideas, while current empiricism affiliates with the truths of religion because it finds in them material to serve for an anthropological generalization. To-day

The Reality of Religion

we seem to be threatened by a theory of origins which ever fails to postulate ground. So far as the theological formulation of religion is concerned, it can be seen that history is not employed in its integrity, because only the Christian religion comes in for discussion, nor is it invested with its spirit of eternal progress. Problems of authorship and authenticity are not problems of essence and character, and the influence of history is not confined to documentary evidence. Higher criticism is only introductory to religion, and it can never occupy any but an eccentric position in theology. It is by no mere chance that history contains the one thing needful in religion, and the emancipation of the human spirit does not depend upon readings of manuscripts.

It is no ambiguous figure which religion presents when it is surveyed historically. Between the forms of rationalism and naturalism there is a constant conflict over the historical moment in religion, as a result of which the meaning of history is lost. Rationalism flouted history because it failed to find therein anything of noumenal significance, while naturalism abuses the ideas of the positive and progress because it glories in the purely phenomenal. The one looks for the ground, and can account for nothing unless it be of a rational source, while the other seeks the origin of religion, and cares not to justify its fundamental principles. In the midst of this conflicting situation we may remember that it is the *essence* of religion which stands in need of philosophical discussion, because we must know what religion is before we can explain its origin or justify its ground. Now the essence of religion is undeniably positive, just as the affirmation of the soul is linked with the one progressive movement of humanity, from the point of view involved in the idea, the precinct of religion, there is no antinomy to be overcome, but only a natural problem to be solved. Religion is historical; such is the actual condition of affairs, and the question, "How can religion be positive?" is a question which can be solved only by scrutinizing the very essence of the thing involved.

The religious conception of history is not confined to the idea of the positive, however valuable this idea may be; it passes from, or through, the positive to the other principle of historical thinking, namely, progress. The positive is a fact; progress is a necessity. At the same time, it is in a peculiar sense that religious thinking employs the term history, by which we would best understand the history of culture with its inward tendencies; for, with the changing programme of outer events religion has little to do. It is the history of culture which embraces religion, because in this we find the perpetual endeavour to proceed from nature, which cannot environ man, to the spiritual world-order, wherein he may find his true home. Not only the general plan of the history of culture, but also its gradation in stages, gives it religious significance, and in passing from the immediacy of nature to the ultimate of spirit, religion and culture carry one common work of emancipation. Only in terms of spirit may progress be understood or justified, and only when it provides a transition from law to freedom may it be appreciated.

The spiritual burden which the human creature has to bear would be intolerable were man only an individual in his egoism, just as the problem which his understanding has to solve would be far beyond his intellectual powers, did not his mind contain implicitly the entire significance of human reason. History is the means by which man approximates to his humanity; its progressive movement gives his existence its bent, and does not fail to point out the possibilities of destiny; its several stages are indications of the advance which is being made. Religion gains by its contact with history. In the instance of Vedanta, where the personal self is identified with the one objective self, there is no apparent means by which the manifest difference between the two extremes may be overcome, although the Vedantist, who has accepted the views of Shankara, may account for the lack of intelligence concerning his absolute self by virtue of Maya, illusion, while

The Reality of Religion

the Yogi may match this theoretical device with the practical expedients peculiar to his disciplinary system. The infinite is found by contemplative renunciation. Occidental thought seeks another method of approximation. It involves nothing precipitate in the soul's relation to God, but declares that only when man participates in the one humanity, whose progressive character he assumes, is he able to sustain genuine relations to the Absolute. It is the function of history to extend the horizon of man's thought, and to reinforce the impulse which animates him to set his being in opposition to nature. The individual is a centre of which history is the circumference, and his will is fortified by the progressive force in the history of mankind.

A philosophic contemplation of the religious does not justify us in considering the manifold forms of ethnic religion, except as these may afford valuable illustration, as in the following division which investigates certain types of world-religion. Nevertheless, the influence of these vast synthetic judgments of human history may be indicated by citing certain dominant facts in the history of Israel and India. In the Hebrew consciousness, nothing was more formative than the memory of the exodus from Egypt or the return from the captivity in Babylon—significant events which bounded the religious experience of the ancient Jew. Like the Hebrew, the Hindu was affected by his separation from the ancient Aryan stock, as well as by his subjugation of the aboriginal Dasyu; and, just as Semitic literature, in psalms and prophecies, celebrated the power of Jehovah to redeem his chosen people from misfortune, so Sanskrit poetry and philosophy looked out from their inner contemplations to recall the triumphant work of Indra and the Deva. Zeal for righteousness on the part of the Semite, and intensity of contemplation with the Aryan, do not forbid these lingering reminiscences of national history, nor do they fail to contain innuendoes of human destiny.

History realizes its mission in perfecting human culture in the form of art, law, and religion. In the soul of the individual there is a native dread of progress, which suggests that man stands in need of improvement, just as it threatens to leave the individual behind in its onward march. Man fears lest his life be only temporal, and history, which so celebrates the passage of time, contributes to this apprehension. Yet history, which involves a greater range than the individual's existence, and a longer course than the limits of his life, is inwardly calculated to allay such alarms, inasmuch as it, with its principles of humanity and the ages, is much nearer than the individual, in his career, to spiritual life and eternity. Historical humanity may, or may not, adjust itself to the religious world-order; it is without question that the personal life of man can never do this. The attitude of the reflective religious consciousness is not that of an isolated spectator, but is the living view of one who thinks, not as a person, but as the human understanding itself, who believes with philosophic thought in general as this has been perfecting itself throughout the course of history.

2. Not only the general view of religion, which reveals the natural connection between religion and history, but the special discussion of the problem as it has been carried on tends to make this connection a necessary one. Thus far we have sought to evince the essential independence of religion, as well as its characteristic nature. The essence of religion, as something affirmative in the form of an active consciousness, signalizes a departure from nature which is made by the soul reacting upon its experience. That which is an affirmation in the soul is progress in the history of humanity, and thus the very essence of religion is unsupportable apart from the historical idea. With respect to the character of religion, which is elaborated upon the basis of the positive in human worship, the same argument will hold good, inasmuch as it is history which, in its development, supplies this living element. A religion which

is not historical is one which is possessed of no character, and a form of faith which does not progress cannot contain the self-affirmation of the human spirit. It is only by the introduction of the historical that religion may assume the proportions of a world-order.

If history has been a burden and a problem, why not consider it an aid in solving a difficult question? How can religion become a world-order? We may answer this by saying religion can become of world-significance only as it develops from stage to stage, and this is possible in history alone. To assert its nature and elaborate its own character, religion must make use of extraordinary means, and when the attempt is made to transform the religious precinct from its narrow confines in nature to the unlimited proportions of a world-order, the religious deed becomes more difficult. Even for the man of civilization and culture, the ordinary programme of religion is almost too great for him to carry out, and it is not without mental and moral struggle that he arrives at sufficient ideas, and approximates to worthy ideals. To comprehend God as an only deity, as monotheism implies, and to conceive of man as having a spiritual destiny, is beyond the thought of the man of culture. How much more difficult are such ideas and such tasks in the case of semi-cultured peoples or barbarous tribes! The relief which is sought when religion strives to see its proper objects and to create its own works comes from the cumulative arrangement of progress.

The principle of development makes possible the independence of religion and the realization of its desires. Again we return to the conception of religion which lies at the heart of this whole work, namely, that religion consists in the total act of affirmation on the part of the soul, which feels that it only exists, and does not truly live in nature. In the beginning of this self-assertion is the deed, whereby the soul as such, and as religious, begins to be. It can readily be seen that the spiritualizing of a human creature is a great task, and one which man, though aided from without, must perform for himself. What is necessary to this inclusive act is history, which must be viewed, not as the mere passing of time, but the organizing of an effort. This effort appears in the form of stages which mark the historical development of humanity, and may be indicated in a threefold manner : first the world of naturism, then the soul of humanism, and finally the world-soul of spiritualism. Religion itself is natural, national, and universal by degrees, and reveals how the human spirit starting from nature employs its own free spirit to arrive at the religion of universality.

Meanwhile the character of religion is receiving elaboration, and the method of spiritual affirmation becomes more manifest. At its inception, the religious consciousness in humanity makes use of art and law as means of support and furtherance, and these are adapted to such a part because they are each of a positive and perceptible nature. Religion may become legalistic, as with the Hebrews, or artistic, as with the Greeks, but it is developing a character which will enable it to affirm its being in contrast to an idealistic and imperceptible morality and metaphysics. Such a position in the scheme of human culture is the result of long growth, and no ethical Socrates or dialectical Plato is able to appropriate religion to his system since religion has grown into an independent form of spiritual life. Man worships God and discerns his destiny before the speculative thinker comes into being.

Finally, the religious world-order is no primitive idea, but a development attained only after superhuman conquest. The ideas involved, the integrity of the soul, the unity of the world, and the reality of the World-Soul are formed slowly as culture and civilization themselves advance. In the case of Christianity, which is the climax of religion, the unity of soul and world appears in response to a religious need which is felt when the soul as self-contained rejects the whole world. The commandment to lose and hate one's life could have no meaning to a savage

The Reality of Religion

living in nature and in conflict with alien tribes, and he could discover no value in the Kingdom of God. Nor could the unity of God be clearly seen before the community of blood and spirit among men appeared, and the dispute concerning Jew and Gentile in the Church was essentially a controversy over universals. The meaning of history and the justification of its programme appear for the first time in speculative thought when the universal in human culture appears; then the true perspective is discovered, and man perceives the unity of spirit, because he participates in a universal life. History, which makes possible the development of this life, also conveys intelligibility, and humanity both feels and perceives its unity of life.

The subjective function of history consists in a cumulative movement which enables the soul to emancipate itself from the environing nature. No special philosophy of history is needed to point out the truth that three leading periods mark the progress of the human spirit from its source to its goal. Man's relation to nature can never be that of the plant or animal, although with them he finds his existence in the immediate world. Human consciousness cannot refrain from contemplation which tends to fuse the various phases of the natural into an order which man alone understands, and which he elaborates in the epic forms of his art. Moreover, the active soul of mankind never takes nature for granted, but enters into conflict with her, and thus discovers her secrets, arranges her process, and perfects her forms in the schemes of science and art. Thus man affirms his independent being in contrast with the mere existence of the external world. Upon the second stage of human religion there is to be found an organization of worship upon the basis of national life. The individual in his isolation is distinct from nature, and how much more so is the state which approximates to the ideal of humanity! When the person becomes a citizen his nature is amplified and enriched to such a degree that he enters into genuine relations with his national deity, just as he may perform duties which have an unwonted significance, inasmuch as they pertain to the total life of a chosen people. The culmination of religion partakes neither of the generality of natural worship nor of the particularity of national faith, but is at once invested with the universality of spiritual life. While we cannot predict the actual features of universal religion, we can affirm that it will involve the soul, the world, and God in universal forms, and, viewed subjectively in the light of religious consciousness, a safe criterion of its character as world-religion will be found in the ideas of humanity, eternal justice, and non-resentment.

On its objective side the nature of history consists of stages of development in the idea of God. Like the periods of progressing religion, these stages of unfolding consist of three leading conceptions of deity. Standing upon the plane of nature, the primitive man offers what may seem to be only another form of the immediate life of the world. He differs from his surroundings only mathematically; where there is nature in general there is human nature in particular. His gods are natural objects, like those which surround him, or ordinary persons, such as belong to his own family, while, as yet, he is possessed of no personality. Yet spiritual life has begun to compete with nature, and the obvious elements of naturalism which enter in are only signs of the place where this conflict is going on. Man meets nature upon her own grounds, and overcomes her. The second stage of religion is marked by individuality, and the god receives positive form and a name, although he still lacks unity. A person, not a natural force, has become the object of regard, in an organized system of polytheism. The founding of universal religion is the culmination of religious progress; it demands an intuition of the unity of the world, the spiritual integrity of man, whence the mind can pass to the idea of the one World-Soul. Only when there is universal religion can there be consciousness of nature and humanity, which is wanting in ideas of diversity and particularity. God is neither one nor many, but All. To evince this truth the whole Orient has laboured for millenniums, and we must inquire into the several claims for universality in religion.

3. *World-Religions*

If the ideas of origin and development in religion seem to be consistent, we may advance to a more definite characterization of the religious world-order, and investigate certain forms of universal religion which stand out as types. To reduce religion to philosophy is to assume that the phenomena of human worship are conformable to a logical plan, just as it is to postulate a unity between the universal in religion and speculation. Three forms of religion, in eastern, central, and western Orient, reveal as many phases of universal religion, even as they manifest successive stages in the development of the universal religious consciousness. China produces the universal in the form of naturism, India advances to intellectualism, while Christianity gives the conclusion as spiritualism. In all three appears the universal as a self-existent principle, and the appeal to the mind is made upon grounds which are independent of interest and authority. The Absolute is presented to the worshipper as though the latter were aware of his absolute self, and the method of life which is enjoined involves the totality of the ego, and implies a negative rather than positive ideal.

The several forms of absolute life are expressed as Tao among the Chinese, Brahman with the Hindus, and the Kingdom of God among Christians. In the light of these intuitions the worshipper reacts upon his immediate surroundings, and creates an independent world-order. With the Mongolian the type of life elaborated is a nihilistic form of quiescence; with the Aryan it is contemplation and renunciation; with Christianity it is self-denial and spiritual progress. The first plan remains fixed in the world; the second reacts upon life, in order to negate it; the last pauses in its natural progress, which it denies, and then proceeds to affirm a higher order of existence. All agree in annihilating the immediate both in nature and in consciousness, just as they all attempt to reach the ultimate in life, and it is by no mere coincidence that they agree in proclaiming non-resistance and the love of enemies. Indeed, this extraordinary principle is a convincing mark of universality and supreme worth in the form of human religion which contains it. The nihilism necessarily involved in the three types of complete religion is complemented by more or less sufficient motives toward a positive life in the religious world-order.

1. Chinese religion discloses the absolute religion in connection with the older religion, which was rehabilitated by Confucius as well as in the Taoism of Laotze. To gain insight into the absolute naturism of the Chinese we may first isolate the scheme of change, as developed in the Yi-King, and as it appealed to the reticent mind of Confucius; then we may perceive the same spirit in the Tao-teh-king. The plan of the Yi is presented in a literary form which at first is bewildering. The work is made up of broken and unbroken lines arranged in the form of hexagrams, wherein the position and mutual relation of the two kinds of lines indicate certain truths of physics and politics, morals and practical life. The symbolism of the sixty-four hexagrams is partially enlightened by corresponding wisdom-verses which subtend the significant lines. In general the broken line indicates the weak and incomplete, while the unbroken one stands for the strong and capable, yet the arrangement of lines may be such as to produce the paradox of weakness in strength and strength in weakness, which results from careless confidence on the one hand, and calm resignation on the other. The lines which are combined to facilitate such a philosophy of religious life serve also to indicate natural objects, as

The Reality of Religion

heaven and earth, fire and mountain, marsh and wood, wind and water, etc.

The complete naturism of the Yi will appear when leading examples from the hexagrams are cited; at the same time the meaning of the Yi-King, as the Book of Changes, should manifest itself:

I. THE KHIEN HEXAGRAM

The arrangement of this leading hexagram indicates strength, while it does not fail to inculcate caution. In the mind of the editor of the work the lines suggest the upward movement of a dragon who, in exultation of his strength, arises from the deep, turns to the field, roams abroad, then leaping up, he rises on the wing only to exceed his proper limits. The lesson is one of reflection and regret. On the other hand, the opposite hexagram proceeds to safe conclusion from negative premises. Here the favourite nihilism of the Chinese consciousness appears:

II. THE KHWAN HEXAGRAM

While this arrangement suggests weakness, it praises docility, and points out how the consciousness of weakness and the recognition of ignorance will produce security and contentment. The tendency toward conservatism and quiescence cannot fail to be noted in this hexagram.

When the strong and weak trigrams are combined as they are in the eleventh hexagram, the contrast is most promising, while the appended philosophy strikes directly at the heart of the whole system of changes :

XI. THE THAI HEXAGRAM

This arrangement points out the certainty of change, and arouses a brilliant comment which is made in the third verse. " The third line, undivided, shows that while there is no state of peace that is not liable to be disturbed, and no departure of evil men, so that they shall not return, yet when one is firm and correct, as he realizes the distresses that may arise, he will commit no error. *There is no occasion for sadness at the certainty of such recurrent changes, and in this mood the happiness of the present may be enjoyed.*" Such resignation is the theme of another leading hexagram, the Ki-Zi :

LXIII. THE KI-ZI HEXAGRAM

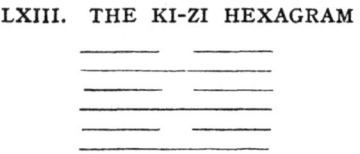

The basis of religious calculation is here founded upon an alternation of strong and weak lines. As a result, we have the idea of constant change. Such a thought produces a state of mind neither optimistic nor pessimistic, but apathetic. The hexagram states : " There has been good fortune in the beginning ; there may be disorder in the end."

In the case of the last hexagram, which ends, at the top, with a strong, unbroken line, the ceaselessness of change is significantly pointed out. " The topmost line, undivided,

The Reality of Religion

shows its subject full of confidence, and therefore feasting quietly. There will be no error. If he cherish this confidence, till he is like the fox who gets his head immersed, it will fail of what is right." The conclusion is failure; such is the suggestion here made. The words of the editor are worthy of quotation : " Some have wished that the Yi might have concluded with the Ki-Zi, and the last hexagram have left us with the picture of human affairs all brought to good order. But this would not have been in harmony with the idea of the Yi as the book of change. Again and again it has been pointed out that we find in it no idea of a perfect and abiding state. Just as the seasons of the year change and pursue an ever-recurring round, so is it with the phases of society. The reign of order has been and has terminated, and this hexagram calls us to see the struggle for its realization commenced."

In the midst of the idea of change there may be found the contrary idea of the invariability of such vicissitudes. Yet we do not discover in this scheme of primitive metaphysics anything like the Stoical $\pi\epsilon\rho\iota\kappa\acute{o}\pi\eta$, much less the modern ideal of progress. The monotony of the plan, peculiar as it is to the Mongolian mind, finds partial counterpart in the recent conception of "eternal recurrence," the "*Wiederherstellung des Gleichen*" of Nietzsche. Inasmuch as the number of natural elements is limited while change is unceasing, it is obvious that the same elements will recur from time to time. On this account the term change is misleading, since the larger logic of the work reveals an implicit trust in the immutability of the courses of nature. The perception of inevitable change is calculated to produce a religious regard, in the midst of which the self-affirmation of the soul occurs. Yet, at this stage of religious history, the result is wholly negative, yet it suffices to render man's regard toward nature less and less naive. Over and above the chain of unavoidable change is the soul, which in this atmosphere can only will to submit.

Taoism advances beyond the philosophy of the Yi,

because it abandons the direct naturism of the theory of changes, and likewise indicates more convincing life-ideals. The Tao-teh is at once speculative and practical, and the implicit naturism of the work involves no such distinction between thinking and acting which a later western philosophy would naturally adopt. To comprehend the meaning of the Tao we may employ the analogy of the Greek λόγος, or we may follow the thought of the Stoics and Spinoza, and use the principle of *natura* to indicate that which is the essence of the world and the aim of human life. Julien translates the title as follows, " Le livre de la voie et de la vertu." Thus the Tao indicates the speculative and the Teh the practical portion of the complete work.

When the idea of Tao is analysed it reveals a conception of being not unlike the principles of identity and the absolute which were fashionable in Germany a century ago ; indeed, the Hegelian declaration that " pure being equals nothing " seems to be anticipated by Laotze, who says, " The Tao is like the emptiness of a vessel. It might appear to have been before God." Under the caption, " The Use of what has no Substantive Existence," the kenotic quality of the Tao further appears. " The thirty spokes unite in one nave, but it is on an empty space for the axle that the use of the wheel depends. Clay is fashioned into vessels, but it is on their hollowness that their use depends. The door and window are cut out to form an apartment, but it is on the empty space within that its use depends." Such figures as these betoken the nihilism which lies at the heart of the system. In its operations the Tao appears in the form of " the equable, the inaudible, the subtle, and the One." It is further styled the indefinable, from which all things are derived. " Man takes his law from earth, earth from heaven, heaven from Tao, the law of Tao is its being what it is." The particular way in which the Tao proceeds is suggestive of the identity-philosophy of Schelling ; it is by contraries, such as ex-

The Reality of Religion

istence and non-existence, difficulty and ease, length and shortness, height and lowness.

> The movement of the Tao,
> By contraries proceeds;
> And weakness marks the course
> Of Tao's mighty deeds.

In Pythagorean fashion it is further declared that " Tao produced one, one produced two, two produced three, three produced all things." In spite of these analogies taken from Greek and German nature-philosophy, Tao remains as an idea peculiar to the Mongolian mind, and indigenous to Chinese culture. This will be seen again when the practical side, or principle of the Teh, is examined.

The Taoist, or man of Tao, is the yielding character whose behaviour is likened to the action of water. " There is nothing in the world more soft and weak than water, and yet for attacking things that are firm and strong, there is nothing that can take precedence of it." The force of this analogy must not appear as that of a fine paradox in nature, but must be appreciated in the religious sense of life's highest ideal. This, like the primitive conception of nature, consists in the nihilistic ideal of " doing nothing." In the Taoist writings of Kwang-tze, the same ideal is proclaimed by saying that perfect enjoyment consists in " doing nothing "; which is after the manner of heaven and earth, whose inaction produces serenity. The Utopia is the " land of the great Vacuity." In more than one place Taoism proclaims non-resentment. In speaking of the " Quality of Indulgence " the Tao counsels one to be good to those who are both good and bad to one, and the climax of this style of reasoning is attained, when it is declared, " It is the way of Tao to recompense injury with kindness."

It may be that this sublime conclusion results from the naturistic nihilism of the whole system, for certainly the fundamental tone is that of quiescence, which leads to the principle of " doing nothing," and the mood of " dumb inaction." Then it would be urged that man should not requite evil in particular, inasmuch as life consists in no form of reaction in general, and the ground would be, not so much love of enemies as a complete nihilism in life. Yet this conclusion is one which Laotze does not draw, and he seems to inculcate non-resentment as a positive principle which has a value of its own. Taoism itself is not so naturistic as to obscure the mind in its view of human destiny, for the use of nature is primitive and nihilistic, and the favourite symbols are those of emptiness and inaction. The Tao negates the world, and denies the value of man's ordinary life with the unconscious result of preparing the way for a living and positive life-ideal.

2. Vedic thought possesses an intellectual character which advances it beyond Taoism, and with more clearness and consistency evinces the supreme element in religion. Taoism has exhausted nature and finds therein only the privative and kenotic; Vedanta, whose naturistic career is the parallel of Taoism, proceeds directly to the soul which it affirms in a positive manner in opposition to the world external and immediate. The attitude of western thought towards Vedanta is not at all direct, and, up to the present time, we have been unable to make use of Aryan ideals in the interpretation of religion. When Anquetil du Perron gave Europe the fruits of Persian and Hindu speculation, they were not consistently received. Kant could find nothing in Avesta, while Schopenhauer was as extreme in the other direction, when he affected to make the Upanishads the be-all of his life and the end-all of his death. Meanwhile, Fichte's conception of the absolute ego was an unconscious tribute to the philosophy of the self as Brahman. In itself Vedanta appears in the *Gotterdämmerung* of Vedic religion, and when faith in the time-honoured thirty-three deities was declining, the Upanishads restate the truth of Vedesin by declaring that the divine is the Self.

Tat tvam asi! Such is grand conclusion in the mind of the Brahman after the primitive and picturesque faith of the ancient Rishi has evaporated. There is in the universe one being, beyond attributes and characteristics, above good and evil, formless and nameless, and " that thou art." And the wise Brahman, who has found the true self, which is not this or that, not mind or sense, not hatred or love, virtue or vice, responds, *aham brahma asmi!* " I am Brahman." Vedanta thus contributes to religious consciousness the principle of objective self, whereby it annihilates the world of appearance, and affirms the soul as supreme. As Buddhism is atheistic, Vedanta is acosmic, which point of view it assumes in order to enable man to find reality in the self alone.

When it is once appreciated that the sacred syllable " Om " stands for affirmation, the " Atman " may be understood to signify the affirmative of the self. The Atman is self which man must reach, by doing away with the various limitations of his narrow personal being ; he accomplishes self-hood by being the self and by knowing the self, that is, by affirming the self. In the Mundaka-Upanishad it is stated that Om is the bow, self the arrow, and Brahman the point aimed at. When thus depicted, religion seems to consist in desire and determination on the part of the self to attain to self-hood. The self is the source of the world, and is the all, which exercises omnipotence and omnipresence over the world, reduces it to Maya, and overcomes it. One who knows self becomes lord and master in all worlds.

The doctrine of the universal self in man finds abundant expression in the Khândogya-Upanishad. As the juices of plants mingle in one, as rivers unite in the sea, as seeds inhabit fruits, as salt pervades the waters, so in all things there is one principle—the soul. This omni-existence of the soul is interpreted in the light of the self in man, and as a continual climax to the survey and summation of natural forms there is brought in the marvellous *tat tvam asi*. " That which is the subtle essence, in it all that exists has its self. It is the true. It is the Self, and thou art it ! "

Still other references from the Khândogya further this striking conception, as, for example, the infinite quality of the ego as it participates in the one self. "The Infinite indeed is below, above, behind, before, right, and left—it is indeed all this. I am below, I am above, I am behind, before, right, and left—I am all this. Self is below, above, behind, before, right, and left—Self is all this." Yet the Brahman does not claim that this self is in our immediate consciousness. As people may continually walk over gold treasure hidden in the earth without knowing it, so they are ignorant of the true self in Brahman. When man finds the Self and says, "I am He," he no longer pines after the body. "Whoever has found and understood the Self that has entered into this patched-together hiding-place, he indeed is the creator, for he is the maker of everything, his is the world, and he is the world itself."

In the Brihadaranyaka-Upanishad, the Brahmanic quality of the self receives characteristic treatment. The genesis of Brahman, if such a suggestion be in order, is stated as follows : " In the beginning this was self alone, in the shape of a person. He, looking round, saw nothing but his Self. He first said, ' *This is I* ' ; therefore he became I by name." It is added also, " Verily, in the beginning this was Brahman that knew self only, saying, ' I am Brahman.' " On this account one should seek Brahman within. True Brahman is not in the sun or moon, in lightning or ether, in wind or fire, in sound or space ; but as the web from the spider, and as sparks from the fire, so all beings come forth from self. Brahman is without cause or effect, without anything inside or outside. The warp and woof of which all things are woven, air and water, sun and stars, Indra and Pragapati, is Brahman ; while of all the forms of nature, both physical and psychical, the self is the indwelling ruler. He who dwells in water, fire, and sky, in eye, ear, and mind, whom these do not know, and whose body they are, and who rules them within, he is the self, the ruler within the Immortal.

The Reality of Religion

Not only the being of the self, but consciousness comes from the one central being. This is shown in the dialogue which develops the theme, the light in man. " When the sun has set, and the moon has set, and the fire is gone out, and the sound is hushed, what is the light of man ? The Self indeed is his light." The particular manner after which the Self supplies this illumination appears in connection with the phenomena of consciousness. During sleep the soul transcends the sensible state and hovers between the two worlds. As a fish moves along between the two banks of a river, and as a falcon first roams about the air, then folds his wings in his nest, so the soul seeks the supreme state of dreamless sleep, when he understands. Then he is able to affirm, " I am He," and beholds the Self as God, the immortal Brahman, unborn, undying.

In addition to this contemplative method of arriving at self-hood, as the essence of religion, there is promulgated a more eudemonistic view of *amor intellectualis*, whereby man becomes immortal by the love of the Self. Persons and castes, worlds and gods, are not dear for their own sake, nor are they to be loved for themselves, but only that a man may love the Self. Caste and worlds, Gods and Vedas, are the Self, and to look for these elsewhere is to be abandoned by them. So far as the Self is capable of definition, it is described by saying, " No, no " ; incomprehensible, imperishable ; he suffers not, he fails not, but goes on to immortality. In the Self, which is free from sin and grief, old age and death, may be found a palace in the city of Brahman, and for him who discovers the Self there is freedom in all worlds, and happiness in the world of persons, the world of perfumes, the world of women, and the world of song. The heart of true desire is as vast as all space, and contains sun, moon, and stars. Such is the basis upon which the Vedanta is developed.

In itself, Vedanta consists in elements found, not in the Upanishads alone, but also in the Bhagavad-Gita and the Vedanta Sutras, whereby the system, if it adds nothing to Brahmanism, tends to advance toward modern thinking. In the Upanishads themselves Vedanta is mentioned in connection with Yoga, as follows: "Having well ascertained the object of the knowledge of the Vedanta, and having purified their nature by the Yoga of renunciation, all anchorites, enjoying the highest immortality, become free at the time of the great end in the worlds of Brahma." When Yoga is observed to signify practice, its ancillary relation to contemplative Vedanta will appear, and in the particular case of Jnana Yoga, which consists in wisdom and knowledge, the Vedantist quality of the system cannot fail to appear in the peculiar element of Self-knowledge. The interpretation of Vedanta belongs to Shankara in the ninth, to Schopenhauer in the nineteenth century, and with both of them may be found an application of Vedantist principles to psychic and cosmic problems. In his interpretation of the Sutras of Vyasa, Shankara discusses the being and knowledge of the Absolute Self in terms of man's limited personality, whereby he is able to indicate for us the religious significance of a system which consists in the speculative affirmation of the soul as an infinitive Self. It is in the second half of the Sutras that we find an anticipation of the Cartesian *cogito, ergo sum*.

Shankara's introduction contains a programme which the Sutras follow; it consists of a discussion concerning ego and non-ego. In reality, urges Shankara, the ego cannot be superimposed upon the non-ego, or vice versa, the non-ego upon the ego; nor can the attributes of the one be superimposed upon those of the other; for subject and object must be conceived of as separate. Nevertheless, there is a superimposition of non-ego upon ego, although this is only natural and relative, and is due to nescience (*avidya*). Knowledge (*vidya*) has the function of discriminating between the self and not-self, and consists in the operation of a knowing personality, which may appear to depend upon the existence of the body with its senses. Human knowledge, which resembles the behaviour of the animal mind, seems to involve bodily superimposition as a necessary element, but it is the aim of Vedanta to reveal the unity of the Self, and thus do away with the false notion that superimposition is essential to the soul. At this point we may glance at the comment upon Sutra II, 3, 7, which seems to contain the Cartesian principle, *cogito, ergo sum.* Here it is laid down as axiomatic that the Self is ultimate and irrefutable. Past, present, and future are united in the Self which says, " I knew, I know, I shall know "; for the knowing subject does not change, and knowledge of the Self is self-established. As " the heat of fire is not refuted by the fire itself, so to refute self-established identity is impossible." Such is the conclusion of Shankara, who may be said to anticipate Descartes in about the same manner that Augustine did.

This psychological principle is not without cosmological significance, which could hardly appear in what was so naturistic as the Upanishads; it involves acosmism. The world is unreal, and the whole combination of names and forms may justly be regarded as an illusion imposed upon the soul in its ignorance. The whole world is Maya, and as one believes a mere rope to be a snake, or a stump to be a man, so he interprets subjective impressions as though they possessed objective validity. Emancipation comes when the thorough unreality of one's immediate surroundings is seen, and the soul finds its inner self in Brahman. Knowledge thus liberates, not only by pointing out the unreality of the world, but by identifying the soul with Brahman. Such perception leads to quiescence, and, in the spirit of Karma Yoga, it is asserted that the real self is not a doer of action, but is possessed of a method which enables the soul to extricate itself from the wheel of action and reaction. It is in connection with Karma Yoga that we find again the ideal of non-resentment which is placed upon other than ethical grounds. He who injures another injures himself, while he who entertains evil thoughts throws open his mind to the fullness of evil which is contained in the mental world.

The practical side of Vedanta is set forth so elegantly in the Bhagavad-gita, that we may turn to its eloquent chapters to pursue this significant principle of non-resistance. To read the twelfth chapter of this work will be to find the ideal of forgiveness set forth in the atmosphere of Yoga, and in a manner which is not always convincing. That devotee is dear to Brahman " who hates no being, who is friendly and compassionate, and who is forgiving " ; such is one eminent phase of the doctrine. Again, the devotee " who is unconcerned, who abandons all actions, who does not grieve and does not desire, who is alike to friend and foe, as also in honour and dishonour, who is alike in cold and heat, pleasure and pain, to whom praise and blame are alike," is dear to the deity. Thus expounded, the doctrine of non-resentment seems to arise in the inculcation of total inaction and non-attachment, wherein it is not single, not *primus inter pares*, but one among the manifold forms of world-abandonment.

For the reason that Buddhism has realized and expressed this sterling idea with such force, we refer to it now, although hesitating to introduce material to which we can devote not even the meagre discussion given to Vedanta. The Buddhist system is twice heterodox, inasmuch as it rejects the Veda and does not include the idea of God. Buddhism has the value of giving a pessimistic turn to religion, which cannot exist without recognition of the evil in the world, and of infusing its own conceptions with the appreciation of humanity. Buddhism advances beyond Vedanta in the way the latter transcends Vedism. For Vedanta, the only God is the objective Self—*tat tvam asi!* For Buddhism, this Self is interior and subjective alone ; hence, atheism. Non-resistance is placed upon a practical basis in a system which is all human, and the Dhomma counsels, " Hatred ceaseth not by hatred ; hatred ceaseth only by love."

3. Christianity is a world-religion which realizes and reveals the essential moment in the self-affirmation of the soul over against the world. As a system it may seem to be wanting in the conceptional forms which we find in Taoism and Vedanta, but this is only because Christianity is a life-system which, like Buddhism, is set upon the redemption of humanity, and the philosophic expression of cogent ideas is a secondary matter. Where philosophy itself is pedantically conceived in the form of theory, school, and the like, a religious system like Christianity may receive meagre treatment, but where philosophy becomes a living system with a culture-content, it becomes reverential toward spiritual life, and finds material wherever the human soul has expressed itself. In another place * I have tried to show how the essence of Christianity is closely connected with our modern philosophy, so that nearly all our problems of living and thinking have a spirit and a setting which they receive directly from Christianity. Here we may content ourselves with an outline of Christianity as a world-religion.

Christianity stands out in sharp contrast to Taoism and Vedanta where Christianity expresses belief in God. Taoism sees a world apart from the soul, which it finds to be empty; Vedanta beholds a Self without a world, and this idea barely preserves its personal meaning. Christianity combines world and soul in the form of a World-Soul, although this idea is not without problem and paradox. The soul of man cannot remain in nature, nor can it repose in the self; it must rather find another self without, which is God. When, therefore, the Vedanta declares *tat tvam asi*, Christianity revises the meaning of the magnificent phrase that it may signify, " That, O God, art thou ! " He, who is not far from any one of us, and in whom we live and move and have our being, is still not we, and Christian thought must reject any notion which, by identifying the soul with God, produces not merely pantheism but nihilism. When

* "Christianity and Modern Culture."

our thought comes to this ontological conception of religion, the formulation of the God-idea will be made according to the Christian method; here it need be pointed out that, like Taoism and Vedanta, Christianity does not hesitate to regard the divine as in some sense an order of things. Accordingly, when man approaches God and becomes like Him, he must abandon the narrow and privative characteristics of his immediate existence, and, in thought and life, fill out the proportions of his absolute self.

Christ was wont to call this the Kingdom of Heaven, or the life eternal, which consisted in the knowledge of God. The juristic moment involved in the phrase was, of course, local and incidental, and the divine realm was regarded as an order rather than a kingdom. For Christ, the Kingdom stood for the ground of the world and the goal of human life, so that man must believe in the existence of this fundamental principle, just as he must strive to inculcate it in his life. The Founder of Christianity did not teach metaphysics or metapolitics, but He presented the idea of God in such a sufficient fashion that we can find nothing more real, nothing more worthy. As we bring our considerations to a conclusion we shall see how the idea of God's Kingdom clears up certain philosophic problems otherwise insoluble, at present. We may add a suggestion or two concerning the way in which the Christian idea of God is to be portrayed.

Let it be noted that the idea of God is no common one which any individual or any nation might discover, but is a characteristic notion which is adaptable to the peculiar needs of the Christian religion. What place could the Christian θεός find in Taoism? How could the monism and intellectualism of Vedanta make room for the Kingdom of God? These systems either have no transcendental needs, or they are self-sufficient in their belief that the Self is divine. It is Christianity which creates and appropriates the theistic idea, and it is this form of religion which must settle the problem which arises. Here it

The Reality of Religion

may be pointed out that the Vedantist conception of the Self as objective, while in itself not final, is a necessary step toward a genuine ontology, and God may be called a " person " only when this personalism is reduced to the absolute form of *tat tvam asi* which relates the world to the soul, and the *aham brahma asmi* which then adjusts the self to the world. From this identity, Christian thought may deduce the idea of the World-Soul.

The particular manner according to which Christianity adjusts the soul to the world is not wholly alien to the cosmic views of Taoism and Vedanta. Taoism points out the essential emptiness of reality, and counsels the soul to relinquish all action, including resistance and resentment. Vedanta denaturalizes the world and reduces it to the Self, for which alone the soul should live and act. This is the meaning of Karma and Jnana Yoga. In the same way Christ points out that life in the world is for ever vain. To gain the whole world is to lose the personal soul, so that the one thing needful is the totality of eternal life which includes both thinking and acting. Christianity is wanting in that intellectualism which possesses Vedanta, as also in the naturalism of the Tao, but the essential remains in the form of eternal life. Strictly speaking, Christianity is not a view, but a type of life ; not a system, but a new conscious process ; yet this life may be reduced to a form adapted to philosophic scrutiny. There is a new system of valuation which produces a characteristic life-judgment.

The Christian philosophy of activity is quite at variance with the " doing nothing " of the Tao and the contemplative inaction of Karma Yoga. It is true that the Christian deed consists in no special performance which might result from sense-stimulus, as in the pursuit of pleasure, or might come from the externality of authority in the form of ceremonialism. In contrast with such specialized performances, Christianity counsels the " doing nothing " as also the freedom from the ceaseless causality of the natural world. Yet the escape is not negative, but positive ; it consists not in doing nothing, but in doing all, and the Christian philosophy of action involves a complete soul engaged in the total work of a free life. This positive view persists in the midst of certain negations. He that loveth his life shall lose it, but he that loseth his life shall find it. Such is the negative-positive view, which rejects the alien only to accept the allied, and calls upon the soul to rouse itself from dumb inaction and attempt the unheard-of.

Another familiar principle of Christianity might be made parallel to the Hindu Yoga, provided we can accept the etymology of the latter as a " Yoke," or harness, put on for the purpose of doing essential work. The method of Jesus was expressed as Yoga in that general sense of the term, and the burden of life which comes from sense and need was one which He would lift according to a method of His own. He had His own philosophy of work, and said, " Take My yoke upon you, and learn of Me." That inevitable burden which the world imposes was not the yoke of Him who said, " Not as the world giveth give I unto you." The unity of the work which Christ imposes is seen in the manifold form which it assumes in His counsels. It is so vast as to include duty toward self, in the case of individual salvation, as well as obligation toward the whole world of humanity. The completeness of the impulse toward humanity is seen in the extremes which are involved in the clothing of the naked and the visiting of the imprisoned, as also in being spiritual teachers to all men ; in duty toward Caesar and toward God, in the love of both Lord and neighbour. Christ reveals the universality of His system, when He calls upon His disciple to abandon the commonplace in life and perform the total deed which belongs to life eternal. What one good thing can a man do to possess eternal life ? There is no single deed, nor series of isolated acts which he can perform, but to inherit eternal life he must abandon all immediate motives and pursue the way peculiar to Christ Himself. Then alone can he find rest, and this obtained, the work of the world-redeemer is ended.

Like Taoism and Vedanta, Christianity has a certain air of finality about it, and marks the climax of religion. With the revelation of the absolute World-Soul, and with the projecting of a world-task, we need look for no further views, but only for new conceptions of old problems. Progress, in which all Christian thinking finds furtherance, is an idea which is bound to be relative, and in the fundamentals of religion it must give way before the idea of perfection. The Vedantist "*That art Thou*" may receive new explanations, and may be superseded by the Christian θεός, but in its own sphere it represents the culmination of the human spirit busied with speculation.

The culmination of religion constitutes a perilous problem concerning the eternal spirit of the world. Where we find a beginning made and progress carried on, we discover also that an end is reached. Yet the climax of religion must not be understood to mean the twilight before the long night of irreligion; it is much better to assume that at last we are in a position to appreciate the eternal and spiritual in those final forms of religion which have too long been shrouded in the purely positive. The law of progress seems to indicate that the higher supplants the lower, so that man has nothing to fear from the progress of humanity. Where naturistic imperialism in China produces Taoism, where intellectualism in India ends in Vedanta, where legalism in Judah becomes Christianity, we may see how eastern, central, and western orients reach their respective goals. The first two forms of universal religion have survived two and a half millenniums and are hardly moribund to-day; the case of Christianity, which in the west is an exotic, is not unlike them. With respect to Christianity it may be suggested that the future may see the realization of our hopes that we shall some day have an "eternal Gospel" which, unlike the Petrine form of Catholicism, or the Pauline form of Protestantism, shall realize in a Johannine form of spiritual religion indeed, neither Catholic nor Protestant, but truly universal. At any rate, the features of Christianity are such that no departures or developments can render it obsolete.

The reality of religion, as we have surveyed it in its history, has now come to its proper culmination, and we are ready to observe its fruit. We have seen that spiritual religion may enter human history *incognito*, and there preserve its intrinsic character as it undergoes development. And historical progress, which goes on of itself, finally reaches perfection in certain forms of universal religion, after whose establishment religion becomes a problem. What, we may now inquire, is the question which confronts religious thinking when it is surveyed historically? It is the question of revelation, which itself involves the problem of communion between man and God. We have seen that religion possesses an independent nature, and an intrinsic character, just as we now see that it is self-constituted in its positive form and self-propelled in its progress. Do such elements of religion forbid or invite such community of lower or higher that we may style religion a revelation?

4. *The Revelation of Religion*

The problem of revelation belongs directly to religion, and is not without its special relation to Christianity. Among the Chinese, who themselves are naturally disposed toward the reverential, the traditions of the ancient, imperial religion were always weighty, and yet we could hardly regard Taoism as though it claimed to be a revelation made to prophets and kings. Of the Aryans, who also emphasize the literary side of human worship, somewhat the same may be said. Buddhism rejects the Veda altogether, and is thus shut off from any connection with historical revelation. Vedanta, however, clings to the Upanishads, whence comes the idea of self-knowledge, and in so far it is Vedic, while it is not calculated to em-

The Reality of Religion

phasize the importance of the traditional thirty-three deities. Where Taoism would neglect the idea of revelation, Vedanta would supersede it, by the introduction of the Self as the source of knowledge, and it is only by accommodation that we may speak of the Taoist of Vedantist revelation.

It is in Christianity that religion and revelation are one. Religion without revelation is like beauty without art, and in the forms of oriental religion which we have examined the religious quality is the free and natural one unorganized by any programme of revelation. Already we have had occasion to observe the importance contained in the idea of a precinct for religion, which is as essential to its nature as the positive form is to its character. Now it may be said that these ideas of the objective in religion assume a more definite cast in the conception of revelation. Like rights and æsthetics, religion must contain more than the singular moment of religious feeling, and must include something fixed, so that as right ends in love, beauty in art, religion must culminate in revelation. Religion itself cannot sunder man from the world unless it attach him to a higher world-order, and just as the first and negative movement rebounds from a nature which is given, so the second and positive one turns to an order of things which is beyond the power of man to produce. The religious act is spontaneous, but not blind, because the vision which indicates the nothingness of nature also views the infinite reality of the religious world-order.

When the idea of revelation is reduced to its ultimates, it seems to contain (1) the communion of the human and divine; and (2) the plan of historical progress. Among the three forms of world-religion which we have examined, only Christianity appears to make use of these in their fullness. Take again the case of Taoism, and we find that the " emptiness of the Tao " renders impossible any communion on the part of the worshipper. It is true that the Tao is better than mere nature, just as the " way of Tao " is superior to common life, and thus in a negative fashion, at least, this naturistic system indicates the goal of religion as a form of spiritual culture. Vedanta supersedes Taoism at precisely this point, inasmuch as it relates the person to the absolute Self, and we may well pass over the rather nugatory form of this in order to appropriate the rich content of this personalism. But something more than personal communion is necessary to revelation; we demand the historical plan which renders such communion an in-living and appropriating idea.

1. The communion of the human and divine is the supreme fact of religion, and it is history which must organize and characterize it. Universal religion has a certain aptness for history, even as it makes revelation itself assume a justifiable form. Religion seeks the absolute and eternal, and the religious consciousness longs for deliverance from subjectivism in the same spirit that the soul seeks salvation; for this reason, the purely anthropological element in religion can never constitute its final form. That which arouses the soul of man, and awakens the desire of desires, can never be thought of as the creation of man's native powers; and that which presents itself as a crisis in his existence can be interpreted only in terms of revelation. What reason can demonstrate and the will accomplish cannot inspire the idealizing tendency in the human spirit, which seeks as the supreme object of its faith that which transcends all thinking and doing. Thus the vanishing-point of religion is found in revelation, wherein all the lines converge, and to realize the meaning of the religious precinct, as well as to understand its character as positive, we must follow the tendencies to their culmination in revelation.

If religion seems to be all-too-human, theology often appears all-too-divine. How shall reconciliation come in? This may not be answered in so many words, but it may safely be assumed that the place where religion and theology find their unity is to be found in the field of universal religion. The science of religion has usually surveyed the religious life upon the low plane of nature worship; evangelical thought has not considered the development of religion at all, but has seized the flowers of faith without asking how they grew. Accordingly, it may be said that science must perform an *anabasis*, theology a *katabasis*, if the ground of human worship is to be secured. This may be found upon the third stage of positive religion, variously called, absolute, universal, or world religion. It is here that Christianity finds its home, and Christianity may be styled a theological religion. In itself universal, theological religion provides a means by which positive worship may become religion indeed; a relation between the immortal soul and the eternal God. Philosophy of religion finds it difficult to assign a sufficient reason why the possessor of positive religion yet regards his worship as having an absolute significance. Theological religion shows the value of historical faith, and convinces man that his religion is not only human but divine. This occurs when religion becomes universal, upon the basis of which positive worship is emancipated and invested with a new meaning.

In this manner instinctive worship is educated, and the art of spiritual life is learned. Then religion assumes a form which is not merely anthropological, but theological. On account of the connection with theology, which appears when religion reaches the final stage of its development, it is misleading to apply the theological idea elsewhere. Primitive religion is wholly anthropological; universal religion cannot exist unless it be in some wise theological. Midway between these extremes, we encounter individual national religions, belonging to self-centred peoples. But we may not speak of this kind of worship as though it were theological; and hence we can only regard it as uncritical when one like Tiele uses the term " Roman theology" to designate a form of worship distinct from Greek mythology. Similar criticism applies to doctrinal thinkers who apply the theological idea to national Judaism. Only in connection with religious conceptions which are outwardly universal and inwardly absolute may we make room for the theological principle in all its superiority. Even there it is necessary for advanced philosophical conceptions to be tempered before they can unite with the realistic ideas of universal religion.

More definite phases of the reconciliation of absolute religion and evangelical theology are found in the ideas of God and redemption; these are thoroughly theological, but they are also native to perfected religion. Indeed, it is in connection with religion that these ideas find their genuine development and most convincing presentation. Purely philosophical considerations of the world and the world's thought about itself, and colourless scientific analyses of nature, both cosmic and human, could never evince the thought of the individual's salvation in the One. Man needs redemption from the world, and he finds it in an only God. Such a movement on the part of the human spirit is produced only by a quickened religious consciousness. Ethical thought may bring out the dignity of life in the world, but it can never account for, much less satisfy, the demand for deliverance from the natural order of things. Metaphysical science may show the rational ground of phenomena and their essential reality, but it cannot provide a means by which humanity may be redeemed. Religion, working within and without, has done this in its own way.

God is such a common word, but such an uncommon idea in itself, that critical views are more than ever necessary. The creature of Theism is not always a worshipful being, and positive religion has ever shown its ability to progress without the presence of any demonstrable deity. Theism, in distinction from monotheism, is in a peculiar position; it is not an essential part of metaphysics, nor is it organic to religion. In the completion of positive worship the idea of God enters in most naturally. Religious consciousness

The Reality of Religion

dawns upon man, not for the purpose of arousing some slumbering psychic function within him, but to lead him to God. In the flowering of the religious sentiment must the connection with theology be found. Reason, which claims to have found out God, and man's relation to Him, can assign no motive in response to which man should seek the divine, and can provide no standard by which religious knowledge can be tested. Revelation, which asserts that the Deity impresses himself upon the mind of man, makes room for no function of receptivity in this indifferent soul. Before the supreme object of religion can be demonstrated, the religious tendency must be assumed. God is primarily a religious conception.

From the religious idea of God the thought of redemption follows quite closely. God is now regarded, not as an object of worship as in the beginning of religion, nor yet a Being whose law must be obeyed, as with legalistic cults, but as One who Himself is inclined toward the world which is His and which He serves. It is upon this third stage that human religion perfects itself and becomes theological. The impulse which leads the soul to affirm itself and negate the world is one which cannot find complete expression unless it be assumed that beyond the world there is One interested in this conflict, which only He can bring to a successful termination. This last moment in psychological religion, when the divine enters, contains at once the principle of redemption and the essence of theology in general. Apart from theology, anthropological religion cannot accomplish everything, but it can make a beginning, conduct the development, and bring about the climax of human life. At last it evinces the idea of mankind's redemption, and its work is done. It is here that theology begins, and at this point it may unite with religion to complete the latter's work.

The religious world-order is neither that of nature nor of spirit, but is found in humanity, which is a synthesis of the two. It is by virtue of the idea of humanity that we are able to fill out our view that religion, which is neither natural science nor rational philosophy, but occupies its own precinct in the world ; now this precinct is humanity as an ever-progressing life. Similar reasoning will justify our distinction between the character of religion and those phases of philosophy which we call logic and ethics, for when it appears that the living and developing humanity invests religion and inspires its consciousness, the taint of a possible irrationalism, or an equally possible, and more dreadful, immoralism, may be forgotten. Now it is the idea of humanity, or the totality of man, within the individual's being and about him in his history, which renders thinkable the communion of men with God, and what cannot be done by the individual, or the sum of individuals which make up the race, can be accomplished by humanity. The Son of Man is also the Son of God, and He makes possible the *communion with* God, rather than a *communication from* Him.

2. The historical form of religion presents a problem which can be solved only when we conceive of history in a sufficient fashion. Within the pale of Christianity this problem has produced its own upheaval in the days of the Enlightenment, but with this controversy removed, even to its final vestiges, we may now consider the larger question of history in the light of universal religion. In this connection it should appear that history, instead of being a burden superimposed upon free religion, is rather a means by which religion may disentangle itself from the nature and attain unto its world-aim. Ordinarily we look to revelation to explain the *source* of religion, forgetting that this is in human nature. What we should do is to regard revelation as the *conclusion* to or goal of religion, which stands in need of postulates rather than premises, which is weak not in " whence," but in its " whither." Revelation does not come to the man of nature in the form of an unrelated idea, but dawns upon the man of culture as the

The Reality of Religion

essential principle which in the history of humanity has been struggling for expression.

History can be conceived of as containing revelation only as history is made organic to the spirit of humanity. To bring about such a conception is by no means easy, yet it is no more difficult than the philosophy of history to which it belongs directly. Accordingly we are not justified in speaking of *a* revelation, much less of several kinds of divine communications, but must conceive of revelation in a generic fashion which preserves the unity of the idea at hand. There is only one history which is coincident with humanity, and there is only one revelation which is the counterpart of the religious consciousness. If we say that history did not become a problem until man became Christian, we may conclude that revelation is a question to be solved, an aid to be employed, and a form of religion which affiliates with the historical method. Revelation is a view so essential that we cannot speak of it as a casual and contingent means of imparting miscellaneous bits of intellectual truth, but must consider it as something absolute and religious.

To make history the vehicle of revelation, let us consider well what the idea of history necessarily involves. In doing this we may ignore several possible views which might be entertained, but which could not bear the burden of man's spiritual life, and seek to advance at once to something essential. History is one eternal present in which temporal and local distinctions are as natural and yet as incidental as are time and space in the real world. It is the history of humanity in which man, as individual and member of an age, participates. These elements of the constant present and universal participation tend to raise history to something like a category. Vedanta and Buddhism refrain from any historical formulation of spiritual life, and content themselves with a belief in transmigration and the doctrine of Karma, or inexorable causality. These conceptions make history, not only unnecessary, but impossible, since they bind past, present, and future together in an imperative fashion, and leave to man no participation in that absolute spiritual life which is present in the world. With Christianity the individual, in spite of his limited existence, is able to enter into relations with the World-Soul, because his personal life is filled with the meaning which accompanies the whole history of humanity.

Revelation thus depends upon the possibility of communion rather than communication, and the means of justifying this human participation in the divine life in the world is found in history. The individual alone, in his isolation, can hardly be conceived of as entering into private relations with the absolute, but when this individual appropriates the vast history of humanity about him, he is in a position to represent man to his Deity. In the same way, it may be added, the immortality of the individual in the singularity of his personal existence is almost too taxing for human faith, but the continued existence of one who, in love, has made humanity the aim of his life, is something which the reflective mind can hardly help thinking. The child of the ages is in harmony with the eternities, and he who is identified with the world of spiritual life will find that God is not far from him. In appropriating his own absolute humanity, man discovers, not only his neighbour, but his God.

Yet the most obvious service of history is that which is connected with time-succession and progress. If God cannot realize Himself in man at once, He can do so at length, because historical revelation provides time and opportunity, and presents a cumulative effort which makes possible an approximation to the Infinite. This is by means of stages, in which humanity passes from nature to man, and from humanity to divinity. Without such stages the idea of history is empty and vain; indeed history itself is secondary to the existence and action of the infinite world-life which follows the historical method, with the result of including man in its scheme of reasonable

The Reality of Religion

and moral blessedness. Mere temporality in history is as negative as mere extension in physical science, and in the case of the savage, whose mental state to-day is assumed to represent that of the original man, we see how time can pass without producing development.

To effect and to justify human and divine communion history unfolds a vast and consistent plan. First of all it provides a variety in point of view which is calculated to reveal the richness of that spiritual life which is man's means of attaining unto God. This is due to types of humanity, both in individual and race, unto whom in various ways of nature and consciousness is revealed the fullness of the Godhead bodily. The manifold quality of humanity could be shown were we to review the total plan of Oriental worship, deduced by Hegel or elaborated by some modern savant in the science of religion, just as it would be indicated by a comparison of Hebrew, Greek, and Roman, whose bloody inscriptions crowned the cross of Christ. Yet it may be as valuable to refer to one other branch of religious life in particular, and thus resume the case of Vedanta. In deriving a convincing idea of God, with whom man communes, we may point out again that Vedanta teaches man to approach the Absolute without by means of the Absolute within, and to find the deity in the act of discovering self. From such a system the Christian can learn that the communion of the soul with God is thinkable only upon the basis of an absolute spiritual life, which God invests with His being, and informs with His spirit, and in which man also participates. Man cannot pass at once to the Absolute, but his inherent humanity, the depths of which his culture and religion have begun to fathom, make it possible for him to approximate to God. In loving the seen he learns to love the unseen, in forgiving injury he feels that God may forgive him of his own sins.

Long is the way from theory to fact, and uncertain is the connection between the absolute and the actual. That which constitutes the quintessence of the problem is the idea of the positive, of which historical religion consists. Positive revelation, the peculiar product of human freedom and mysterious constraint, from without is the content of the Bible. What this book contains is no scheme of abstract thought and no play of mythology, but a succinct account of events in Israel's history, and the performance of Christ in Galilee and Judea. Such a direct conception of revelation belongs especially to the present, begun as it was in the nineteenth century. How significant a fact is it that not until this period did Christian thought produce the biography of Jesus Christ! In the same way the critical history of Israel did not appear until this larger present set in. How, then, could there have been any sense of revelation, that is, in the form of living history? But now, with the psychological and historical colouring given to Old and New Testaments, the manifestation of religion may be seen. Laying aside for a moment the question how revelation is related to religion, let it be asked, how shall we esteem the career of Israel and the behaviour of Jesus Christ? One, we may say, perhaps, was so much history; the other a certain biography; but such explanations, having to do only with the form of the Bible, are superficial. Apart from the idea of a divine manifestation, no sufficient reason can be offered for the Bible; and even if one does not see his way clear to justify the claim of a divine revelation, he can offer no more satisfactory explanation of Old and New Testaments. These works are self-evident manifestations of a religious life, and their use is confined to the service of this.

The position which the idea of revelation occupies in philosophy of religion will depend upon the manner in which the historical method is appreciated. When it is once seen how vital is history to human worship, and how valid is the conception of revelation, then it may be shown that Christianity especially is fitted for the character of a revealed religion. For itself, religion is an historical phenomenon; in Christianity the unity of history and

The Reality of Religion

religion is a singularly perfect one; for Christianity is essentially an historical world-religion. For the realization of the cardinal ideas of Christianity no method is more apt than the historical one. Eternal life, in the sense of Christ, is not future life alone, but belongs, by all the rights of spirit, to man's present existence. The mediator between temporal and eternal life, by virtue of which the transition becomes less abrupt, is the historical process. Likewise the idea of the Father's Kingdom. If, hereby, Christ showed how accessible is the nature of God, He did so by using, again, the thought of progress; the Kingdom is a development in time. Thus to emancipate the soul, and bestow upon it eternal life, to manifest the Father and establish the Kingdom were spiritual processes requiring time and inner development. Progress and spiritual achievement, which are organic to Christianity, are likewise vital to the theory of revelation.

Abruptness, however, spoils this conception. And it is here that traditional theology has had its own difficulties. It has been imagined that revelation consists in the direct communication of abstract truth; but this is alien to that which goes on in social history. There it is primarily life which rules, and not thought. But theology has not always asked, What is the nature of religion, and what method does history follow? By following these ideas the principle of revelation is found. Revelation which consists of acts, rather than thoughts, is a living thing, rather than a theoretical exercise. In the case of the New Testament, where our interest centres, is such especially the case. This religious production was not brought about by means of imagination or intellectual work, but was made up of observed results in humanity's history. When one reads the Gospels and Epistles, he sees that something has happened; in this event is the revelation to be found. When Christ, the author of these deeds, is surveyed, He can only be considered as a manifestation of God and the spiritual world-order.

The educational idea has more than once been employed to ease off the abruptness which has resulted from theology's failure to work out a philosophy of history. This appears in St. Paul, in Origen, and in Lessing. Education takes hold of the mind in its incompleteness, makes use of a gradual method, and supplies the intellect with the materials to be dealt with. Science discovers new phenomena; philosophy grasps its truth at once by following logical steps. But education, in individual and race, is a more deliberate procedure. The pedagogical analogy, however, serves only in connection with method, and does not touch the matter which is to be imparted. It gives as the idea that, although the complete principle be known to the educator, the soul to be educated must gradually approximate to this. So, likewise, in the case of revelation, where the law acts as a schoolmaster to lead us to Christ. But the more essential idea is that God, as the schoolmaster, makes use of the law as a primary method of instruction to prepare for the higher education of humanity.

Lessing's conception of revelation was expressed in his work, "The Education of the Human Race," and refers almost exclusively to the Old Testament and the career of Israel. This revelation consisted chiefly in two articles of religion: the unity of God and the immortality of the soul, which ideas, while not native to Israel, were gradually brought out in its development. Lessing may be criticized for emphasizing the element of *knowledge* of God and of immortality, as though divine education were a scholastic achievement. Since the days of Lessing the emphasis has been changed from the abstract truths of reason to the actual truths of history, indeed the whole setting of the problem assumes a different guise in an age like our own which is steeped in the historical both in matter and spirit. No longer do we consider the truths of history as though they were *contingent*, no longer do we estimate absolute truth as the peculiar property of *reason*, for our idealism has succeeded in overcoming the breach between mere sense and

The Reality of Religion

sheer understanding, just as it has risen above the conflict between isolated events and syllogistic arguments. The single case of Hegel is sufficient to show how such a problem as Lessing's can be solved and forgotten.

Above the conflict between the contingent of sense and the eternal of reason appears the idea of the religious world-order which inheres in the thought of a revelation of God in man. When it is seen that God can reveal Himself to the totality of humanity in its history, it will further appear that this living realm of spiritual life assumes the form of a *Heilsordnung*, or realm of redemption. This German term suggests the happy historical fact that German thought has never really stumbled at the difficulties of a revelation, and this is probably because its idealism ever involves something like a realm of grace, which Leibnitz placed above the realm of nature, while Hegel postulated a world of spirit which grew out of the system of immediate existence, and both of them pledged their faith in the idea of development. It is just this thought of a realm of redemption, which seems to follow from the independence of the religious precinct as well as from the characteristic nature of religious conscience, and that which justifies the existence of such a realm is the historical programme which uses humanity in order to develop its character. Above the domain of both sense and understanding is the world of humanity, which produces its historical effects in a manner superior to either physical necessity or ethical freedom. Within the realm of redemption humanity is able to effect the communion of man with God, and the revelation which is the fruitage of this union is no extra-product, but a native part of man's religious consciousness.

On the part of man revelation has the advantage of securing for him the idea of something *given* from without, but received by man in the spirit of his own humanity. It was in this spirit that Lipsius used to speak of the Christian conception of the Kingdom, as though it were both

Gabe and *Aufgabe*, a divine gift, as also a human problem. This dual conception of religion has also been expressed by Von Hartmann in the form of a consciousness of *Gnade* and *Glaube*, the grace of God and the faith of man. It is by means of such fuller conceptions that religion is saved from subjectivism, as a man may be saved from his friends. That which man fears is, not his shadow, but his God, and that which he seeks is not only the realization of the self, but the revelation of the World-Soul. No sensation, however bright, could manifest His presence, no inference, however perfect, could convince us of His existence. But the living synthetic judgments of humanity's history have a vastness which makes possible the appearance and influence of the Soul of the World itself.

PART IV

THE RELIGIOUS WORLD-ORDER

UNDER the caption of the "Reality of Religion" we discussed the phenomena of human worship in their historical significance, from the remote origin to their culmination in revelation. This inquiry has made necessary a final one, which concerns the truth of religion, or the credibility of a religious world-order, which idea has been implicit in all the foregoing, but which has thus far waited for direct expression. The considerations which are involved in this concluding phase of the subject include an examination of traditional theism, which must be adjusted to our conception of the religious precinct, as well as a contemplation of the world of humanity, in which finite and infinite may commune. Without something like an ontological point of view, the nature and life and history of religion are developed in vain, yet it is only in a consistent manner that the substantial ground of human worship may be deduced. Better is it to abandon all religious thinking and fall back upon instinct and tradition, than to erect a sentimental conception of religion upon what naive realism calls the "World-Ground."

The truth of religion, however, is an idea which need not be renounced in an age of culture and humanism; it made possible the production of Herbert's "De veritate," whence followed the development of modern religious thought. Nevertheless, it must be remembered that truth does not consist alone in the formal agreement of subject and predicate, or in the correspondence of thought and thing. We arrive at the idea of the fundamental in religion by some other means than by premising some logical idea or postulating some ethical principle. The world-harmony of æsthetics and the ideal order of rights are conceptions which prepare the way for the world-order of religion. In the formulation of this view our thought must be content with insight where system does not appear, yet it is hoped that the ontological treatment of religion will realize some of the possibilities of human faith. Having reviewed the chief argument for theism, we must see how human culture corroborates by certain affirmations the abstract idea of the Absolute; thence we can see how religion culminates in a world of humanity whose ideals make possible the unity of finite and infinite.

1. *The Religious Value of Theism*

The humanistic and historical method which has guided our examination of the religious precinct forbids that we should turn aside to the path of rationalistic theism. When it is seen that religion is a spiritual fact in the life of mankind, it can further be observed that the idea of God, instead of having waited for theistic demonstration, has already appeared in the study of religious consciousness as in the review of universal religion. It remains only to examine the idea of being in order to see how it accords with the living culture of man; to do this philosophy of religion must appropriate an idea which has habitually been employed by naturism and apply it to the realm of humanism. The idea of God which has been relegated to the world of natural forces must now be transformed to adjust itself to the world of human values. What is sought is not a concept, much less a conclusion, but a new realm which we style the religious world-order.

1. The idea of being has a certain affinity for religion, just as theology is often included among the divisions of metaphysics. To determine the relationship between the two we must subject the whole problem to the test of

The Religious World-Order

religion. The ancient, who had no religious problem, developed the general idea of substance under the term οὐσία, employed by Xenophon, dignified by Plato, and systematized by Aristotle. In discoursing upon being, the ancient elaborated the distinction between being and not-being, τὸ ὄν, τό μή ὄν, all this being done after the manner of logic and a theory of ideas. In medieval-modern times, where ancient realism, or idealism, was first adopted and then abruptly transformed, the significant term is *realiter*, as it was used by Abelard, or *realitas*, as found in the writings of Duns Scotus. While the medievalist, with his new term, continued to employ antique methods of consideration, as he affirmed *universalia sunt realia*, the modern has given the idea, reality, a new philosophic value in the form of that which is different from phenomena. The modern is psychological in his method, and thus presents the contrast between reality and appearance. There were ancient realists then, and there are modern realists now, but the term realism is exactly the reverse of what it was in classic speculation.

To understand being is a task no less, and yet no more, difficult than to evaluate life ; yet we may assume that the world does have existence and life does possess value, while we proceed to inquire wherein these consist. Genuine reality is spiritual, and the form of this consists in a world-order. The ancient conception of substance usually found expression in the form of a cosmos, while the modern, with his instinct for physical and logical law, responds to this with a conception of order in nature. No truer notion than that of a world-order is likely to be found, and the metaphysical conception which is to be the support of this fourth division is that of an ever-present and all-convincing realm of spiritual life. Logical criteria of universality and necessity, metaphysical categories of substance and causality, are but suggestions of a world-order, which invests reality with its essence while it enlightens it with its intelligence. The essence of religion, which culminates in the affirmation of the soul, the character of religion, which seeks expression in history, as also the positive in religion, which advances to the idea of revelation, all bespeak the existence of a world of religion, as the realization of the religious precinct.

The philosophy of theism, which has ever contended against irreligion, but which has never sought to relate itself to religion, is an imperfect expression of the world of religion. Where religion is rendered independent of empirical science and speculative philosophy, and where its character is distinct from logical and ethical views, there is no place for a theism which, from Descartes to Lotze, has been an argument from thinking to being, while from Butler to Martineau it sought to combine causality and conscience. Thus far in its history theism has not been put upon the basis of religion. Theists are not necessarily religionists; religionists are not always theists. To exalt the being of the Absolute is a philosophic project which often belittles the human ego, in which religion reposes, and an ontology, whose metaphysical perfection prepares the way for the Deity, is vastly different from a psychology which takes man as it finds him. What genuine religious thinking demands is a universal realm in which the supremacy of God and the destiny of man may live in eternal communion; this we call the world of religion.

To realize the essential moment of religion we need not speak slightingly of "metaphysics in theology," as Ritschl has done, but we are justified only in so far as we separate a false metaphysics from living religion. There is a truth *in* theism, although theism is not religion any more than religion is theism. The metaphysical view of the Godhead has overdone a matter falsely conceived. It has made the belief in God so logically complete that a living and growing religion has found no place in it, and among the various antitheses which beset our modern thinking, not the least harsh is that between religion and theism. To extricate ourselves from such a difficulty we must proceed from the religious point of view, whereupon we shall see that the idea of God is not to be deduced from any category, or produced by any ethical maxim, but springs spontaneously from the religious consciousness of humanity, so that philosophy of religion is not confronted with a *tabula rasa*, but with a mind quivering with religious possibilities. Those who have done the most for philosophy of religion—Kant, Hegel, Schleiermacher—have said the least about theism, while those who have laboured to demonstrate the being of God—Anselm, Descartes, Cudworth—have done the least for religion. As Kant said, " I had to destroy knowledge in order to make room for faith," so to-day one might say, " I must destroy theism in order to make room for religion." Theism is to religion what geometry is to art, what mathematics is to music, what geology is to the landscape. A demonstration of the divine existence is an *idée fixe* in our theology, because the intuitions of religious consciousness have never been consulted. Where the older theism was metaphysical the newer one is moralistic, and where causality once sat supreme as the judge of Deity, conscience now enters for a share in the claim of theistic adjustment. Such an opposition between intellectualism and voluntarism seems to open the way toward a third system which consists of the world of spirit wherein the idea of God does not propose but solves problems and answers questions which come not from, nor are directed towards, the understanding.

The affirmation of religion is the affirmation of redemption, and the impulse which leads the soul to negate the world is the same as that which inclines it toward God. Perfect pessimism turns to perfect optimism, for where the world of nature is reduced to nothing, the world of spirit is regarded as everything. Man rejects the whole world and similarly accepts God in this divine integrity, while Jesus said, " I have overcome the world," and did not fail to add, " My Father and I are one." Thus the reality of religion depends upon the reality of God, and if man begins by disclaiming nature as his world, he ends by affirming the existence of the One, in whom he lives and moves and has his being. Consciousness of the spirit within is consciousness of the same spirit without, and in the light of Deity do we see the meaning of humanity. If naturistic thinking determines man by his environment, spiritistic views must magnify man by many diameters as it relates his being to the world of spirit. Man must have some world-interpretation; shall it be of a lower or of a higher order? Shall we return with science, or advance with culture? From the conception of divine, characteristic, historical religion as we have entertained it heretofore, we must proceed to the world of humanity, revealed in the spirit of culture.

Not only the consciousness of the human spirit, which well knows how to distinguish spirit from matter, but in the deed of humanity, which affirms soul in opposition to world, does the implicit unity of spiritual life in man and God appear. It is no easy, no usual, task which, in the dawning of culture, the human soul has before it; to negate nature and affirm spirit is a world-work, worthy of a god. The magnitude of this task is well appreciated in the course of human history, wherein man has performed the one deed of time and eternity in his passage from the low to the high. Man is not only the one who looks up, but the one who strives upward, looking for redemption from on high. In the performance of this gigantic deed the idea of God arises as a necessary element in the consciousness of the human being, who has courage, if not audacity, to know. Grades of development surely come in, and the man of nature worships his fetish where the man of culture adores his Deity; yet the one supreme moment of soul-affirmation, world-negation, and communion with the Godhead, cannot remain concealed. Where man is spontaneous to impulses from within, he is also sensitive to impressions from without, and his religion deepens into redemption where man and God are one in their infinite work.

2. How does theism regard the communion of finite and infinite? Current theism ignores the rich content afforded by positive religion, and proceeds to the immanence of the World-Ground. In most quarters, where this idea is entertained, the setting which accompanies it is so naively realistic that the philosophic significance which might result from speculation is lost. Where nature in her immediacy is made the interpreter of God, the view assumed must be that of the artist, and not that of the logician, whose abstract purposes the temporal and spatial can never serve. And, for itself, what does religion seem to need? Not nature, but culture and humanity; not the world of things, but the world of persons; not the World-Ground, but the World-Order. It is from the world that man is trying to escape; why do you then put upon him the yoke of a World-Ground? To invest religion with the idea of a World-Ground is to repeat the error of the Enlightenment which made of nature a Deity and a Deity of nature.

Apart from any unfitness which the idea of World-Ground may be found to possess, it may be noted that in itself this idea is lacking in logical consistency. First, upon the conceptional side, the theory that God is so immanent in nature that the various features of physical activity may be identified with His will, is such as to run counter to our fundamental principle of reasoning: *principium identitatis*. The law of identity forbids that we should pass from nature to Deity and thus say, *deus est natura*, because the very concepts involved make it necessary for us to say God is God, while nature is nature. The judgment of immanence is rejected, not because it is a judgment, nor because it is synthetic, but because it attempts to join dissociated ideas. For the judgment, *deus est natura*, there is no sufficient reason, and in the face of so fixed a principle as that of identity one would hesitate to deify nature or to naturalize the Deity.

In addition to this logical scruple, which we manifest

against the idea of theistic immanence there is the question of experience. For the sake of experience logic may suffer some of its doubts to be overcome, as it yields to the testimony of the actual, and bows before the might of synthetic relations. Yet experience does not urge us to identify the alien realms of nature and spirit, so that he who would find the immanent action of God in the manifold forms and courses of nature must explain, and explain away, the abiding difference between our experience with the world of things without and our experience with the realm of feelings within. To perceive with the senses is not the same as to intuit with the unity of consciousness, and the principle of existence is one thing, while that of value is another. Experience is not capable of such an extension into the world of spirit, and even where the distinction between lower and higher is disregarded, the empirical testimony concerning nature affords qualities intrinsically different from those evinced by an experience of Deity, if such indeed there can be. Where the novel idea of the immanence of God in physics and ethics receives encouragement from the naive enthusiast who assumes no metaphysical or moral responsibilities it can only encounter serious obstacles at the hands of the logician who takes understanding and experience for what they are justly worth. Our own conception of the character of religion, as that which, distinct from logic and ethics, forbids us now to adopt a view which, indulging in the sentiment of "immanence," reduces religion to metaphysics and morality.

The theistic demonstration has never been able to represent the totality of religion without or its essence within, so that if religion can be atheistic, theism can be irreligious. Theism has been a tendency, and has been of such a particular nature as to have produced a theistic school, as though there could be any other. Yet it is significant that general philosophical thought has not hesitated, in certain of its particular precincts, deliberately to depart from these traditional views. And this has

The Religious World-Order

been done, not in the spirit of atheism, but rather in a sober manner, by men of sincere piety and intellectual character. Witness the examples of Grotius and of Fichte. At the expense of theism a science of rights and a science of knowledge were consistently wrought out. Convinced of the intrinsic sanction of natural rights, Grotius went on to say, though with appropriate hesitation, that the principle would be valid, even though there were no God, *non esse deum!* When, a century later, Vico corrected the error in Grotius' fundamental principle, of an anti-historical *jus naturale*, he completed his own view, by introducing the idea of God, now conceived of in a more vital manner than anything which the idea of *deus* may have meant to Grotius. It was as "an historical demonstration of Providence" that the Scienza Nuova was founded. In Fichte's philosophy of knowledge the fundamental principle of life was developed in strict independence of the theistic thought. Yet that philosophy was a spiritual one, and seemed to point to the presence of a religious world-order.

What is the significance of this? Do not our modern systems break with the theistic idea, because it does not represent the living God? Is it not remarkable that there can be a discussion of religion, its nature and the conditions of its development, without there being any consistent view of the Divine Soul? Traditional religious thought has ever been nothing but a theism; philosophy of religion has been hindered because such theism was urged speculatively, and not religiously. The natural result has been sure to follow; the current method of considering religious questions is not in the direction of, but away from, the thought of a divine life. Where we still insist upon a bald theism, confusion arises in our thought, which is pervaded by the historical element. But, just here, the monotheistic interpretation, because it is at once religious and historical, has decided advantages. At the very least, monotheism may be regarded as entering in to aid an unsteady philosophy of theism; thus the former tends to render religious thought more credible. It is natural to expect that such an overpowering sentiment as that which religion evokes should culminate in some positive creation. Where the religious sentiment is a thorough conviction it can only become universal.

It would seem, then, as though the true idea of God were the product of historical religion, although the bearing of this is not easy to realize. In conceiving of the independence of religion in man, as well as in distinguishing between the God of thought and the God of worship, no modern thinker has been of greater service than David Hume. His service, however, was that of the critic only ; just as he advanced beyond the shallow deism of his day, so his own imperfect thought must in the present be transcended. The questions which challenged Hume's attention in religion were these : the foundation which the sentiment has in reason, and its origin in human nature. In discussing the latter phase of religious inquiry, Hume's contributions were somewhat more than those of a negative criticism. He perceived at once that, in actual history, an imperfect and polytheistic form of religion was the original one. From this, monotheism was developed, and that by the following method. The train of ideas in man's mind was not a logical one, but was rather psychological. By virtue of some circumstance, one of the many gods seems to have been regarded with the most favour, as most beneficial to man's well-being. To this one prayer seems to be most effectual, and he now becomes the god of gods. Thus, by ascribing to a particular god more than ordinary praise, his worshippers elevated him to perfection, ascribing " unity and infinity, simplicity and spirituality." That such an idea of God should correspond with the cosmic theism produced by reason was, in Hume's mind, merely a matter of coincidence.

What is gained by such a notion of development in religion ? The particular result is in its value limited, but the method pursued is more than suggestive. For his

The Religious World-Order

own part Hume found in this monotheism an unstable produce, no more valuable than but rather inferior to polytheism. Yet religious thought gains by applying such a method, for it is seen that the monotheistic idea has its origin in human nature, and according to the latter's principles must it be explained. For reasons which the religious consciousness itself assigns, man believes in the unity of God. In the history of human worship this proposition has been insisted upon, as the only method of preserving the perfection of the divine idea in religion. God is an only God; any other view would consider Him, not only as another being, but as an inferior one. Perfected religion perceives that it is neither in Gerizim, nor yet at Jerusalem, that God is to be worshipped. Where worship is true God is seen to be a universal spirit. Such a conclusion on the part of the religious consciousness is not a speculative idea, but a vital concept, wrought out only after a continual struggle, within and without.

The idea of God, which has thus been brought out, is not a metaphysical one; the historical unfolding of human faith has not followed the steps of theistic demonstration. Yet religion, as such, independent as it is of metaphysics, possesses its own thought of God, which, if it be not theistic, is none the less monotheistic. As a fact, monotheism must be admitted; to account for its origin, as well as to verify its essential form, appeal must not be made to theistic reasoning. For reasons which are in no wise scholastic man believes in God. When the aroused religious consciousness sees how alien is the world to man's personal needs, appeal is made to that which is more than human. The earthly condition is felt to be unsatisfactory; the present life appears too limited and insecure; upon humanity there rests a burden which, by earthly means, cannot be removed. Stung by the contrast between inner need and the vacuity of the outer condition of things, man breaks with the world, and in some way looks to that which is divine. Where reason may enter in, it is not

Q

through speculative considerations, but rather because the wish is father to the thought. But, in the " Absolute " of theism we do not care to believe.

But something more than the mere fact is to be taken into consideration. It must further be assumed that the idea of God is necessary to the life of religion. When it is said that religion can exist without the idea of God, it can only be said that such faith is godless and in vain. Unless it culminate in the divine principle, the religious life can only end in despair. In this way it becomes necessary to construct some such system of thought, as that which theistic natural religion has ever aimed to produce. But this kind of religious thinking must not be pursued in a traditional way, as though religion and its divine object lived solely for the sake of filling out man's metaphysical conceptions. Has it not been shown again and again that theism, with its concern for things rather than for spirits, is unequal to the demands of the religious life in humanity ? Creating the proper atmosphere, religion corrects this tendency and turns our attention from nature to the soul. It desires to find God, that it may content the demands of man's spiritual nature.

Over monotheism theism has some advantages ; it has not failed, by explanation and argument, to justify itself. The monotheistic idea has thus far been only an obscure one. Where thought has taken hold of it, it has been chiefly in the phenomenological science of religion, where the idea of God is a psychological rather than a philosophical one. As a reality the belief in one Being as an only God has been produced at the cost of a spiritual struggle far beyond anything, in the way of actual gain, that might come from sheer speculation. Humanity has at last learned to revere God as alone divine ; He is no longer the abstract *deus*, but is a living God, upon whom man may believe. Here a study of the divine idea may well begin ; not with a bit of curiosity about the world, but with a mighty concern for human life. This is the cardinal motive. That the world has had a first cause is not so much an inspiration as that man's life has a divine destiny.

Heedless of the demands of religion, the theistic department of metaphysics has continued adding proof to proof. Has this departure made possible any connection with that belief in God which has been the destiny of historical religion to produce ? The advocate of theism has of late observed that actual religion, with its idea of God, may in some way claim his attention, but, as in the case of a recent writer, has dismissed the testimony of history by styling it the "archæology of theism"! Yet to-day, where historical science and philosophy is so pre-eminently in advance of metaphysics, it may be well to show more deference to the archæology of theism ; without it religious thinking is altogether vanity. When the customary proofs of the divine existence are reviewed the religious *motif* may perhaps appear, and thus may be made possible an easy transition from thought to life, from theism to religion. In examining them our purpose is not to inquire into their validity for thought, but their value for the religious life. In the heart of man religion lives and develops ; if it can make use of these "proofs," well and good ; but if not the loss is on the side of philosophy, not on that of worship.

3. Theistic demonstrations seem to have sprung from the practical side of human life, as well as from the speculative instinct in human thought. They relate to life and to the world ; life in the most general and natural usage of that term, the world as given to the senses. But these teleological and moral arguments for the divine existence are necessarily limited, depending upon some more fundamental determination, to which, however, they add vividness and character. It is to the ontological and cosmological arguments that we must turn, to find a complete system of demonstration. Of the two, the former seems most in harmony with monotheistic faith.

The cosmological argument is strangely concerned for

the world, from which latter the religious consciousness invariably turns away. In the natural order of things, the soul can find no profit. That culmination of divine and human activity, which is called the Kingdom of God, is " not of this world " ; the founder of this Kingdom felt that He had " overcome the world." Thus independence of the world, deliverance from the world, victory over the world, are cardinal ideas in universal religion. In clearly defined opposition to the natural order does the religious consciousness move. Human destiny is conceived of as directed from nature, as given in experience and speculation, to something higher. The contingency of the world is no real problem for philosophy of religion ; here the all-absorbing question is redemption from the world. How, then, shall we reconcile this religious aspiration for the supernatural and divine with the speculative concern for the natural and cosmic?

Where the religious idea is made supreme the ontological argument would seem to represent a more perfect form of transition from theism to the religious world-order. In the case of Anselm, as also with Descartes, such a method of argument was conceived of in the spirit of religion, and in connection with personal Christian life. This is seen in the respective points of departure of the two systems. Anselm's motto, *credo ut intelligam*, was parallel to the sense of Descartes' method, which might have been expressed by the words, *dubito ut intelligam*. In either case the faith, here affirmed and there at first denied, is made the source of speculation ; as a result, appeal is made to a definitely religious principle. In the case of the Schoolman from Canterbury this is obvious ; with Descartes it was none the less direct and forcible. Initiating a searching scepticism, which climaxed in the denial of all knowledge save an original " cogito," Descartes passed at once to the idea of God as the essential correlate of human thought. In so doing he laid more emphasis upon the humanistic and psychological elements in the process than on the

The Religious World-Order

metaphysical. For this reason it is possible to regard the method as in some sense a religious one; although the general method of both Anselm and Descartes was intellectualistic, the idea of spirit did not fail to make itself manifest. At the same time the religious consciousness, which had turned away from the world, now came in contact with essential truth, and it was seen that religion was possessed, not only of value, but of validity.

The medieval formulation of the ontological argument had the effect of establishing realism, yet in addition to this scholastic tendency there accrues the general result of the spiritual as a universal order. On the side of the modern treatment of the problem Cartesianism was calculated to show that man, in his inner consciousness, participates in the one spiritual life whereby communion with God becomes possible. What is needed to-day is not a rehabilitation of the ontological argument, but a realization that there is an ontological or ontosophical order of spiritual life which makes religion possible in human experience and supremely valuable in human life. The humanism of Descartes surpassed the scholasticism of Anselm, and now spiritualism must take a third step and seek God in the religious world-order.

The way from theism to religion is thus indicated by the ontological argument whose religious value cannot be denied. As to the several forms of demonstration, teleology is necessarily limited to perceptible nature, cosmology cannot pass beyond the world of things, but ontology, with all its intellectualistic form, involves a conception of being which is more than theistic. Whatever may be said of the success of these demonstrations, it is reasonable to assume that the argument from being is the only one which can appeal to spiritual religion, and the ontological demonstration has the value of indicating how philosophy may pass from the highest in thinking to the highest in life. That which is here involved is not the faculty of reasoning, but the totality of the human spirit which embraces both the living and reflective forms of man's being. Accordingly, the idea of God is not as demonstrable to the understanding as it is acceptable to the spirit of man, and where theological calculation may be baffled, religious consciousness proceeds undismayed.

It is the religious order which is the unity of religion and theism, and just as Christianity speaks of God in immediate connection with the Kingdom, so the religious consciousness finds sufficient consolation only when it invests its object with universal proportions. In all this the truth of the personality of the Absolute may be maintained, when it is seen that even the human soul cannot confine its being to narrow particular limits, but must construe its life as universal, and conduct its course as integral. Man belongs to an order which is none other than that of Absolute Life, or God. If the more familiar ideas of the Deity seem to be masked by this idea of the religious world, it must be remembered that traditional theism has been so zealous to demonstrate Deity that it has failed to redeem man from his human distress; so that anything unhappy in the utterance of independent religion is really due to a contrast, not with living belief in God, but with a rationalistic theology. We need not refer to the absence of the idea of God in Taoism, much less to the antipathy toward it expressed by Buddhism, to observe that a universal religion is not necessarily theistic, and in the all-important case of Christianity it may be assumed that if the idea of God be the same as the theistic conclusion, it is due to coincidence rather than to calculation.

Theism, which is thoroughly intellectualistic, must not be supplanted by a lower naturalism, but by a higher spiritualism. The essence of this is found in that world of spirit which religion itself has created, and the highest truth concerning man or God is expressed in the form of an order of being, instead of in an isolated thing. Egoism and subjectivism in man are intolerable and undefensible;

The Religious World-Order

in God they are unthinkable. Personality is an idea so rich in its significance that we cannot degrade it to the plane of mere ipseism, but must elevate it to the realm of what Eucken has called the "Personalwelt," and which he further regards as the essence of Christianity. Such a conception was not wanting in expression in the earliest forms of Christian thinking, as we find from a glance at the neo-Platonic idealization of Christian values under the pen of Plotinus. Here appears in reverential fashion the idea of that which is "beyond being" and "beyond thought," under the guise of which the religious principle of spirit enters in to surmount and out-top reason, as reason itself ascends beyond sense. Toward this realm the ontosophical principle simply points, while of it theism is but the dim outline.

2. *The Affirmation of Absolute Life*

It is not something less than theism which religion demands, but something more. When we remember that the intrinsic character of religion makes it necessary for our thought to abstain from logical and ethical formulations of human faith, we can realize that the foundations of such belief cannot rest upon metaphysical and moralistic proofs. The living method, which ever keeps in the shadow of human history, can only regard theistic demonstrations as eccentric methods of realizing the religious world-order. Independent in its essence, complete in its character, and positive in its form, religion need not resort to inference when it seeks to postulate its ultimate ground; and in the real presence of Absolute Life faith forgets the arguments drawn from the rationale of natural forces or the morale of human motives. The ontological argument, however, does contain a nucleus of truth, whereby we are encouraged to search for evidence of the unity of the world, not in mere abstract thinking, but also in the manifold forms of spiritual life. Ontology, which does assume a very enviable position in modern thought, is almost as valuable to positive religion as to speculative theism, and our loyalty to the older form of religious thinking need not be doubted when it is observed how we seek to exalt the valuable idea of being-for-self. Logic and æsthetics, ethics and rights, contain implications which cannot be fathomed unless our thought assumes an ontological form. The pursuit of this idea in its fourfold form will evince certain evidence of an Absolute Life in the universe.

1. Logic demands a principle both formal and real, in whose light it may reduce the law of identity to fundamental validity. The *principium identitatis* thus realizes itself when it assumes a constructive form, and only as it is invested with ontological significance may it inform man of its own inherent certainty. To be assured of the sufficiency of this principle we find it necessary to return to the consciousness of self, so that the thinker is able to declare " A is A " only as he can say " I am I." Vedanta with its belief in the Self, Socrates with his γνῶθι σεαυτόν, Descartes with his *cogito, ergo sum*, point to the common path travelled by sound thinking and exalted living; and all genuine metaphysics finds the self-evident to consist in the self-conscious. Nominalism, with its concern for the individual, and realism, which reposed in the idea that only the universal can be permanent, prepared the way for a living conceptualism, which turned from the outer world of phenomena and noumena to the inner realm of spiritual life, and Abelard, who gives us the significant word *realiter*, shows how humanistic our thought must be in order to have consistency.

Thought possesses real, and not only formal significance, but this real quality need not be considered to come from metaphysics alone, but also from the realm of spiritual life. Not only the canon of logic, but the impulse toward culture, should be understood under the head of knowledge, and the intellectual act which expresses the Soul's being springs from the deepest source of Absolute Life. With Plato it is the " eros " and " mania " of the mind ; with Aristotle it is the " energy of contemplation." Kant calls it *Interesse*, while Schopenhauer describes it as " knowledge of the will-to-live." Thought is both an act and attitude, and neither can be understood until it is interpreted in the light of the One Life which is everywhere self-active. While Herbert of Cherbury was at once dogmatic and naive in discussing religion under the head *de veritate*, he does not fail to suggest that the appetite for truth is an *instinctus naturalis*, which at heart is the essence of religion. The pursuit of fundamental truth, like the principle of ultimate thought, is itself religious.

2. Upon the side of æsthetical considerations the same yearning for ultimate reality appears ; art does not serve religion out of mere sympathy, but works with it because both seek the One who is the life and beauty of the world. Beauty contains the universal in the serene form of contemplation, and it is because of its ability to surmount the common conflicts of human life that it makes possible the communion of man with God. Art creates, not in mere imitation of nature, but after the manifest spirit of that process which is apparent in the world. Those who speculate upon the mystery of art return with the message of infinity and unity. Plato speaks of the " sea of beauty," while Plotinus follows æsthetics on to the " supernal realm " beyond both thought and being. Bruno pursues the beautiful till it leads him to the one life of the world, and Shaftesbury traces the æsthetical into the realm of world-harmony. Schelling finds in art the means by which the human spirit transcends both morality and metaphysics, while Schopenhauer sees in the intuition of beauty a form of pure contemplation, through which the pure subject surveys the world in its entirety.

The obvious difference between religion and culture need not discourage attempts to find in the latter something of permanent significance. Both depend upon the supersensible which is internal and ultimate in human existence, but culture seeks the mere psychological *idéal*, which rises superior to sense, while religion advances to the ethical *idéal*, whose pursuit is imperative. But, like logic, culture with its æsthetic attitude implies some kind of participation in the spiritual world-order.

Culture involves the totality of the universe which it expresses in a convincing fashion. All culture is fundamental, and cannot be perfected apart from belief in the destiny of man and the existence of God. Where common experience impresses upon man his actual situation in the world, culture awakens within him the thought that his essential being is not purely natural, but is possessed of humanity. To obey the voice of culture, and with the spontaneity of consciousness create works which are of no practical utility and no phenomenal validity, is a task which can hardly be accomplished by an individual or a race which is not already permeated with the idea of spiritual life. " He who works for sweetness and light works to make reason and the will of God prevail." The despair of culture, which Schiller bitterly expresses by saying, *"Das Wissen ist der Tod,"* is religious despair to be cured only by faith in the humanity of man and the reality of God. Ethics cannot permit, much less can it forbid a culture which in the end is an affair of faith and religion.

The æsthetic attitude, which precedes the creation of the artistic, and which may be assumed by him who is wanting in talent for æsthetic work, cannot conceal the gleams of the Infinite which constantly make their shining presence felt. If religion in its superstitious moments has sought the presence of divine power in the witch or possessed person, appeal may be made to the exalted, and ecstatic moments of consciousness experienced by sensitive souls who perceive both beauty and significance before them. Beautiful scenes will react upon beautiful spirits in a manner which they alone understand, and those who cannot participate in their hallowed feelings may yet recognize the influx of the Absolute into the recipient forms. Prophets were ofttimes recognized by their frenzy, and he who perceives any substantial trace of the Absolute is likely to display emotions which are extraordinary.

The ecstatic moment, implicit in the perception of the spiritual realm, reveals the power which humanity possesses to sever temporary connection with the world of time and space; it can be found in the significant word as well as in the beautiful deed, and it invests æsthetic criticism as well as artistic creation. In the ecstatic mood described by Plotinus, philosopher, lover, and musician, fleeing from sense and dissonance, ascend on high to the supernal realm which lies beyond both reason and reality. He who is able to intuit the vastness of nature and the elegance of art, is unable to withstand the sense of awe which surges in upon his perceiving mind. Newton becomes ecstatic as he sees the majesty of physical law, while Winckelmann's eyes are cast down in reverence when he first beholds the art of antiquity. Schopenhauer's gloomy soul is stirred to intellectual joy as he reads the Upanishads, in which he finds solace in life and consolation in death. Wagner's description of Beethoven's musical mood in composing his symphonies bears the same weight of evidence for the retreat of ordinary life before the presence of the Infinite. In the spirit of self-contemplation this master of gloom exercises the power of clairvoyance which made the profoundest world-dream his own. " A glance has shown him the inner life of the world; he awakens and now strikes the strings for a dance, in such a way as the world has never yet heard. It is the dance of the world itself; wild delight, the lamentation of anguish, ecstasy of love, highest rapture, rage, voluptuousness, and sorrow; when, suddenly, lightnings quiver, the angry tempest growls, and high above all, the mighty player, who exercises, and forces, and proudly and securely conducts everything from the whirlwind to the whirlpool, to the abyss—he smiles at himself, for the incantation was to him, after all, only a play. Night beckons to him. His day is finished."

In a manner more intimate and human does this same ecstatic possibility appear, and thus is found a new meaning for the expression, *pectus facit theologum.* The immortal Veda, which aspired to guide man to the Infinite of pure contemplation, did not fail to add the promise that he who thus found the Self should also attain to the " world of perfumes " and the " world of women." In such a pleasing fashion does the ineffable One, described by Plotinus make itself apparent, not only to the philosopher in search of unity, but also to the lover who is agile in the pursuit of beauty. In the romance of Abelard and Eloise was found a fine mingling of humanity and divinity, and the glorious union of these ardent souls was effected by their common participation in the Infinite Godhead. How significant are the sonnets of Petrarch ! His " Contemptus mundi " implies a hatred of life, but his verses breathe forth the love of Laura. He makes his penance for his sin consist of the praise of her beauty, and he sinks into an abyss which her absence creates ; her gentleness has made him great. Dante's sentimental salvation at the benign hands of Beatrice is the central theme in a grim work called "Divina Commedia," the divine quality of which consists in its humanity. The drama of " Faust " reveals the same mingling of love and faith, only here the influence of Marguerite is more active than anything accorded to the sweet will of Laura or Beatrice. The amorous atmosphere of " Martha's Garden " does not stifle religious inquiry, and, to the catechizing of his adored one, Faust replies with questions of his own.

> Misshor' mich nicht, du holdes Angesicht !
> Wer darf ihn nennen ?
> Und wer bekennen :
> Ich glaub' ihn ?
> Der Allumfasser,
> Der Allerhalter,
> Fasst und erhalt er nicht
> Dich, mich, sich selbst ?

The Religious World-Order

Marguerite, who in priestly fashion hears this confession of faith, finally exercises the function of salvation and stretches out her hand to save Faust, while the *Chorus Mysticus*, with its theme of womanhood eternal, echoes the concluding words of the whole work :

> Alles Vergangliche
> Ist nur ein Gleichness
> Das Unzulangliche,
> Hier wird's Ereigniss ;
> Das Unbeschreibliche,
> Hier ist's gethan
> Das ewig Weibliche
> Zieht uns hinan.

In the same spirit do we follow the romantic irony of Friedrich Schlegel in the letters of Julius to Lucinde, wherein the base and noble are strangely united. For them, their love is the eternal union of their spirits, not only for this or that world, but rather for the infinite and nameless universe, as well as for their entire life and being. In this erotic consciousness, every thought stands out as vividly as a living personality, and in the extraordinary moment of unwonted clearness, these living ideas mingle into one vast intuition, which unites all elements of time and reduces life to a single thought or feeling. As blood of one plant and leaves of a single flower, both souls are seen as one common spirit, and their union of life which they had looked forward to in hope appears to have been history. " Like an oriental sage," says the lover, " I was sunk in holy brooding upon and calm intuition of the one substance, especially thine and mine." Such was the spirit of Schlegel, but even a Schleiermacher found the essence of religion in the midst of romantic speculations. What shall be done with these warm phantasies ? Shall we relegate them to the memories of Eden's garden, or simply style them bits of " amoristic superstition " ? Religion is human and lays hold on man as he is in nature, so that in the early stages of faith, as well as in the survival of these primeval traits, the beautiful may have been confused with the holy, just as yearning may, at times, have clung too longingly to the life of sense. But true art and genuine ecstasy, like profound thinking, are not foreign to a faith which seeks both grace and truth.

God is not merely an idea but a pulsating reality, in whose presence our human faculties cannot remain dormant. Religion arises in keeping with such an ever-living fact of human consciousness, whose warmth and richness have been overlooked by intellectualism. Art, which itself reveals the extra-sensitivity and over-spontaneity of the soul, is not alien to that central act of self-affirmation which makes religion what it is. Culture also exhibits that striving of humanity with nature, which in religion is the conflict of the animal individual with the spiritual self. Every genuine effort of the soul is religious. Man has ever sought to abandon his terrestrial condition; for his art, his religion, and his love cannot rest content with the present objects of time and space. Action now becomes a total deed of the soul in its desire for self-realization. Yet the artistic alone cannot reveal man's affirmation of the Absolute Life.

3. From the more ethical point of view, the same line of reasoning may be carried out, and just as the striking moods of the mind disclose the presence of an Absolute all-surrounding, so the ideal deeds and deep moments of remorse of mankind reveal roots which descend as deep as the final reality. This appears in the conduct of life, viewed from the standpoint of ethics, rights and religion. At this point, ethical imperatives are valuable and influential only as they indicate the union of ideal with reality. Thus arises the metaphysics of morality, which was whole-souled in Plato, honest in Aquinas and still confessed in the halting and hypocritical forms of " absolute morality " with Spencer, and the " social organism " of Stephen. When ethical philosophy is understood, it is seen to be, not merely critical, but constructive, whereby

it indicates, not only what should be, but what is in reality. It may be urged that ethical theory, as we know it through its history, does not warrant our departing from the purely normative function for the sake of that which is more realistic, and where such theory consists of an antique " Good " accompanied by a fixed happiness, or a modern " Duty," which glances off into pleasure and utility, such an objection may obtain ; yet let the ethical be interpreted in terms of " Value," and the constructive feature of the moral cannot fail to appear in the form of a world of values. In the light of this conception, we may instance the presence of the ethical as evidence for the existence of an Absolute Life which uses morality as one of its chief tendencies.

Not only the thought of the ethical is able to suggest in convincing fashion the existence of a spiritual order, but the consciousness of him who awakens to his position in that realm is even more perfectly fraught with high intelligence. The most striking instance of the vast ethical relation which man sustains to the universe appears in the phenomenon of remorse. Herein we discover an ethico-psychological fact which bears the impress of Absolute Life. Let us view the rare quality of this sentiment and then relate it to its proper position in the spiritual world-order. Remorse arises as an " infinite compunction " and cannot be identified with any sense of mere mistake, however humiliating and painful the latter may appear to be. The domineering personality of Napoleon was expressed in characteristic fashion when, called upon to pass judgment upon some case of moral wrong-doing, he exclaimed, " It was worse than a crime ; it was a blunder ! " To see how intense and far-reaching may be the consciousness of fatal error, one has only to review that famous stanza in Tasso, where the genius of the poet is finely consecrated to the description of Tancred's agony when, by mistake, he kills his beloved in the form of the masked Clorinda.

> Vex'd by just Furies, anguish, grief, and care,
> A wand'ring maniac must I live—to run,
> Shrieking, from phantoms with which sleep shall scare
> My soul, when Night her orgies has begun ;
> To hold in horror and in hate the Sun,
> That did my fatal error show ; to eye
> Myself with fear, and strive myself to shun :—
> Evermore flying, evermore to fly,
> While hell's pursuing fiends are ever howling nigh !

It was this single stanza which stood out so vividly in the mind of Rousseau that he declared the whole poem, which was so symmetrical that it could suffer the loss of no verse, or line, or word, without suffering complete ruin, could easily dispense with the one in question, because it was so totally unique and unrelated that it could be applied prophetically to the misfortunes of the rhapsodist himself. Yet genuine remorse sinks deeper than the mood thus celebrated by Tasso's verse and Rousseau's criticism.

What is the cause of such infinite compunction ? Evolutionary doctrine has rendered only a superficial estimate of this emotion. Darwin stands midway between Leslie Stephen, who carried out his suggestions, and Schopenhauer, who anticipates the whole problem of the evolution of conscience. Stephen regards conscience not as an isolated faculty expressing some mysterious view of man's conduct, but as the complete judgment of the whole person in his social relation. Having related man to something outside of him, Stephen calls conscience a sense of shame, which itself is due to a perception that the individual is out of harmony with his social environment.

To trace the view back to Darwin, we may note that with the author of the "Descent of Man" conscience is not simple, but compound, since it is made up of a combination of sociability and reflection, as it arises in a dramatic fashion when reason asks the meaning of the wounds which the social nature suffers at the hands of self-love. Fully to comprehend the value of Darwin's theory, we must read into it some well-known principles of psychology. Man, who is acted upon by both egoistic and social feelings, observes that the one is a passion marked by intensity, the other is a sentiment characterized by duration. The furious onslaught of egoistic passion, in the case of anger, is such as to overcome within the individual his native social sense. Yet the altruistic sentiment, while weak, is enduring just as the instinct of self-love is necessarily brief. When anger is expressed it is likewise voided, and the wounded social nature, which in its mildness has been overcome, now reappears above the threshold to offer strange contrast to the violence of the original passion. The intensity of passion is its weakness, and anger itself subsides before its expression passes off, as the tide begins to ebb along the banks of the river before the flood in midstream has ceased. Nature has so secured man in his social capacity that even the violence of egoistic passion fails before sociability. Such is the point in Darwin's valuable theory, and so long as we consider him as a psychologist who sought to explain emotion and its expression, we do neither him nor conscience any harm.

Yet a deeper view is necessary in order to comprehend conscience as also to receive the benefit of its ontological suggestion. Before Darwin's science came Schopenhauer's speculations. As we have added to the former by means of psychological discrimination, we may subtract from the latter by eliminating the unnecessary orientalism. Schopenhauer's point of departure is the individual in his philosophic capacity as *principium individuationis*. In itself, the world is one will to live; in appearance, there are many such individual wills, which in phenomenal fashion are separated from one another by the veil of illusion. The remorse of conscience rends this veil in twain and man's narrow egoism stands out in strident contrast to the whole of the world; thus the individual in bitterness realizes that it is the one will in all creatures now turning its weapons against itself. " The bad man sees that he himself is this whole will; that, consequently, he is not only the inflicter of pain, but the endurer of it, from whose suffering he is only separated and exempted by an illusive dream." We need not affirm or deny the validity of Schopenhauer's voluntarism to see that a profound truth is contained in these words. Deeper than the sense of shame, or the survival of the social instinct, is this invincible affirmation of the will-to-live which protects itself from destruction by turning its entire force to the individual who opposes it. Remorse of conscience thus affords most penetrating insight into the ever living and ever active Absolute life behind phenomena. Conscience then becomes a knowledge with (συνείδησις) the Absolute, for good or bad, while compunction has its source in the awful contrast between the vicious egotism of the individual and the ineffable sublimity of the One.

4. Such a profound apprehension of the depths of remorse leads to an idea which carries us ever into the constructive and real domain of rights, where we discover the idea of eternal justice. Grotius' enthusiasm for the rational *jus naturale* led him to declare that the same would be valid *non esse deum*, yet more consistent and less enthusiastic reflection will lead one to see that at last justice is eternal because God is an ever-living principle. *Dieu et mon droit* is an expression which unites ultimate humanity with essential divinity; man believes in the superhuman when his rights are threatened. To believe in the *jus humanum* is to believe also in eternal justice, and to believe eternal justice one must descend to the ontological construction of the universe. No consideration based upon experience can convince the studious observer that vice will end in misery while virtue will be crowned with its deserved recognition, yet no righteous man can live without such a belief. Man's genuine life is not lived among phenomena, but among essentia, wherein is found the idea of universal justice. Here it is that we may, perhaps, follow Schopenhauer in his application of the Vedantist, " *tat tvam asi*—that art thou," which suggests, nay more than suggests, that such is the unity of the real world that to do wrong is to suffer wrong, while to follow virtue is to attain to happiness.

The bad man finally discovers that the difference between him who inflicts suffering and the one who bears it is valid only in the world of appearance, and in the excitement of egoistic passion he is like a beast which "buries its teeth in its own flesh, not knowing that it is injuring itself."

The Christian religion has secured man from moral doubt, and consequent despair which would follow upon noting the apparent vanity of righteousness, by inculcating belief in the Kingdom of God. In the mind of Christ, this Kingdom consisted of a spiritual order so fundamental as to represent divine design and human destiny, so practical as to reveal the presence of eternal justice implicit in the manifold of human existence. It was this which led Christ to transcend the political and forensic, and to proclaim a Kingdom not of this world, and a life eternal marked by the absence of both lawlessness and legislation. It was in this spirit that he revealed God as the Father of human spirits, and the Judge of all men.

That which naturally follows from the principle of eternal justice is the maxim of non-resentment and love of enemies. To assure ourselves of the presence and power of these principles, we must pass from rights to religion, just as we proceeded from ethics to rights. All religious ideals are metaphysical; holiness is impossible apart from the belief in a God who is holy; renunciation is empty where the subject does not fall back upon some eternal principle in which he trusts; the love of enemies arises from a motive which is supernatural; while the essence of vicarious suffering involves the unity of mankind as well as the eternal presence of God. Indeed the whole range of religion involves the ontosophical, and it is on this account that, having observed its essence, character, and world range, we now pursue the thought of its ultimate nature. In this particular connection, where we glance at the logico-æsthetical evidence for an Absolute Life, and seek the same principle in ethics and rights, we turn to religion, not in general, which is our theme throughout this whole work, but refer only to two salient features of faith which seem to be particularly rich in ontologic suggestion. These features are, the ideal of non-resentment and the theory of vicarious suffering.

The maxim of non-resentment is not wholly new to the essay which is here nearing completion, for we made use of it as a test in deciding which forms of ethnic religion were to be deemed universal. It was because Taoism, Buddhism, and Christianity made theoretical acknowledgment and practical use of the principle of non-resentment that we felt justified in styling them spiritual and cosmic. What is involved in this postulate of non-resentment? First of all, it may be assumed that the principle is constructive, and not merely normative, because otherwise we cannot understand the extraordinary attitude of the religious subject who is led to forego his native resentment. He who follows non-resentment as a life-ideal has measured the meaning of human life with its *jus humanum* and has found something more real and more valuable in the principle of eternal, divine justice. In addition to this consciousness of something above nature and beyond man, there is the practical attitude of life which only adds to the total argument. To follow non-resentment is to believe in eternal justice, and to believe in eternal justice is to believe in God, although not necessarily the empty, characterless Deity of theism. He who thus loves his enemies does something more than reveal nobility of human character; he becomes as an actor who plays his part in a life-drama; he is no longer a person, for he has identified himself with the Absolute Life of which he is the prime evidence. Nature can give evidence of nothing beyond itself, and so far as man is merely natural, he is of no value in the universe, but when man transcends nature and becomes the spiritual super-man, he evinces the existence of the spiritual world-order. In the vicissitudes of nature and the changes in human history, the real is found in the permanent—ἀγάπη

The Religious World-Order

μένει, and it is not in nature, but in the Godhead that we live and move and have our being.

What is the ground of resentment, *lex talionis*? It is the ego in his isolated capacity as natural being. What, then, is the basis of non-resentment? It is the person, who perceives his proper position in the spiritual world-order. Such an attitude is convincing, and St. Francis with his holy love is more of an argument for God than Anselm with his ontological proof. He who deliberately abandons the principles of *jus naturale* and native resentment, not only affirms his belief in an order of things not of the empirical world, but actually transposes himself to such a realm, whose reality can no longer be doubted. Logicians may seek to demonstrate God, seers may indicate traces of His shining presence in the world, but saints who are with Him reveal his Being directly. It is this exalted form of religious life manifest in those who repose in eternal justice and refrain from retaliation which constitutes the real ethical proof of theism.

Just as the principle of remorse is explained as the influx of the Infinite into the mal-adjusted individual's consciousness, and just as non-resentment becomes possible only upon the conviction of eternal justice, so the problem of evil is now seen to involve that peculiar relation of individual to individual which ultimately consists in their common participation in the one Absolute Life. Here we find another trace of the Infinite which is as ineradicable as the intellectual interest which argues from creation, design, and the like. When general ills appear and stifle human faith in all its innocence, the problem concerning the origin and ground of human suffering becomes a spiritual predicament indeed; but when, in addition to this, the particular ill falls upon the head of the righteous, while the evil-doer seems to escape, the problem becomes a burning question which produces the worst form of mental danger conceivable, namely: moral doubt. Purely speculative scepticism, which may lead even to vehement denial concerning the validity of our most essential beliefs, is nothing in comparison with that form of moral poisoning which declares that righteousness is in vain, while sin marks the path of success and honour. Among the legalistic writers of the Old Testament, there prevailed a positive belief in an eternal justice, active and apparent in the affairs of individuals and nations, yet there were not wanting instances, like the drama of Job and the seventy-third psalm, where the incompleteness of such an empirical programme was painfully propounded, although the only solution suggested by these wisdom writers was that which is contained in the idea that finally justice will be done to help the righteous to harm the evil-doer.

Among the prophets, however, an extra and almost metaphysical element is added, when it is pointed out that such inexplicable suffering has a vicarious value, and thus understood, the innocent who were said to suffer *instead* of the guilty are now declared to suffer *for* the guilty. He whose acquaintanceship with grief won for Him the title of " Man of Sorrows " bore this suffering in a significant fashion, so that the beholder could see the purposive character of His pain. It is in the isolated case of a world-person like the Man of Nazareth that the quality and meaning of sorrow make their most direct appeal. It was as though the whole creation were expressing its grief with groanings which could not be uttered, and in this world-sorrow all individual cases of suffering are merged. Thus that which is inexplicable upon the basis of the individual and his own experience becomes clear in the light of an Absolute Life, which so unites humanity that it is possible for one to suffer for another, or for one in particular to suffer for the whole world, as is the case in the career of Christ. Man foregoes his native resentment just as he suffers his remorse of conscience because of his relation to the totality of spiritual life, and in the same way he suffers for another who is not unlike himself and who, participative in the one life of the world, is not unrelated to him.

Yet not only these rarer moments in human consciousness, which are appreciated only by selected souls living lives of isolation, but in the general life of humanity which reveals only the more obvious forms of spiritual perception, does this demand for fundamentals reappear. Here it is revealed in the common feeling of need, possessed by the man who neither strives nor cries. This is a feature of consciousness which involves no gifted artistic activity or trained speculative power, but depends wholly upon the individual's ability to suffer. What man commonly calls need is a superficial feeling which lightly screens from him the possibility of profound feeling. Hunger and privation suffered by reason of circumstances, or produced ascetically by one who aims at self-discipline, are not as significant as the inevitable withdrawal of ideal needs; when these reveal abysses in the soul of man, he is prepared to hear deep calling unto deep, and from the depths he himself puts forth his voice to declare, " Now I know that no one being in the universe is either willing or able to help another." Human need in its purely human aspect points out the fact that it is to the Infinite he must make his appeal.

From these general considerations what seems to follow? We have seen how the profundity of human thought and the ecstasy of human feeling suggest the presence of an Absolute Life, which constitutes the ground of intellectual perception. In the same way a supreme act of nature as well as the remorse of conscience have no other explanation than that which we find in the thought of the inflowing Infinite. Likewise belief in eternal justice and the practice of non-resentment unite with the doctrine of vicarious suffering to evince the inevitable presence of something more than man. Consciousness of finitude and the pain which follows therefrom seem to force the conclusion that humanity cannot be understood without everywhere postulating the presence of one Eternal Life.

3. *The World of Humanity*

Thus far, our contemplation of the religious world-order has resulted in evincing certain gleams of intelligence and fragments of thought incident upon those occasional manifestations of Absolute Life which occur in exalted thinking and living. Insight has thus been obtained, but system is still lacking, and it is with the hope of reducing these scattered elements to a scheme of philosophic thinking that we take up the problem of humanity. In itself, this is a question the meaning and merit of which have only begun to dawn upon us, and the solution of the humanity-problem seems to be impossible apart from an ontological principle. Man must be invested with world-significance, and our thought must advance beyond the metaphysics of nature to the metaphysics of humanity. Since we have already found it possible to construct the character of religion without having recourse to the intellectualism ordinarily expressed in logic and ethics, we need not hesitate to pursue the system of humanism which has been implied throughout this entire consideration of the religious precinct. Certain it is that religion cannot be contained in nature, and when man himself endeavours to provide a realm for his faith, the substance of things hoped for, he must abandon the ego, shun the mere aggregate, and postulate the world of humanity. Genius in the individual out-tops mankind in general, because it reveals new qualities in the soul, and the genius of humanity lifts man out of time and place.

1. When one considers the history of the problem, he discovers that the idea of man's unitary nature is not primitive, but secondary, consisting of a most advanced philosophy. In the religious consciousness, the notion of humanity does not appear until history has brought to light the allied ideas of nature and Deity, and in universal religion the world-whole, the unity of God, and the order of humanity are principles which stand upon an equal

footing. The practical maxim of non-resentment, which invariably accompanies world religions, signifies something more than a civilization which has abandoned savagery; it indicates a culture which lives and moves in the august idea that humanity is universal and absolute, for which reason all retaliation is blind and in vain. It is within such a metaphysical realm that the precinct of religion is discovered, and it is only as our thought postulates an order of relations that its problems can be explained. At last, man looks himself in the face and his humanity inspires him to affirm his soul over against the world of nature. Since the idea of humanity is so essential to spiritual life, the various steps which philosophy has taken to reach the universal in man are worthy of consideration.

In the Oriental world, where the idea of Deity seems ever to mask the consciousness of man's humanity, the world of mankind does not fail to receive recognition. This is in reality the subject which the Sankhya philosophy pursues in its doctrines of Tamas-guna, Rajas-guna, Sattva-guna. These Gunas are qualities of ignorance, passion, and illumination respectively, which act as so many cords to bind man down to certain degrees of existence. Instead of being mere physical qualities or psychical temperaments, the Gunas constitute Prakriti, which is the one substance of the world, and, in Aphorism sixty-one, Kapila, who founded the school, declares: " Prakriti is the state of equipoise of goodness, passion, and markness." From another point of view, namely, that of emanation, the Gnostics distinguished pneumatical, psychical, and hylical men. The intellectualism of Vedanta does not forbid the formulation of a humanistic doctrine, because the objective Self in which man really lives consists of a realm in which all individuals participate, and it is in the consciousness of this that the devotee refrains from hate and retaliation. Buddhism is everywhere invested with living humanitarianism and Karma and Nirvana, the be-all and end-all of human existence in a system which believes neither in God, nor the world, nor the individual soul, and which can be interpreted only upon the basis of a world of humanity.

In the Occidental world, which made a beginning in Paganism and then renewed its efforts in Christianity, there arises the consciousness of humanity. Among Greek poets and philosophers, the terminology of humanity is taken up and the way prepared for a direct presentation of the problem. The word φιλανθρωπία occurs in Æschylus' Prometheus, where it indicates the attitude of love which the gods sustain toward men, and it was because of his ardent philanthropy that Prometheus was punished. In the same exalted sense we find the term employed by Plato, while Aristotle, as also Polybius, adds to it the cognate word συμπάθεια. Diogenes Laertius refers to the common law of mankind and distinguishes its peculiarly human quality from common nature. As the practical term philanthropy comes from these Greek writers, the Latin, through Cornificius and Cicero, furnishes us with the word "humanitas." So reassuring is the testimony of language that we pursue the career of the humanistic ideal throughout the development of modern culture.

As early as the days of Notker, German thought employed the equivalent of the term "Gesellschaft," while, later, Eckhart introduces the words "menscheit" and "miteliden." The discovery of humanity belongs properly to Vico, who employs historical considerations to the end of creating a new view of mankind represented as a "Scienza Nuova." The constructive portion of Vico's work consists of fundamental distinctions, by way of grades, in the history of humanity. Herein are revealed three natures: the poetical, the heroic, the moral; three kinds of language: divine, heroic, rational; three forms of government: theocratic, aristocratic, democratic; three stages of jurisprudence: mystical, heroic, human. The principles which guide humanity involve the ideas of God and immortality, while the scheme which embraces the ensemble

The Religious World-Order 251

of humanity leads Vico to say, the "'Scienza Nuova' is an historical demonstration of Providence." Schiller made the idea of humanity the central theme in his system of culture, where it stands midway between the Goethean model of sense and the Kantian maxim of duty, and unites grace, the expression of a noble soul, with dignity, the expression of a lofty mind. The æsthetic education of humanity is possessed of a means by which mankind may pass from the low plane of mere sense to the higher one of sheer virtue. It will appear, then, that Schiller indicates a threefold scheme of humanity and history whereby he assumes a position by the side of Vico, while both of them complete the scheme suggested by the Sankhyan and Gnostic doctrines of the triple cord which binds humanity to its several stations.

Having thus glanced at the steps which philosophy has taken in its attempt to indicate the meaning of mankind, we may now turn from this historical reference to note how distinct are antique and modern ideals of humanity. With the ancient, the humanity of man related to himself or his superior nature, and was represented in a perpendicular fashion which emphasized the difference between higher and lower. The spirit of humanism and the study of the humanities are thus in keeping with the classic ideal, the manifest aim of which was to separate man from the brute, as well as the civilized man from the barbarian, while it signally failed to establish any rational relation of humanity between individual and individual. The modern conception here appears in striking contrast, when it is asserted that, ethically, all souls are equal before God, while, practically, they evince this equality in the presence of law. Added to this doctrine of rights is the moral principle which declares that man has a duty toward others, in the performance of which he reveals the virtue of benevolence and the attitude of altruism. In contrast with the ancient view, modernism is thoroughly horizontal and everywhere manifests the tendency to put all men upon a common level. The ideal is sympathy, not superiority. At the same time, the modern indulges in a thought which is even more alien to the sufficient and aristocratic conception of Paganism; this is the evolutionary scheme which unites the various degrees of social progress, from savagery to civilization, in the programme of social evolution, and even goes so far as to advance the theory that mankind is descended from the animals. This may suggest an altruistic ideal, but it does not enhance the alleged aristocracy of the human species, and no Greek could have accepted an hypothesis which lowers culture to nature, and degrades humanity to animality. These are present-day dilemmas.

2. A sufficient doctrine of humanity seems to lurk in a view which combines the superior and aristocratic in antiquity with the sympathetic and altruistic in modernity. That which is implied by such a combination is, not merely some higher order of individuality or a more appreciative attitude toward others, but a world of humanity, an idea which completes the doctrine of man, just as it is itself fulfilled by the idea of the Godhead. The endeavour to realize man involves considerations drawn from the history of humanity, which cannot be understood until its ontological significance is made out; while the desire to find God cannot be satisfied by magnifying the individual by an infinite number of diameters, but must first be permitted to seek nourishment from the idea of the totality of spiritual life in mankind. From this minor metaphysics of man, the path to the major metaphysics of God is not difficult to find. When man is known as one who participates in the world of absolute humanity, his relation to his fellows will appear in a manner at once engaging and convincing, for each will look upon the other as a mirror of the one spiritual life, whence it will follow that all men possess the aristocracy of humanity for which reason sympathy must be extended toward them.

The ontological view of mankind involves views which

The Religious World-Order

are both static and dynamic, here we encounter humanity, there its history. So far as terminology is of value, it may be suggested that the term "world" is capable of a dual significance, and no consideration of such a vast idea can speak of the world of objective things while it neglects the subjective world of persons. The reality of the latter appears more strikingly in the phrase "history of the world," which can exist and exert its influence only in the realm of humanity. The world of nature is no more and no less demonstrable than the world of mankind ; in each exists a manifold which finds its unity in some higher principle as causality or custom. Only the world within can comprehend the world without ; that which they have in common is the Absolute without which neither can obtain universality or necessity. There must be a metaphysics of life as well as a metaphysics of thought, and only as man is made to assume world-significance can he become the measure of all things. The spirit of the world is, none the less, to reveal itself to man as to matter, and why seek we the living among the dead ?

In a complete system of metaphysics, ontology relates and imparts itself to both cosmology and psychology, and there is no reason why a doctrine of being should confine itself to the forms and the courses of nature when the living soul is so responsive to the idea of being-for-self. The ancient may regard man as a microcosm ; the modern views nature as a macanthropos. So far as man is concerned the participation in the Absolute can receive no sanction until the individual does not lose, but finds himself in his implicit humanity. But when the attributes of man are apparent in him, as the principles of reality appear in things it will be seen that the world of persons and the world of things together make up a cosmic order. Individualistic systems, like those of Leibnitz and Fichte, carry out the same idea, and for this reason, the monadology of Leibnitz, which is based upon the thought that the universe is a combination of spiritual atoms, is capable of a sociological interpretation, while Fichte's notion of the ego in its opposition to the non-ego was by him applied ethically to the relation of man to society. If nature can no longer be humanized, humanity must be viewed, like nature, as possessing a world-significance. Now, individualism, which is as common to nature as to man, is no necessary bar to universality, and if Kant can doubt the existence of things, we can believe in the reality of spirits. Yet the spirit in which we would pursue this investigation is not only one of negation, but consists of a sincere and positive aim to ascertain whether humanity is significant of reality.

From the point of view which is occupied by religion, the significance of the world of humanity appears as something disclosed within upon more profound examination. The world of phenomena, which is sufficient for perception, cannot wholly contain or completely mask the world of noumena; yet within and beyond the world of speculative noumena is found the world of living pneumata, by virtue of which these others stand or fall. Here it is that religion lives, and with dignity occupies its proper precinct; and hereby does religion receive its sufficient justification in the world. Substantial is the bond which connects individual with individual in the one world of humanity; time and space do not prevent its operations, and in the spirit of humanity and history the person who to-day occupies the moment of present being sees that his life is unified with the totality of human existence. Problems of the past still confront us; virtues of former days still inspire our hearts; sorrows of those who long since have been laid in their graves arouse our sympathies. We weep for Hecuba, and, in joy, listen to the story of "the love of some dead man for some dead woman, whose hair was as threads of fine gold, and whose mouth was like the pomegranate." If such sympathy eternal be not religion, it is a phase of spiritual life without which religion cannot exist. What in the common world is usually styled friendship is as fleeting as chaff in the presence of the wind. One is

The Religious World-Order

a friend only as he sees in the other, not the empirical ego, but the intelligible person, which viewing and valuing he furthers in a fashion which is in keeping with the proper vocation of man. He distinguishes the features *de mundi sensibilis et intelligibilis* and, while he realizes that the average man is hemmed in by his surroundings, he can guide him to the one world of humanity, in which all spirits dwell. Oriental world-despair can only counsel man to mark the falcon as he folds his wings in his nest, or to behold the tortoise as he withdraws from the world, but Christian thinking does not exaggerate the possible benefit of self-retreat, for it calls upon the ego to abandon his own and take his place in the world of persons.

In the world of spirits, then, obtains the law which declares *universalia sunt realia*, and the individual need not complain when philosophy of religion relegates him to the world of humanity whereby his being is invested with universal significance. Far from suggesting annihilation, whether the first and moral Nirvana of renunciation or the second and metaphysical one of extinction, the world-life of man really creates the individual, just as it informs him that, apart from participation in the one life which inhabits the world, there can be no knowledge of being. The realization of humanity within is the pre-requisite of the perception of nature without; and world confronts world, as man mirrors the universe. Only under such conditions of universality may man assume to have knowledge of God, or commune with Him; but when he abandons his anthropomorphic methods of representing the Deity, he need not relapse into the abstract, but may advance to a view which sees God through the totality of humanity, whereby man in spirit and in truth may worship Him who is filled with truth and grace.

The world of humanity provides a place for persons, who are thereby enabled to find themselves; meanwhile the limitation of the ego in his individuality is a fact which, by contrariety of reasoning, evinces the supremacy of the religious world-order. In addition to the usual arguments against egoistic living, which, by the way, must to-day be put upon some new and more convincing basis than that which the ethics of altruism affords, there is the metaphysical conception of humanity which cannot tolerate the atomic and aggregative view which ordinarily prevails in the consideration of mankind. Individualism is hopeless metaphysically, inasmuch as the isolated person is unable to represent the being and significance of the world. So vast is nature, that humanity must be its interpreter ; so manifold are her forms, that a plurality of individuals must enter in to exhaust the richness of her life. When man knows himself he knows nature, and thence he may advance to knowledge of the Godhead. Thus it is seen that humanity is more than man, while God is more than humanity. History is richer than time, while eternity exceeds and excels history. The historical world of humanity becomes a sure means of discovering the presence of God in the world ; certainly it provides a condition necessary to all sincere contemplation of the Absolute.

The world of persons is Utopia. But must we then conclude that it is a Nowhere, and say that the world of humanity is the realm of non-existence ? Far better is it to assert that the spiritual world has no particular places of " here " and " there," or times of " now " and " then," and to see that the true view of humanity is metapolitical, in that it informs the concept " man " with significance and invests the calling of mankind with world-power. Such a view is not Utopian, but Pantopian, since it treats of that which is beyond space and time, and superior to the influence of matter and causality. Pantopia is a realm in which exist all the active ideals and rational forces which are destined to guide humanity to its proper goal. To make a citizen, the ancient Aristotle declared man to be a political animal—ἄνθρωπος φύσει ζῷον πολιτικόν; to conceive of him as a creature of rights, Grotius made the social one of his human attributes—*homini proprium sociale*. In either case, the individual is related to an order from which he receives his political character.

The problem of man's relation to the Deity is no particular problem of religion, but is the general condition which prevails in all culture and reflection ; it is religion which realizes the predicament and which aspires to place all human affairs in their proper light. According to the Vedantist conception of the world, there prevails everywhere the principle of Maya, illusion, which acts upon the mind of man with the result of creating a false belief to the effect that it is the individual in his own world which constitutes reality. Under the influence of Vedic reflection, however, man is enabled to cast off the illusion of finitude both in himself and in nature, and in this exalted state of contemplation he suffers the world of things and the body of sense to evaporate before the presence of the one Self which abides in the world. In a similar, yet more guarded fashion, we may call attention to the illusion of individuality which besets the ego, and which prevents him from justly participating in his implicit humanity. Christ refers to the person only as the soul which outweighs the world, and which accomplishes its destiny only as it submerges its natural self for the sake of attaining to the self-hood of the Kingdom. Under such auspices man is viewed as supra-human, while yet he remains infra-divine.

Man's consciousness of his humanity is relative, and the minimum of personality which ordinarily invests the individual stands out in unspeakable contrast when, in historical or poetical climaxes, the possibility of man is realized. The courage of a Leonidas, the consecration of a St. Francis, the gifted humanity of a Schiller, are but indications of the height to which humanity may rise. Courage among the ancients and philanthropy among the moderns do not overawe the easy chivalry of medieval life, which was so celebrated among the poets of the Italian Renaissance when that spirit was fast retreating. Ariosto portrays a fine picture of this in the opening book of "Orlando

Furioso." The fair Angelica, who had been the source of discordant jealousy between Orlando and Rinaldo, is doomed likewise to precipitate the duel between the Pagan Ferrau and Rinaldo, whom he attacks in furious combat. As the conflict continues, the maiden flees, so that the conqueror is confronted by the idea of an empty victory, in the loss of Angelica. Here "sweet reasonableness" possesses the minds of both Christian and Saracen, and they decide to seek the flying virgin, and, one deprived of helmet, the other in want of his horse, they mount a single steed in the common amorous pursuit. It is here that even the poet, as Schiller suggests, marvels at the picture of chivalry so fair to behold in an age so foreign to its spirit:

> O noble minds, by knights of old possessed;
> Two faiths they knew, one love their hearts profess'd;
> And still their limbs the smarting anguish feel,
> Of strokes inflicted by the hostile steel.
> Through winding paths, and lonely woods they go,
> Yet no suspicion their brave bosoms know.
> At length the horse, with double spurring, drew
> To where two several ways appear'd in view,
> When doubtful which to take, one gentle knight,
> For fortune took the left, and one the right.

The ground of sympathy is to be found in the world of humanity. He who participates in the sufferings of another exercises this holy function by virtue of the one humanity which arches over individuals, who share each other's feelings only as they assume their proper attitude toward the totality of spiritual life. He who indulges in the luxury of grief does not pity the personality of his own private soul, but by virtue of his own sorrow he enters into sympathetic relations with all mankind and breathes the atmosphere of absolute humanity. It is the benediction of Mizpah between *tuum* and *meum*, and is an open confession, that individual can sustain vital relation to individual only as both are reflected by the Absolute Life of the world.

No human plight can quite compare with death, yet this

The Religious World-Order

most obvious incident in human experience is habitually relegated to the domain of unconscious life, where it takes up its ambiguous abode in the sombre portion of man's existence. Reason knows as much of death as of life, but no more. Opposite views and varying grades of appreciation are to be found in the art and philosophy of past and present, of Orient and Occident. Eve with the body of Abel, and Mary with the figure of Jesus before her, present conflicting spectacles. The primitive mother, who finds her son slain, can scarcely apprehend the fact of death, with its closed eyes, upturned face, and straightening limbs, and her sorrow is unconscious and unintelligent; the Pietà, however, has had preparation for the fatal end which beset her Son, and her sorrow is so human that one must say, "Surely this was grief." As past and present so differ, also east and west in their thanatopses. The Oriental thinks that to die is bad perhaps, but not to die is worse, accordingly he shuns reincarnation as intensely as the Occidental seeks the resurrection. What advances must culture make, what inwardness must humanity assume, to produce unanimity of opinion concerning the death-problem! Only then may we hope to reach the borderland of the vast world of humanity; meanwhile, to set life in the one sphere and death in the other is by no means a simple attitude of mind. Man may not overestimate its significance in his own case, but he does underestimate its meaning in the instance of others; for a man confronted by his own death feels that all existence is at an end, while in contemplating the death of another he regards it as of consequence to him alone and as ineffectual in the real world. This warped view, which exaggerates the ego and deprives the alter of his proper sympathy, is due to the absence of the world of humanity from the mind of the reasoner. A profound spirit surveys the loss of another saying:

> This losing is true dying,
> This the lordly man's down-lying,
> Star by star his world resigning.

While another, who lived in the world of spirits, strove to drive back the sympathetic tears of them that were beholding and bewailing His death by saying, "Weep not for me, daughters of Jerusalem, but weep for yourselves." Sorrow is here idealized, and being no longer individualized it is ascribed to humanity in general, so that the particular victim is :

> As one, in suffering all, that suffers nothing,

since he abandons his private misery to embrace the sorrow of the world. No one liveth or dieth unto himself, since each of necessity exists in the one human world which surrounds all finite spirits. The world of humanity is a spiritual fact and form of consciousness whose reality cannot be denied.

3. There is still another consideration which enters into the idea of a world of humanity, and that is the active principle of destiny. This appears in the plan of human history, and is what Vico had in mind when he spoke of the function of "Scienza Nuova": "It traces the eternal circle of an ideal history in which revolves the real history of all nations." If man is more than man, history is more than history: the one is humanity, the other is destiny. The static view of humanity shows that the world is too vast to have its meaning and value exhausted by the individual, while the dynamic view should now indicate the method according to which humanity realizes itself. This is the genial programme of history.

At first sight, history seems to be a snare in which the individual is trapped, and even a worse predicament is brought about when we see how the idea of eternity suffers at the hands of progress. Nevertheless, we no longer live in the barren Enlightenment, which made of individuality, as well as of eternity, an *idée fixe*, and we can see to it that history shall help and not hinder humanity in its self-realization. The dynamic view of humanity, involving the idea of a destiny which mankind must realize, is capable of constituting and considering history in a fundamental fashion. Therefore we need not fear lest the individual be left behind in his age, and eternity be never attained in the relatively perpetual flux of time. The individual, instead of losing, gains by the historical view, which affords a speculative ground and a practical means of relating him to the Absolute Life. To adjust the isolated individual to the eternal is in itself impossible, to attempt this adjustment by the interposition of the history of humanity is an undertaking fraught with the hope of possible solution. Hence the problem of progress, while difficult, is easier than the static scheme of the Enlightenment, which suffered such signal failure in its attempt to regard nature *sub specie aeterni*, and man *sine die*.

In the dynamics of humanity, history must receive metaphysical treatment, and this means that our thought must transcend space and time. At this juncture, the genuine service of history appears, and like art and law, which in the second part of this work offered such timely assistance, we see that here is a scheme which descends to the level of man in the temporal and spatial phases of his individualized existence, and yet raises him to something which is beyond time and space in the realm of Absolute Life. The Athens of Olympiad 88 cannot claim Plato any more than the Florence of the Cinque-cento can contain Michel Angelo; history, which localizes them, also lifts them to their positions on high, where they are admitted to the constellations, and while each retains the character of his day, these are but the garments of his fair personality. History has a calling to which it does not fail to respond; it provides a means by which the individual may participate in the eternal in the form of a living present, and its superlative worth appears the moment we contrast the savage, who to-day is about what he was ages ago, with the man of civilization, who has been made by the historical spirit infused throughout his soul. Each individual in history accomplishes his own destiny in a characteristic fashion, and need not complain that he was born too early or too late, for the whole plan of dynamic humanity shows that, apart from the totality of life, no individual is made perfect.

Religion does its intrinsic work in connection with the destiny of man and the design of God. Yet apart from his humanity the individual can have no destiny; where, however, he is adjusted to the whole of which he is a member, and is related to history where he occupies his position, his calling as man appears in the form of the world of persons. History here performs a double function: it indicates what is to be the end of human life, and supplies the practical means whereby this is attained. The isolated person, who lives in a particular period, could not discover his destiny, much less realize it, but when the particular problems of the individual's life are viewed through the lens of history, the position and importance of mankind are seen. The ideal history of humanity appears in the real history of mankind, and just as humanity is raised above the particularities of time and space, person and circumstance, so humanity hastens on to the domain of Absolute Life. It is by such reasoning that religion realizes itself; and when we see that over man is humanity, it will appear that above this is the world-order which barely falls short of the Godhead.

At the same time, the idea of God receives certain elucidations when it is interpreted through the world of humanity and its historical expression. In the complete history of man two different conceptions of being have sought to express the relation which God sustains to the world. Aryan culture reveals a certain confidence on the part of the human intellect which aspires to represent the beauty of the world and the majesty of the Deity; as a result, pride of intellectualism ends in the perfection of an immanental view, which invests the whole world with the presence of God. In contrast to this is the Semitic view, which magnifies the distinction between man and the Creator and marvels at God's gracious concern for his creatures. This sense of reverence thus produced a transcendental view of the problem and elaborated, not an ameliorating pantheism, but a stern deism. Poetry brought Brahman into intimate relations with the soul; piety separated Jahveh from the domain of ordinary existence, so that the priest must stand between the soul and God, while the prophet represented the divine mind to the sons of men. This contrast between Sanskrit and Semitic forms of theistic belief continued until the union of the two tendencies at the inception of Christianity.

The Christian theory of redemption restores God to His world in such a manner as to unite the principles of immanence and transcendence in an original manner. This is made possible by virtue of a new view of the world, which is no pragmatic fact to be found directly by means of observation, but consists in an ideal which thought itself must construct. Thus understood, the world of naturism with its forces fades in the presence of the world of humanism with its values, and the world-aspect of the Deity is expressed by saying, God is immanent in the world of spirits, while He transcends the world of things. Buddhism does not fail to distinguish the " world of humanity " from the " world of Nirvana " and the " world of the gods," while Christianity elaborates the idea of a divine Kingdom in which all spirits live.

4. *The Unity of Finite and Infinite*

To bring this examination of the religious precinct to a suitable conclusion, we must meet a problem which has lain implicit throughout the whole of this work; it is the problem of finite and infinite. When it is asserted that religion affirms its independence over against the world, maintains its own character in contrast with logic and ethics, and develops its positive existence in the history of humanity, it is implied that the human spirit is approximating toward an independent realm of Absolute Life. Such was the significance of the first three parts of the study which lies before us. Having just seen that, on all sides, mankind posits an Absolute Life as the basis of the world of humanity, we must now seek to render man's participation in the Infinite, an idea which, if not perfectly demonstrable, is not to be rejected. The unity of spiritual life, which has been lost to science and philosophy, reappears in religion, wherein it consists, not in a return to nature or a life according to reason, but in a harmony with the ideal. It is the fate of religion to reveal the peculiar plight of man, who is last in nature and first in spirit; and the secret of all human distress and error is found to consist in the dual capacity of mankind with his naturism and spiritism. In the total analysis, this dualism involves the contrast between finite and infinite.

The commingling of lowest and highest is inevitable in the human mind, which determines one principle in the light of the other, but it does not follow that this immediate synthesis is wholly intelligible. To reduce it to acceptable terms of theory, we would best assume that the unity of finite and infinite is not an external one toward which our thought vainly strives, but consists rather in an immanent relation which life itself renders more or less tenable. The whole course of life and its arts, the constant trend of philosophy with its problems, made manifest the thought that apart from some representative relation to the Absolute, human living and thinking can neither be justified nor explained. Significant situations which art discovers in human existence, as well as flashes of insight which philosophy habitually discloses, involve the unity of spiritual life in such a determined fashion that we cannot help relating man to a higher order than that of ordinary life. This inevitable relation makes its presence felt in logic and other forms of speculative philosophy, as also in ethics and more general conceptions of human life. Here, it appears in the reconciliation of spirit and sense, of conscious and unconscious, of temporal and eternal; there,

The Religious World-Order

it affirms the oneness of subject and object, freedom and fate.

1. All sincere philosophy postulates the unity of spiritual life. Much of the confusion, and consequent distrust, caused by philosophy is explicable in the light of the fact that academic reflection is often more concerned about method, whether empiricism or rationalism, hedonism or intuitionism, than about a *view*, and it is in the development of the latter that genuine philosophy becomes representative of the human mind. Plato's idealism surmounts all bickering contrasts. Plotinus advances to spiritual existence which is at once hyper-real and hyper-rational. In the religious dialectic of Scotus Erigena, the search for finality ends in the conception of " That which neither is created nor creates," a Being which transcends both activity and passivity. Above both phenomenon and noumenon there is the realm of spirit which is known by means of intuition.

To perfect the unity of finite and infinite, appeal must thus be made to a third form of knowledge in which humanity and divinity may participate. Knowledge which arises from the senses, and that which is elaborated by the understanding, do not prevent a third form of knowledge of an intuitive order. In the strict monism of Spinoza, this tertiary and intuitive kind of reason finds its place in a system which premises the absoluteness of the Deity, while it postulates the freedom of the human mind. Over and above the knowledge which springs from sense and that which arises in reason, there appears a third form, which is intuitive. "*Praeter haec duo cognitionis genera datus, ut in sequentibus ostendam, aliud tertium, quod scientiam intuitivam vocabimus.* Besides these two kinds of knowledge, there is, as I will hereafter show, a third kind of knowledge, which we will call intuitive." The discussion of this intuitive form of knowledge, thus promised by Spinoza, is carried on in the fifth part of the work, which treats of human freedom ; and here it appears in conjunction with two other notions, which are highly prized by the faithful reader of Spinoza's "Ethica," namely, "The intellectual love of God," and "Knowledge under the form of eternity." "*Summus mentis conatus, summaque virtus est res intelligere tertio cognitionis genere.*—The highest impulse of the mind and the highest virtue is to understand things by the third kind of knowledge." The religious value of this view appears in the statement made concerning the Deity. "*Ex tertio cognitionis genere oritur necessario amor dei intellectualis.*—From the third kind of knowledge necessarily arises the intellectual love of God." Added to these propositions, concerning intuition and intellectual love, is a third, number thirty-three, which introduces the view *sub specie aeternitatis*, to form a triune statement of the problem before us. "*Amor dei intellectualis, qui ex tertio cognitionis genere oritur, est aeternus.*—The intellectual love of God, which arises from the third kind of knowledge, is eternal." In thus discerning the unity of spiritual life, Spinoza's thought is more convincing than in the first part of the work, which is based upon the idea of a substance which is constituted by itself and conceived of through itself, and the conflict between the formalistic and realistic views of substance and attribute loses its significance in the light of Spinoza's own intuitive synthesis of the necessary and contingent, of eternal and temporal.

The problem of finite and infinite stands in need of just statement as well as of adequate solution. In one sense, there is a noetical equality, inasmuch as one half of the disjunction weighs as much as the other; yet, when viewed inwardly, the finite must assume a secondary and derivate position, whence it is able to affirm and accept, not to deny and reject. Assume the view, then, that finite and infinite are both problematical, and may we not see that one stands as much in need of justification as the other? Atheism is a possibility, but equally so is acosmism; man may doubt the existence of God, but he can also question the

The Religious World-Order

identity of self. Such is the logical poise which the formal question assumes. The human merits of the case, however, require us to abandon this artificial device and survey the finite as the slow and painful ascent to the infinite ; and hence the difference appears no longer to consist of the distinction between separate qualities, but of certain degrees of lower and higher, which, in the history of humanity, appear in the form of stages of development.

To this approximation of finite to infinite religion is wonderfully adapted. Here it brings its realistic and positive character to bear upon humanity's approach to the Godhead, and its whole plan involves a living reconciliation of sense and spirit, which are abandoned by logic and ethics. Religious intuition is a third form of knowledge which is neither abstract nor concrete, just as holy love can never be confused with desire or duty. In the total view of religious intuition, the claims of empiricism and rationalism are adjusted and no longer need reason to calculate from data or demonstrate from grounds, inasmuch as it finds in religion the possibility of an entire view of the world. When such a view is made the maxim of human life, individual desire which finds its seat in the body, as well as the strain of character which follows upon the expression of duty, are both ameliorated by an artistic impulse which, in all serenity, goes forth to find the Highest.

In the fullness and richness of its own nature, religion perfects the unity of finite and infinite in the blending of conscious and unconscious expressed by every holy act. Saints, as well as artists, rise above natural instinct, while they do not turn aside to the devious ways of inference ; in all spiritual integrity, they create their living intuitions. And in the totality of human consciousness, as in the unity of human activity, both alert choice and blind constraint fall below the presence of the One Being of the world. Unconscious activity on the part of the soul is habitually referred to genius or to inspiration ; religion invests it with a new meaning, when it is ascribed to the presence of Brahma-Nirvana or to the Holy Ghost. It is only by courtesy or common consent that such a condition of mind is styled unconsciousness, which here should signify, not descent to the plane of instinct, but elevation to the precinct of spiritual life. In a broader and yet less valuable fashion does art employ these extremes of conscious life in the intrinsic work of genius. All æsthetic contemplation raises both its subject and its object to a level where the unity of the soul is reflected in the unity of the world.

In this tertiary form of knowledge, which, inwardly viewed, consists of intuition, there is further involved the thought of culture, which itself posits the unity of finite humanity and the infinite Godhead. Concrete experience, when neither analysed nor appropriated by man, is vastly different from perception, and when the dualism between these is projected outwardly it arouses the conflict between finite and infinite; thus it is that the secret of the antinomies of cosmology, as inflicted by Kant, is found in the inevitable contrast between sense and understanding. It is the vocation of culture to surmount the elements of this dualism, and in the progress of the human soul, from the domain of sense to the realm of spirit, the perfect synthesis of finitude and infinitude is found. Culture dwells upon neither the abstract nor the concrete, but projects a third form of spiritual being which has neither the formlessness of sense nor the void of mere understanding. Nature and reason, instinct and reflection, the particular and the general, are opposites which are securely unified in living culture; and in the historical development of the human spirit these opposites readjust themselves from a horizontal to a vertical position, where they assume the form of ascending stages.

That which makes man also unmakes him; it is his individuality. Himself a part of nature, his mind reflecting its most significant phases, man transcends animal existence, as the beast surpasses the plant, and the plant the stone. By means of his culture, he opposes knowledge to nature,

The Religious World-Order

humanity to animality. All culture is humanism; all humanism is individualism. This condition is the reason why the value of human culture is at times brought into question; for when we realize that man has been sundered from nature, in which he has his actual existence, we are inclined to doubt the expediency of a spiritual system which turns man's attention from immediate necessities to remote interests. Then, the individualizing tendency of culture produces, not only the exaggerated ego of the genius, but the isolated personality of the average man, and the naturistic in man is wounded by the humanistic in him, when the individual opposes the world. Individualizing culture thus precipitates the problem of finite and infinite.

In the midst of this dilemma, we discover the idea of a world of humanity, because we have seen that man ever relates himself to some appropriate system, and never abandons the instincts of a world-life implicit in his origin as a natural being. When it is observed that, in addition to the empirical ego, which dwells in the world of time and space, there is also an intelligible ego, which must find its realm elsewhere, it can be seen that a world of humanity is as necessary to perfect man as was the world of nature to produce him. From nature to the individual, from the individual to the world of spirit—such is the complete plan of human destiny; and having found his place in the finite, man can find it also in the infinite. Such is the metaphysical view implicit in the conception of religion which has been expressed in this work; when man affirms himself as a spiritual being, he declares that the intelligible person cannot remain in nature, and must hence ascend to its proper place in the world of humanity.

Upon the human side, the conflict between finite and infinite makes another appeal to the mind in the question concerning immortality. Metaphysics and ethics have each had their chances to demonstrate the proposition concerning the continued existence of the soul, and where one has proceeded upon the premise of the soul's eternal essence the other has advanced to the postulate of its immortal value. To these views, which contribute neither proof nor disproof, may be added a third based upon the total culture of the human spirit, which advances man to such a plane of being that the contemplation of eternal life becomes less and less alien to human existence. Culture fills out the life of man to something like its just proportions, and however vast the delineations of eternity may be, the child of humanity is able to survey them. No matter how loftily the temple of eternity may arch above man's head, its windows are adapted to his eyes as its steps are fitted for his feet. The history of man, which reveals the path from finite to infinity, shows that if humanity cannot advance to spirit, it cannot remain in nature, if it cannot become infinite, it is in no wise able to remain in its immediate finitude. History so lengthens and deepens the meaning of man's life that under its tutelage he becomes half-immortal and inherits a part of eternity.

To return to nature would be to abandon abruptly the plan laid down in the history of human culture, and while it is still difficult to advance to the spiritual unity of finite and infinite, the actual progress of mankind forbids that we should continue to employ, in our thinking, the immediate unity of man and nature. The dualism which obstructs the passage from the temporal to the eternal acts negatively also in the contrary direction, and the retreat to nature is as hopeless as the advance toward the world of spirit. No longer may we assume that man is a creature of nature, for the view of naturalism stands in need of the same form of argument which is usually found in the quarters of spiritualism, and in determining the status of a being whose nature is problematical, culture is possessed of more worthy arguments than those afforded by nature. Meanwhile, the idea of immortality stands in need not so much of demonstration as of appreciation; it should pass from logic and ethics, with their grounds and motives, to culture and religion, with their ideas of destiny and value.

The usual life of man in nature reveals in fragmentary fashion the union of finitude and infinitude which is involved in the doctrine of the soul's immortality. Within the consciousness of the individual, the total life of humanity arouses a sense of man's true position in the world, and the gleams of insight and throbs of holy love which animate the human heart suggest the character of the cherubim, who are as exultant over knowledge as the seraphim are ardent in affection. Man's happiness consists in knowledge —*C'est le bonheur des hommes, quand ils pensent juste*— and in moments of ecstasy, he forgets all time in the thought that he lives for ever. The exalted state of mind, which reveals the striking truth of some inner sentiment rather than the reality of an external relation, is unattainable under purely finite conditions. If man is not destined to be spiritual, he is not to be thought of as merely natural, for in the course of his religious development, with his ideas of God and humanity, he has outdone himself already. The elevated frame of mind which must be the despair of all ordinary naturistic thinking cannot remain long concealed in such works of art as the "Apollo Belvedere" and the "Dead Slave." The one expresses an immediate tranquillity of mind in the gaze which is directed outward toward the world; the other wears a sadder demeanour, as he reveals, in death, an acquired peace which the world cannot give, but which comes only after continued conflict when flesh rests from its struggles while the spirit sublimely acquiesces. Standing side by side, the slave is more divine than the god, while both silence all objection to the sentiment that finite and infinite may enter into communion.

While it perfects these symbols of spiritual achievement, religion ever tends to realize them in flesh and blood. In moments of self-effacement, the devotee rises to participate in the One Absolute Life, and thus realizes what the artist merely indicates. The weighing of one's self, as well as the disposition of it according to an ideal, is an integral deed by which the soul finds its own unity ; and he who has exchanged the narrow personal life in nature for the infinite life in spirit transcends both life and death as he says, "ζῶ δέ, οὐκ ἔτι ἐγώ—I live, yet not I." An uninspired account of such self-abnegation may be found in the "Confessions of a Beautiful Soul," which occupies the interim of "Wilhelm Meister," where the egoism of the first period is about to change to the altruism of the final phase of the work. For herself having weighed the finite of the world against the infinite of the soul, the fair saint is struck by the strangeness of the spectacle which she has herself created, and expresses her self-consciousness by saying, "My story had been noised abroad, and many persons felt a curiosity to see the woman who had valued God above her bridegroom."

From such considerations drawn from logic and æsthetics, we venture to express the conviction that the human mind, when left to its own powers and confronted by its peculiar problems, does not hesitate to raise mankind to an unwonted height of speculative contemplation, which reveals the presence of God in the life of man as well as an accompanying sense of the soul's immortality. Immediate experience, further fettered by the prescriptions of empirical science, stands in the light of such insight only in the case of those who are addicted to nature and consecrated to its ways of viewing things. But all genuine culture, which, by way of illustration, may be said to repose in the third quality, or "Sattva-Guna" of Sankhya philosophy, is pledged to a view of man which does not exclude the religious consideration. What speculation puts upon the level of possibility, life advances to the point of necessity, and further study of the problem at hand will show that essential existence cannot be conceived of apart from an interplay of spirit and nature. Socrates may gaze into the burning sun and not feel dazed, but the average man receives his vision in the light and shade of ordinary life.

Nevertheless, genius and common man cannot reason apart from the presence of the absolute spirit, whereby we see the poetic and religious truth of the wise and worshipful sentiment, " In thy light do we see the light," an idea embodied in the Occasionalism of Father Malebranche, which declares that " we see all things in God—*nous voyons toutes choses en Dieu.*" Thus the idea of God, which in its isolation as something to be demonstrated is with difficulty maintained, now appears as the unity of sense and reason, of conscious and unconscious ; indeed, as the first and last principle of all speculative thinking.

2. When applied to the ethical side of human life, the unity of finite and infinite assumes the form of freedom and fate. Here, in bringing this consideration of the religious precinct to a conclusion, we must face a problem which, in theory as in practice, has perpetually grieved the spirit of man. And what shall religion say to one who puzzles over this never-ending question of inner freedom and outer constraint ? Religion, whose independent nature and intrinsic character have long since made their presence felt, may now assume that it is possessed of a method which will, perhaps, afford reconciliation in the unity of humanity with the Godhead. Art has always done this, and in how secure a fashion ! The Homeric epics reveal θεοί and ἄνδροι participating in one life, while Greek tragedy forgets the problem of fate and freedom. Thus the bad man is so hemmed in by the Divine that he never really harms the universe, while his evil deed becomes ill desert ; the good man, on the contrary, may pass through conflict, yet eternal justice so supports him that he never truly falls. King Œdipus and his daughter Antigone reveal the force of a fate inevitable and inscrutable ; King Lear and his daughter Cordelia act under the inspiration of freedom, while external circumstances reveal the weakness of old age and the power of youth. Sophocles premises a fate which circumscribes all freedom ; Shakespeare postulates a freedom which is influential within the realm of

T

fate. The crass conception of law which is peculiar to the domain of physics, as well as the bald ideal of liberty which is vaunted in the science of ethics, are both set aside by this religious conception of life which intuits fate and freedom as one total act of spiritual life in the world. At times, philosophy, as in Fichte's dialectic and Froebel's pedagogy, has found it possible to include liberty and necessity, while religion everywhere unites the two opposites in the complete calling of mankind. Nevertheless ethical thinking proposes a problem which seems insoluble where the religious sanction is wanting.

In the problem which lies before us, there is one place where even the security of the infinite seems to stand in danger, and that is where the free individual is invested with the moral law as a duty which he imposes upon himself. How, then, can the supremacy of duty consist with the sovereignty of Deity? When this essential Christian problem occurred to the scholastic thinker, he promptly raised the casuistical inquiry, "Is the good good because God wills it; or does God will it because it is good?" The first view was taken by the Franciscan, Duns Scotus; the second, by the Dominican, Thomas Aquinas. The implications involved in this dilemma are such as cannot escape reflective thinking. If God, by an act of will, creates the moral law, He may preserve His sovereignty; but He destroys the sanctity of the moral law, which, being dependent upon His will, may consist of the vicious as well as the virtuous. On the other hand, the view of Thomas is not without destructiveness; for, if it be affirmed, that God merely recognizes a law which is beyond His power to create or destroy, the perfection of morality is established upon the ruins of theology.

It is to be expected that such contrary views should not be without their own individual weaknesses, especially when they are elaborated in defiance of the unity which obtains between finite and infinite. Scotism, which enhances a supreme yet arbitrary will, can attribute no *standard* in accordance with which this should create the law of righteousness, and thus presents the unhappy spectacle of an infinite genius who ignores the canons of criticism and the ideals of artistic construction. Something more than power is requisite. Thomism falls into a void no less deep, because it calls upon the divine intellect to choose the self-constituted moral law, without attributing to His æsthetically indifferent nature any *motive* which should naturally lead to such a choice. Will stands in need of guidance, while understanding is wanting in moral impulse ; hence, any separation of functions can end only in a contradiction which forbids progress. The moral law, which is the one means by which the finite can hold out against the infinite, is best understood in a living form as that which involves the being of humanity and divinity.

On the side of moral sanction, the problem of freedom and fate now appears and sets the total question in the same light. Where man is ethically conceived, where his nature is viewed in the form of freedom, the finite is able to assert his spiritual dignity, although he would not be found to fight against God. Rather is it that when man rises to such a moral pitch that he is in a position to understand his proper relation to the Absolute, ethics proposes a problem which religion must solve, just as it aligns an ideal which religion must objectify. In the question concerning the sanction of duty, the dilemma involves—here, the freedom of man, there, the sovereignty of God ; and how shall reason choose between them ?

As in the previous predicament we decided that both views were wrong, here we declare that both are right, and need only their respective forms of perfecting to meet upon a common plane. God's sovereignty is not the inexplicable tyranny of an Oriental monarch, for such a view, abhorrent in itself, would involve the difficulties of Scotism. Better is it to ask, Wherein consists the value and purpose of such sovereignty ? Whereupon it may be replied, God is sovereign in order that His *righteous* will may prevail in the establishment of the moral world-order. In the same calm spirit may we interpret human freedom and invest it with that ethical purport which it was first called forth to realize. Why should man be free ? Not to affirm any fantastic or vicious will of the sensuous individual, but solely for the purpose of achieving moral destiny, the end of which consists in participating in, and furthering, the holy interests of a realm of righteousness. Such was likewise the end of holy omnipotence, and in the precinct of religion—call it Brahma-Nirvana, Tao, or the Kingdom of God—the design of God and the destiny of man unite in expressing and advancing the supreme interest of spirits, infinite and finite.

It is when man attempts to participate in the infinite that the consciousness of this unity appears as the one ideal of life. No better representation of this problem can be found than that which is afforded by the drama. Where, according to Aristotle, the term poetry comes from the Greek "poiein," to make, the cognate verb, "dran," drama, signifies to do, and dramatic poetry thus represents the dynamic element in human life, as well as the unity of subject and object, and the relation of man to the world. The epic with its grand theme and majestic verse stands out in contrast to the lyric, which speaks from within for the personal soul ; one is objective and vast, the other subjective and intense. Midway between the two is the drama which endeavours to relate the lyrical subject, who now no longer speaks for himself alone, to the epic situation, with its realm of historical forces. Here the temperament of the individual strives to accommodate to itself the tendency of the world of affairs, just as the mind of the subject endeavours to set up representative relations with the Absolute. Apart from some such ontological interpretation, the ideal sufferings of an imaginary character can have neither significance nor influence, and it is only when religion is allowed to interpret the situation that we are able to comprehend the meaning of tragedy which is never a purely human affair.

In the tragedies of Sophocles and Shakespeare, the attempt on the part of the subject to adjust himself to the world produces the dramatic situation as it also conveys the philosophic lesson. In " Œdipus Tyrannus " mere man cannot play against fate, while in the " Antigone," a youthful mind cannot solve the problem of duty. Among other things, the " Electra " reveals the finitude and incapacity of humanity, which is subject to the limitations of sex. Macbeth's vaulting ambition overleaps the bounds of justice, and conscience collapses in the presence of remorse. Hamlet's reflecting, academic nature suffers from *folie du doute* and shows how meditation unfits man for action. Othello's energistic soul is incapable of loving wisely. These tragic failures portray the ideal life of man, which consists in a complete adjustment to the infinite, which habitually imposes too great a burden upon the soul of man.

The participation of the finite in the Absolute, in addition to its being a speculative problem as difficult to state as to solve, produces practical difficulties also, and man learns that the entrance of the Infinite is not without pain. The chorus in " Antigone " places this matter in a sombre light when it declares :

   τό τ' ἔπειτα καὶ τὸ μέλλον
   καὶ τὸ πρὶν ἐπαρκέσι
   νόμος ὅδ'. οὐδὲν ἕρπει
   θνατῶν βιότῳ πάμπολύ ἐκτὸς ἄτας.

" And through the future, near and far, as through the past, shall this law hold good ; nothing that is vast enters into the life of mortals without a curse." In spite of the uncertainty of the reading of πάμπολύ, we may adhere to the text, as also the translation of Jebb, because the entire spirit of " Œdipus " and " Antigone " indicates how weak are flesh and blood in the presence of such vast things as fate and law. The essential ground of suffering is traceable to man's relation to the Absolute, and emotions like fear and wonder, surprise and anguish, are unintelligible in themselves, just as they would probably be unconscious in their passage through the mind, without the immanence of Absolute Life in mortal man. Ideal pain is but the shudder and awe felt by man in the real presence of God, while all genuine suffering is due to man's inability to commune with the Infinite. Strictly speaking, there is no human tragedy; it is rather the total life of the world, expressed by means of fate, or even circumstance, which imposes the burden which is felt in the form of world-sorrow, and it is the Infinite Spirit which speaks with groanings unutterable.

In his matchless essay on "Naive and Sentimental Poetry," Schiller uses this distinction to indicate the difference between poetics antique and modern, whose metaphysical contrast he expresses as follows : "The power of the ancients consists in compressing objects into the finite, and the moderns excel in the art of the infinite." Apart from this valuable bit of criticism, the poetic theory of Schiller expresses the idea that when man departs from nature he cannot rest until he rests in the ideal. Thus it is that the finite seeks repose in the infinite. The idea of God, which is implicit in these views of life, assumes the form of unity, which is the essence of personality and spiritual life ; and the conception of the world which is involved in such a view is that of an Absolute Life which eliminates the distinction between finite and infinite. It is essential to all genuine religion that it should involve finite and infinite in a consistent unity. Common acts of faith and worship involve human nature in its simplest form, yet do not fail to include the essence of the Godhead. Outwardly man lives for the time being ; his source is found in nature while his career is an affair of history. Yet he has the feeling that the life of immediacy is not all of his being, so that above the facts of daily life and the deeds of the hour, there is a higher vocation which is none the less, but all the more, his own. This is an open secret in all spiritual religion, which never dreams of separating the finite from the infinite, but in simple passivity declares the One Being of the world. The world of nature reveals the implicit unity of spirit, and why should we shrink from such an idea in connection with the world of humanity ? No isolated faculty can account for the forms of human action or thought, which are due to the entirety of man's nature. Man himself cannot live or be understood apart from humanity, while humanity itself rests upon the basis of the one spiritual life which inhabits the world.

As for man, the substantial aim of his life is finally seen to consist in abandoning the eccentric position in which nature has placed and left him, and in performing an integral deed calculated to lodge him in a centric place. This is the spirit of that conception of religion which has been discussed in the foregoing—the self-affirmation of the soul. Such an adjustment of humanity to the world is the proper work of religion, which, in its universal forms, involves the totality of the human spirit. And it is here again that the conception of a religious precinct assumes its just significance, inasmuch as it strives to represent the wholeness of man's spiritual nature, as it affirms also the independent character of his religious culture. Religion is not as broad as culture itself, but it is more intense in its search for the fundamental in thought and the final in life ; and it is for this reason that we suffer it to speak for that sense of human destiny which does not leave man until it has placed him in the world of Absolute Life.

www.ingramcontent.com/pod-product-compliance
Lightning Source LLC
Chambersburg PA
CBHW062004220426
43662CB00010B/1221